AF560772

Hamara Rahul

Hamara Rahul

A Tribute to Rahul Bajaj

Edited by
Tarun Das
and
Kiran Pasricha

JUGGERNAUT BOOKS
C-I-128, First Floor, Sangam Vihar, Near Holi Chowk,
New Delhi 110080, India

First published by Juggernaut Books 2024

10 9 8 7 6 5 4 3 2 1

P-ISBN: 9789353459468
E-ISBN: 9789353453800

Typeset in Adobe Caslon Pro by R. Ajith Kumar, Noida

Printed at Manipal Technologies Limited, Manipal

For Rahul Bajaj
(10 June 1938–12 February 2022)

Contents

Foreword

My earliest encounter with Rahul Bajaj's influence was during my growing-up years in Andhra Pradesh – the iconic Bajaj scooters and three-wheelers were for us symbols of mobility and aspiration. My journey from a middle-class upbringing to being a faculty member at Harvard Business School (HBS) brought me closer to Rahul's world. Our paths crossed, and a professional acquaintance blossomed into a personal connection. Rahul, who introduced me to Tarun Das and the Confederation of Indian Industry (CII), was instrumental in enriching my research on India and facilitating for me dialogues with key business leaders.

In my role as the senior associate dean for international development at Harvard, I relied heavily on Rahul's help, advice and guidance in the launch of the HBS India Research Center. When Rahul visited Boston or I visited Pune, I always looked forward to our dinner meetings to hear his thoughts on India, the world and HBS. I always left feeling fortunate to have experienced his kindness, warmth and wisdom.

Rahul Bajaj's impact on the Indian landscape is immeasurable, touching the lives of millions every day. Bajaj auto rickshaws are a ubiquitous sight on Indian roads, ferrying countless numbers of passengers. Bajaj two-wheelers, often a young Indian's first vehicle, symbolize freedom and progress. Bajaj Finserv, under Rahul's aegis, became a cornerstone for the financial well-being of the middle class, offering them access to consumer finance, wealth management, and health and life security. Rahul's visionary leadership and strategic foresight in steering the Bajaj Group have crafted an enduring legacy that resonates with hundreds of millions across India.

But Rahul's impact on India goes way beyond his leadership of the Bajaj Group. As a vocal leader of the business community, as the two-time president of CII, in 1979 and in 1999, and as a member of the Rajya Sabha from 2006 to 2010, Rahul played a critical role in shaping the liberalization of the Indian economy. While he was one of the early voices calling for liberalization, championing the opening of India to global companies and investors, he was also a fierce advocate of domestic business, playing a leading role in building modern India. In recognition of these contributions, he was given the CII President's Lifetime Achievement Award in 2017, the Government of India's Padma Bhushan award in 2001 and the HBS Alumni Achievement Award.

More than his business acumen, it was Rahul's human touch that set him apart from the rest. He nurtured a culture of mentorship and progressive leadership at Bajaj Auto and Bajaj Finserv, ensuring that his pioneering spirit would live on through the next generation of leaders. His approach to business was not just about profits but also about people – about making a difference in the lives of employees, customers and the broader community. As a father, friend and mentor, Rahul's legacy extends beyond the boardroom to the countless lives he touched with his generosity, his passion for excellence and his unwavering commitment to making a positive impact. Rahul Bajaj, in his journey, mirrored the aspirations and achievements of a rising India, leaving behind a legacy that will inspire and guide many future generations.

KRISHNA PALEPU, *Ross Graham Walker Professor of Business Administration, Harvard Business School*

Preface

Some people cannot be contained in a book. Especially a person like Rahul Bajaj.

This is not a book about Rahul Bajaj, the outspoken Goliath who, till recently, straddled the Indian business world. It is about Rahul, the man, as he lives on in the memories of those who knew him well. Since the popular narrative does not do justice to his multihued personality, we decided to ask people who knew him well to write their personal stories and anecdotes about him.

This book does not intend to be a commentary on Rahul Bajaj. Instead, these pages are meant to give a glimpse of the man behind the name and image, and to celebrate him through the memories he left behind.

The idea of compiling people's recollections of him seemed like a good one until we actually started making a list of possible contributors. It was then that the complexity of the task hit us. Rahul had rubbed some people the wrong way. But there were many more who were fond of him, who felt they owed him acknowledgement and who wanted to tell the world that he was much more than his public persona. To have all of them contribute would have resulted in a tome, which is why a shortlist was created, which kept growing as work on the book progressed. Eventually, we closed at seventy-nine contributors, including Rajiv Bajaj, Rahul's elder son, who has written a very personal poem. This poem was shared by Rahul a day after he received it from Rajiv.

The contributions poured in; reading them was like getting to know Rahul all over again. The anecdotes showed him in so many different lights – sometimes obdurate, usually generous, but always patriotic and never ever a walkover.

This book captures his multiple dimensions – from his passionate commitment to everything he did, to his wide-ranging interests (and friends), his support to institutions he cared for and his philanthropic activities.

This is a tribute to our friend Rahul, who was a unique person, a role model to the world, who believed in India. He was an ambassador for India internationally long before it was in fashion. His values and ethics in business were extraordinary, and he was fearless in expressing his beliefs. It was for these reasons, and several more, that we wanted to put this book together. It is our 'thank you' to the Rahul Bajaj that we had the honour to know over several decades.

TARUN DAS and KIRAN PASRICHA

James Abraham

I first met Mr Rahul Bajaj after becoming a fellow of Ananta Aspen Centre's India Leadership Initiative (ILI). We met in his office in Pune, where we talked about this new fellowship and what he expected from the fellows.

'Fearlessness!' he said. 'We need leaders in India who are fearless. Fearless to chase ambitious dreams, fearless to stand for what they think is right, fearless to do what is necessary for this country.' His voice boomed across the office. I grew up in the church, so I'm used to sermons from the pulpit, which are academic and lack personal risk. This was different. Mr Bajaj lived by the creed he was preaching.

During our board meetings, Mr Bajaj would pay special attention to the growth of the fellowship, and particularly what the fellows were doing in service to India. At a critical moment, unprompted, he stepped in and provided the necessary funds to provide for a decade of stability and growth. Asked why, he said, 'I have seen what they are doing, and I have faith in the fellows, if we have enough of them, [they] can be a force for good for our country.'

As a principal donor to the fellowship, Mr Bajaj had the choice to name it, and he chose his father's name, Kamalnayan Bajaj. He said, 'For me, my father was the first fellow. He was successful in taking our business through troubling times. More than that, he risked his life and fortune during our country's struggle for independence. I hope the fellows, like him, will risk themselves for this country.'

Our fellowship is now called the Kamalnayan Bajaj Fellowship, a reminder of the fearless service that is needed. Though I only knew Mr Bajaj for a short time, his lessons in fearlessness, faith and service resonate through the fellowship, as it does through my own life.

JAMES ABRAHAM, *Founding Partner, Boston Consulting Group, India, and entrepreneur in renewable energy and climate technologies*

Anu Aga

Tarun Das, who started the Confederation of Indian Industry (CII) and later brought Aspen to India, requested me to write about my experiences with Rahul and I readily agreed. Though Rahul and I both lived in Pune, I had not met him except on a few social occasions, and we did not know each other personally. It was only when I became active in the CII that I came to know him well. Though, in many ways, we were very different people, we admired and liked each other very much.

In 2002, when the Gujarat riots took place, I was the chairperson of the CII Western Region, and Gujarat came under me. I openly condemned the atrocities. Rahul took me aside at a party and said I had done my bit and for the sake of my company and family I should not say any more and that he would speak and write about this cause. He kept his promise. This was one of the many occasions when I experienced Rahul's warmth and care.

Anyone who knew Rahul would know of his candour and of his being unafraid to speak his mind. Tact was not his strong point, but in the corporate world very few have the courage to go against the establishment, and hence his frankness was a breath of fresh air.

Rahul was well known all over the world, and of course across India, for being a very successful, ethical and philanthropic businessman. He came from an illustrious business family that took part in our freedom struggle. He did an MBA from

Harvard University, married a lovely and beautiful lady named Rupa, and they had three wonderful children.

He was very active in the CII and was the only member who was asked to be president for two terms, and he was a very effective president. He will be remembered for being very vocal and for making each meeting interesting and fun.

I am not going to elaborate on his various achievements but would like to talk about how I experienced him as a friend whom I knew for twenty-two years. I will miss his openness, his frankness, his generosity and kindness, his warmth and care, his zest for life and his loud, argumentative nature.

Rahul and I enjoyed a few things in common, and yet there were areas where we were very different. Rahul loved to go to Davos and was a very regular visitor there. I, on the other hand, was not at all enamoured by Davos, and though I had an opportunity to attend, I stayed away.

Rahul was elected to the Rajya Sabha and very much enjoyed his term in Parliament, and after his retirement always went to the Central Hall of Parliament to visit his friends when he was in Delhi. I was nominated to the Rajya Sabha for six years and did not enjoy the experience. And since my term ended I have never entered Parliament. Rahul very much enjoyed his two terms of being president of the CII. When I was offered the CII presidentship, I declined it.

Rahul invited me to be a member of the Jamnalal Bajaj Foundation council of advisors that gives annual awards to outstanding people in India and abroad who follow Gandhian values. It was then that I realized what an enormous amount of philanthropy has been done by his illustrious family. He personally took a very active interest in the matters of the foundation and attended every single meeting to select the awardees. Every year, he would meticulously plan the main awards function in Mumbai.

Being Rahul, he could invite anybody in India or abroad to be the chief guest, whether the invitee was a senior politician or a religious guru. I am not aware of anyone who refused his invitation.

The council had a process by which each subcommittee went through the nominees and selected a few to be brought to the council meeting. At one of the council meetings, a member suggested that a nominee who had not been vetted by the subcommittee should be considered because he had been nominated by the governor of the state. Rahul was willing to concede to the request, but I strongly objected because we were not following the laid-down procedure. There was a heated argument over whether exceptions should be made. I felt that if we did so, it would be a mockery to have a subcommittee. To Rahul's credit, he saw my logic and agreed to defer consideration of the candidate for the award for the next year.

I have in the past asked for his support for the NGOs I am involved with, and he has always been very generous. He found it difficult to show his soft side, but behind his loud talk and objections there was a caring, warm heart. He was the founding trustee of the Ananta Aspen Centre, and along with Tarun Das helped it to flourish as a great institution that encourages leadership. At Ananta Aspen too, I was touched by Rahul's generosity in supporting the Young Leaders Programme and the Kamalnayan Bajaj Fellowship.

Rahul was a fun-loving person with a great sense of humour. He would express opinions without mincing words, but he gave his friends the same freedom to differ from him, and sometimes he conceded defeat too. If Rahul was in a meeting, you could be assured it would not be boring, since he would liven it up.

I recall an incident that is typical of my friend. I had invited him for a small sit-down lunch at my house. He was the first guest to arrive (he was never late for any event). He asked to know who else had been invited, and when I mentioned a particular name he said to me, 'Don't you know we are no longer friends?' My response was that I was not aware of this and now that I had invited both of them, he should behave himself and not make any rude comments! Rahul was civil, as requested, but totally ignored that other guest.

Rahul's birthday falls on 10 June and I have fond memories of his birthday celebrations, plus of the annual winter party at his house at Akurdi. Rahul, like me, enjoyed dancing and we had a lot of fun.

I will cherish these memories. I miss my friend and I pray that he is happy wherever he may be.

ANU AGA, *former Chairperson, Thermax Ltd.*

Michael Alpert

Introduction

I knew Rahul for over sixty years, and my wife Sandy and I were very close to him. We regard ourselves as part of the Bajaj family, which we have remained close to, up to and after Rahul's untimely death. I feel that I have lost a brother.

We all know that Rahul was an Indian patriot; a very successful Indian industrialist who was honest and outspoken about what he believed in and built, who led an incredibly successful business group; and who was a philanthropist who cared for all Indians and served in many roles when called upon by senior-level government leaders to do so. I could go on and on. However, we all have read many of the tributes paid to him by Indian government leaders, Indian industrialists and many others. All these tributes recognize his amazing character, the energy he brought and the contributions he made to his country, his businesses and his many friends.

However, I want to focus on Rahul as a cherished friend and as a person who loved his family and could provide, when necessary, advice to keep the family together. He was proud of Rajiv, as he built Bajaj Auto, and of Sanjiv, when he started and built Bajaj Finserv, the pillars of the Bajaj Group of companies. I was impressed that he let each of them manage their own companies, even when, as chairman, he disagreed with some of their decisions. In the following account, I relive many memories and stories from our sixty years of close friendship.

Harvard Business School (HBS)

I remember the first time I met Rahul. It was in September 1962, and I was with my room-mate Tom Beach. Our room shared a common bathroom with three other rooms at the McCullough dorm. We heard an unusual noise in the bathroom, and Tom and I both got up to find out what was happening. The noise was Rahul, with his unmistakable strong voice.

We introduced ourselves, and that was the beginning of a sixty-year friendship. I spent time with Rahul and learned that he was a vegetarian and that his wife, Rupa, was coming to stay with him during the latter part of the year. The first-year class was divided into sections. Tom and I were in section A and Rahul in section F. Even though we did not spend time in classes together, our friendship continued to develop and we did discuss some cases together.

When Rupa arrived, Rahul moved out of the dorms and into an off-campus apartment. As I remember, we didn't see as much of each other as before, but somehow our friendship and respect for each other started to blossom. I do remember having several meals with Rahul and Rupa in their apartment. At one of these occasions, Rahul gave me something to taste, with Rupa looking on disapprovingly. It was an incredibly hot pepper, which burned my mouth, and I had since always been careful when he offered me anything to taste. During this time, I also got to know Rupa better and learned how much she influenced Rahul.

After the first year at HBS, Rahul and Rupa took a tour around the US and we met again at the beginning of our second year. The classes were no longer divided into sections, and thus Rahul and I did have the opportunity to go to some classes together. I remember that we both took a final exam in a course called 'management of new enterprises'. The case was about a decision as to whether to buy a radio station. When we both walked out of the exam, Rahul turned to me and said, 'I wonder which idiot did buy the radio station.' I said, 'You are looking at that idiot.' In the end, we both got the same high grade!

This is another example of how HBS teaches you to think. It was more about the assumptions you make, about understanding the facts of the case and about the logic of your thinking. Rahul and I always joked around together, and when we met Rahul's friends I told them that I got Rahul through HBS.

At our graduation, I met Rahul's father (Kamalnayan Bajaj), a very distinguished man who was a member of the Indian Parliament, and a disciple of Gandhi who was imprisoned during the Indian Independence movement. Rahul's grandfather was Jamnalal Bajaj who, I learned, was considered Gandhi's fifth son. Rahul always considered both Shishir, his brother, and his cousins, Madhur, Niraj and Shekhar, as his brothers. Over the years, I became Rahul's fifth brother. After our graduation, my parents invited Rahul, Rupa and Rahul's father to our home in New York for a celebratory dinner. As I have said many times, one of the most rewarding parts of my experience at HBS was my friendship with Rahul.

My first trip to India (May 1965)

After my graduation from HBS, I began my two-year military obligation as an officer in the army. At the first possible opportunity, I took a military flight in May 1965 to visit Rahul and Rupa. The flight, which originated from Charleston in South Carolina, landed in New Delhi after stops in Spain, Saudi Arabia and Pakistan. Rahul had forgotten to tell me that May is one of the hottest months in India, just prior to the monsoon.

When I got off from the rear of the plane, I thought the pilot had forgotten to turn off the engines since there was a lot of hot air blowing on me. I then realized the engines were off and it was the hot Delhi air that I was encountering. I remember going to the Ashoka Hotel and jumping into the pool, hoping it would cool me off, but it was like jumping into a warm bath. Honestly, I have forgotten how I arrived at Rahul's home in Akurdi (Pune). It is in close proximity to the Bajaj Auto factory.

This was the beginning of a wonderful ten-day stay with Rahul and Rupa. There are several memories of this trip that stand out to me. Next to their original house in Akurdi was a tennis court. I asked Rahul if he wanted to play, and he agreed. It was one of the shortest sets I have ever played.

Rahul was a good player, but every five minutes one of his secretaries would appear on the court asking him to sign or review some papers. We then decided not to continue. I think this was the last tennis match Rahul played. Subsequently, the court disappeared and it was replaced by an area where children could play cricket. Another of my favourite memories was a trip to the Gir forest, a national park and wildlife sanctuary, at Rahul's suggestion. Rahul took time off from work to join us and we had a wonderful time. I still have a picture of the two of us at the Gir forest, Rahul with binoculars around his neck. I ate with Rahul and Rupa, and after a particularly wonderful meal, which I thought consisted of veal cutlet, I told Rupa that she really didn't have to do this for me. Rupa then told me that it was a vegetable cutlet! It is amazing how tasty a variety of Indian spices can be. I had ten days of vegetarian meals and didn't miss beef or chicken at all.

During part of the time that I visited, Rahul took me to his office and to the manufacturing plant for scooters and three-wheelers. We had a good time going over his current business, which, due to government regulations, had an eight-year backlog in orders at that time. I told him we never had a case at HBS showing the difficulty of managing a company with this long a backlog. We both had a good laugh.

Rahul then arranged for me to visit the Ellora and Ajanta caves accompanied by a friend of his. We drove a relatively long distance to the caves, one of which is famous for a small village built into solid rock and the other for its cave paintings. It was extremely hot (114 degrees F/45 degrees Celsius), but the car was air-conditioned and we had adequate water. However, outside the car it was stifling hot.

At our last stop at the Ajanta caves, I took a bottle of water and asked the merchant selling drinks to please put it in ice so it would be cold when I finished the tour. Unfortunately, he did not do this, and while I was in the cave I was dreaming of a cold glass of water. When I got out, I was so thirsty I made a big mistake and asked the merchant to give me a glass of ice. I then poured the water over the ice. It tasted so good. You will see the implications of this later. We drove back to Akurdi, and during the drive I was so exhausted from the heat that when we got to Rahul's home, I drank a six-pack Coca Cola, which I had brought from the Army PX.

As I was recovering from this trip, Rahul told me that his uncle, Ramkrishna, had arranged for me to escort Miss India to an Indian wedding the next day. I was very excited, but during the trip from Akurdi to Mumbai, I started to feel bad. When we arrived in Mumbai, Rahul and I had lunch with Miss India 1965, Persis Khambatta. She was beautiful, charming and very nice. It was a memorable lunch and all I could think about was escorting her to the wedding. But after lunch I started to feel even worse. Finally, in the afternoon, I told Rahul I could not go with him. Rahul went to the wedding with Persis, and I stayed in Rahul's apartment in Mumbai. He had one of his staff staying close by me, and finally I asked him to give me a thermometer. I could not believe it when I read that my temperature was 105.5 degrees fahrenheit. I had the staff member call Rahul. He immediately returned from the wedding with Persis and a doctor. I was sick in every possible way, and Rahul and Persis stayed with me until the medication started to work. So, instead of me attending an elaborate Indian wedding with one of the most beautiful women I had ever seen, I ended up with Persis putting cool compresses on my forehead. She later played Lt. Ilia in the feature film *Star Trek: The Motion Picture*. Unfortunately, she died at the age of fifty in Mumbai. Rahul was with me the entire time until I felt better and was able to get out of bed and walk around the apartment. This trip with Rahul and Rupa further strengthened the bond we had had at HBS and served as another foundation of our sixty-year friendship.

1965–1974: the transition

During this period, my two-year army obligation was completed and I took a job at Pan American World Airways working for the treasurer, who was the son of Juan Trippe, the founder of Pan Am. While Rahul was successfully building Bajaj Auto, I was starting my business career. As we both focused on our careers, there were times when we didn't speak for months together. However, the connection we had remained, and when we did speak it seemed as though we had just spoken with each other the previous day.

During this time, Rahul and Rupa began raising their family. Rajiv was born in 1966, Sanjiv in 1969 and Sunaina in 1971. I followed them as they married, had their own children and attained success in meeting their personal and business objectives. It was during this time that I was introduced to other members of the Bajaj family. I remember meeting Ramkrishna and Vimla Bajaj, Rahul's uncle and aunt. At that time, Ram was at the forefront of social change.

During this period, Rahul's brother Shishir and his wife Minakshi, along with Rahul's cousin (Ramkrishna's son) Shekhar, and his wife Kiran, came to New York and studied at New York University. We kept in touch with them during their studies, and when Ram visited them in New York, Sandy and I took them on a tour to see the fall colours in New England. I still have pictures of all of them in our den at our New York apartment. We saw Sunaina and Manish when they visited New York. We also appreciated the time spent by Niraj, another of Rahul's cousins, and his wife Minal, when they hosted a good friend of mine who was visiting Mumbai.

In 1974, I took Sandy on her first trip to India. On this trip, we also visited Rome and then Israel. We were fascinated by Israel and decided to stay another two or three days. I knew Rahul was expecting us earlier, so I sent him a telegram, which he never received. When we finally landed, there was a car for us, and it took us to our hotel. We arrived very early in the morning, at about 4–5 a.m., and were very tired.

At around 8 a.m., I received a phone call from Rahul, whose first words to me were, 'What the hell is the matter with you? I sent a car every night to pick you up!' At that point I knew nothing had changed between us. Rahul arranged for our transportation to Akurdi (Pune), to his home, and we stayed with them during the entire course of our trip, except during the side visits we made. During this time, we met the rest of his family. We took many side trips from Akurdi to Pune and Mumbai. Rahul and his family made sure that we saw not only the lifestyle of the wealthy but the poverty of the poor and the challenges that India faced in moving from a third-world country to where it is today. The highlight of our trip was India, and Sandy's love for Rahul, Rupa and the rest of the Bajaj family and for India began on this trip.

Highlights of the ensuing years (1974 onwards)

As you can tell from the previous sections, I have spent a lot of time describing the foundation of the sixty-year friendship between me and Rahul and why it endured all these years. As I am sure you are aware, it is difficult to remember the chronology of the events of the next forty-eight years. However, there are certain memories that I will never forget. I will highlight many of them. Some might be out of chronological order, but all were memorable.

Four Indian weddings: Sandy and I had the opportunity to attend the weddings of Rajiv and Deepa; Sanjiv and Shefali; Sunaina and Manish; and Sargam and Adi. Rajiv and Deepa were married on 18 December 1994; Sanjiv and Shefali were married the next day, on 19 December 1994. Sunaina and Manish were married on 29 December 1995, and Sargam and Adi on 28 December 2006. Sandy and I were fortunate to attend all four weddings. At either Rajiv's or Sanjiv's pre-wedding celebrations, Rahul helped Tom and me 'break into' the henna ceremonies for the women. We had a fun time, and both Tom and I got henna 'tattoos' on our arms, and Suzy Beach and Sandy both had beautiful henna 'tattoos' on their feet.

During the weddings and the receptions, we met many wonderful Indian families and we still stay in touch today. After the back-to-back weddings, there was a fabulous celebration at the Bombay Turf Club. I was in touch with Rahul before each wedding and he helped us to arrange tours to places in India, some of which we had not visited.

These included Agra (the Taj Mahal), New Delhi, Jaipur, Udaipur, Jodhpur, Jaisalmer, the Thar desert, Pune, Bangalore, Chennai (formerly Madras), Mysore, Goa and other places whose names I cannot remember. Rahul arranged for us to stay at wonderful hotels, but one of the best we ever stayed at was the Umaid Bhawan Palace in Jodhpur. During these tours, I spoke with Rahul many times. While we were in Jaipur we rode an elephant, and after this adventure Sandy's leg was very swollen. We called Rahul, who immediately responded and he sent us to a hospital which was very different from any we had seen. Rahul personally talked to the doctor many times, and after these calls Rahul told us it was safe to go back to our hotel. We met many Indian people and families at these weddings and on our travels. This increased our love for not only the Bajaj family but India too.

Celebrating New Year's Eve in India: Since all the weddings described above were in December, Sandy and I spent New Year's Eve at least three times in India. I remember one of them, when Rahul arranged for a group of us to be driven at least an hour or more, heading up on what I thought was a mountain road to a beautiful resort setting. I think it was a relatively small group, including some of our HBS classmates and friends of Rahul and Rupa. The setting was ideal, and everyone had a great time. I specifically remember Rahul and Rupa on the dance floor, moving like they were at least twenty years younger. It was a memorable evening, as well as the drive home, arriving early morning on 1 January.

On another occasion, we celebrated New Year's Eve in Pune. Rahul, as usual, made the arrangements. It was a joyous evening for all of us. When we were not together, Rahul and I had our own traditions of celebrating New Year's. Sandy and I typically went to the opera on New Year's Eve and then had a late dinner celebration. When we got home, and before we went to bed, I always called Rahul to wish him a happy and healthy New Year, when he and Rupa would be having a late breakfast or brunch on New Year's Day. Now that Rahul is not with us any more, I have continued that tradition, but now I call Sanjiv.

Medical issues that brought us even closer: On 6 June 1996, Rahul had a prostatectomy at Johns Hopkins Hospital in Baltimore. Prior to his operation, Rahul and I had many discussions. He selected a renowned surgeon, and I spoke to the doctor several times to learn about the surgery and the recovery, and helped Rahul prepare for Rupa and other family members accompanying her to Baltimore. Sandy and I were in Baltimore every day prior to the operation to help (it was a short drive from Washington DC to Baltimore), as also on the day of the surgery and after. The surgery was successful, and the family stayed with Rahul, with some returning to India after some time while Rupa and some others were with him until he was ready to fly back to India.

When Rahul was ready to leave the apartment they had rented, we took a short walk around the area. Rahul had to pick up a prescription at a CVS pharmacy. I went into the store with Rahul and the pharmacist looked at the prescription and at Rahul and said, 'Are you the real Rahul Bajaj?' This started a thirty-minute conversation between the two. It was so typical of Rahul, to treat everyone the same no matter the position or class of the person to whom he was speaking. It reminded me of one of my favourite poems, 'If', by Rudyard Kipling. Here is a section that I think exemplifies Rahul: 'If you can talk with crowds and keep your virtue, Or walk with Kings – nor lose the common touch.'

Not many people have this wonderful trait, and Rahul is one who did; Chuck Dolan, chairman and founder of Cablevision and my former boss, is the other – both extraordinary individuals. Rahul and Chuck met several times while I was still at Cablevision, and they were glad they met each other.

The second set of medical issues revolved around Rupa. As many of you who knew Rahul are aware, he spent a lot of time on the phone doing extensive research to determine the best solution for Rupa. Together they decided that the best option for Rupa was the Cleveland Clinic. On 28 October 2004, Rupa had an aortic valve replacement. Sandy and I travelled to Cleveland to be with Rahul and his family.

Rahul was extremely worried and nervous before the operation. I remember standing with him and holding his hand as Rupa was taken to the operating room. Rahul and the rest of us were so relieved when we learned the operation was successful. Rahul was very happy with the result, and as Rupa recovered Sandy and I flew back to Washington. This was another indication of the soft side of Rahul. In business, he was strong and tough, but he had a heart of gold and a very soft side for family and close friends. For those he loved, he was always there to help them, whether it was a serious medical issue or something minor. His primary concern was, as always, for Rupa, his children and grandchildren. For example, I remember something Rajiv said about Rahul leaving his work and being with the family at a veterinarian's by the side of their beloved family dog.

1999 cruise on the Celebrity Millennium: This trip was an enjoyable adventure! Rahul invited Sandy and me as well as Tom and Suzy Beach and at least twenty of his friends to join him on this cruise. The ship was big and could accommodate 2,000 guests. However, as a group we stayed somewhat together. I think Rahul arranged for an Indian chef and we all ate dinner together. One night, there was a formal dinner where Rahul and Rupa arranged for the four of us to wear Indian clothes. Sandy and Suzy were dressed in beautiful saris, and I remember that when they came to dress Sandy they had to start from the hallway to wrap the sari around her (our room was not that long). Tom and I were wearing white Indian jackets with the appropriate pants. I still have pictures of us from that night in our living room.

On one of the evenings, Rahul had rented a room where we all got together for drinks and appetizers. I cannot remember whether or not we had dinner in that room, but I do remember that a group of Rahul's friends put on a skit. It was very funny, but the highlight of the evening was when one of his friends imitated Rahul's unique character and way of speaking and organizing things. He did a great job and at times we were almost convinced it was Rahul. Everyone there had a wonderful time.

One day, Tom and I went with Rahul to the spa and we tried to get him to work out. Those of you who knew Rahul will not be surprised to learn that our efforts were not successful. However, Rahul did inquire from some of the female attendants about various massages and facials. Tom and I were laughing very hard while he was speaking to the attendants – in a way that was uniquely Rahul. He finally chose a facial. I think everyone in the spa knew Rahul by the end of the cruise.

For many of us, the highlight of our various ports of call was Alexandria in Egypt. While working for a Saudi Sheikh, I had already been to Cairo to visit the Pyramids, the Sphinx and the Cairo museum. After that visit I thought to myself that I wanted Sandy to have the same experiences.

We all travelled in several buses to Cairo, and we all took many pictures of ourselves riding on camels in front of the Pyramids and the Sphinx. After this adventure, we went to the Cairo museum. Most of us thought that it was one of the best museums we had ever visited. After the visit, we all got into our buses and headed back to the ship. When we arrived, the locals had put up stalls selling souvenirs, carved wooden boxes and other items. Unfortunately, Sandy wanted to buy something for her parents but wanted to change first. This was the beginning of the next adventure.

I waited and waited for Sandy to come down to the souvenir stalls and was getting concerned that she was not showing up. So I decided to go to the pier to get a better view to see if Sandy was coming down to the stalls. I started to get a little annoyed that she was taking so long. I started walking away from the ship, and suddenly it happened. It felt as if the sidewalk had disappeared and I was going into a free fall. I then found myself hitting the water between the ship and the pier. When I realized what had happened, I started to shimmy up with my back against the ship and my feet on the pier.

During this time, one of Rahul's friends called him and said, 'Your crazy American friend has jumped from the ship into the water.' Rahul went into action and called the emergency team, and before I could do anything to come out of the water myself, there were sirens, firemen and ship emergency crew trying to help me by sending ropes down and pulling me up, I was finally on dry land, and aside from being soaked in the bad-tasting water, I felt okay at the time, but did not fully realize what had happened. The crew immediately took me to the ship's clinic.

I saw Sandy and asked her why she hadn't come down earlier. She said she was about to when there was an emergency and everyone had been stopped from leaving the ship. I told her that I was the emergency, and she then followed me to the ship's clinic. Before they were able to give me a tetanus shot and other medications, someone from the crew came in and said there was an important call for me. The call was from Rahul, who wanted to know of my condition. When I told him I was all right except for wet clothes and sneakers, he was relieved and gave me a short lecture, of the sort one would only get from a very close friend. When Sandy and I got dressed for dinner, we met Rahul and the rest of our group. When they knew I was fine, I received a lot of good-natured grief from all of them. However, most of Rahul's friends remembered this incident for a long time, and at one of the New Year celebrations in Pune, when I took a walk in front of a small water fountain, three of Rahul's friends escorted me away from the fountain so I wouldn't jump in!

HBS Alumni Achievement Award: In 2005, HBS announced that Rahul was one of five recipients of its Alumni Achievement Award. This is one of HBS's most important honours. The recipients are chosen for their significant contributions to their companies and communities while upholding the highest standards in everything they do. The five award recipients were to be honoured at HBS during a class reunion. This gave me another chance to get together not only with Rahul but also with many members of his family who attended this event. Tom, Sandy and I attended this event and had a wonderful time with Rahul, his family and friends.

Other trips to India to visit Rahul: Aside from the four weddings and our 1974 visit, I made at least seven more visits to India, mostly with Sandy. One or two of these were short business trips where I went alone, thanks to Rahul's connections. During these trips we always stayed in Rahul and Rupa's beautiful new home. We were also able to see Rahul's grandchildren growing up. I can honestly say that I cannot remember the details of all our visits, but there are a few memories that stand out.

I visited Rahul in his office many times. The office was large and impressive, with a very big portrait of Rahul behind his desk. Computers were just becoming standard office equipment, and I told Rahul that I was impressed with the computer in his office and asked if he knew how to use it. He said, 'Of course, I do.' I said, 'Okay, show me.' Rahul immediately pressed a button and Mohan arrived and turned on the computer, and we both laughed.

The next memory relates to a prank I developed with the help of Rajiv and Sanjiv. I asked to have someone take a photo of the three of us, with me in the middle. We then blew up the photo and had it framed like Rahul's portrait and put it next to it in his office. Under Rahul's portrait we wrote 'The Present', and under the photo of the three of us we wrote 'The Future'. When Rahul returned to the office, he laughed to see it, but with appointments scheduled in his office, our picture did not have a long time for viewing.

During many of our trips, Rahul showed us not only his factory in Akurdi (Pune) but also the newer plants nearby. We visited a hospital that the Bajaj family had built in Aurangabad. We also learned much more about Rahul's family and the philanthropic initiatives they undertook to help the poor in India. I also had opportunities to ride the Bajaj scooters and motorcycles. I wasn't very good with the motorcycle, so Rahul made sure someone was around since he didn't want to lose a motorcycle or to abet in any injuries that might occur.

When some of our classmates visited India, we went to a Gandhi museum and Rahul had a guide who gave us a wonderful tour and explanation of the objects and photos in the museum. We also went to a Bajaj showroom, where we learned more about the scooters and motorcycle distribution chain.

During all these visits, Rahul and I had many deep conversations about personal issues regarding our families. I remember the time when he disagreed with some of Rajiv's decisions, but after speaking to Rajiv about his point of view he decided to let Rajiv implement his recommendations. Further, he decided that Sanjiv would lead a separate company, basically taking over the financing part of the Bajaj three-wheelers, scooters and motorcycles. Many Indians were not able to pay the full price of the vehicles upfront, and Bajaj Auto provided them financing. It was the beginning of Bajaj Finserv. As many of you may know, Sanjiv was incredibly successful in building this business. Rajiv created the strategic business plan for Bajaj Auto, which focused on not only the efficiency of the manufacturing process but also considered the changes in the market and made preparations to face additional competitors who were building small cars or electric cars. Thus, Bajaj Auto and Bajaj Finserv are now the primary wealth centres of the Bajaj Group.

Rahul and I also had many discussions about my growing consulting business. On one of his visits to New York, he did not like the temporary apartment in which we were living as I transitioned from Washington DC to working directly for Chuck Dolan. Rahul made his opinion very clear to me, and Sandy and I visited many apartments and found one we liked and purchased – a co-op at 910 Fifth Avenue. It was a long process to get approval from the co-op board for the two of us, and then the rest of the long-drawn-out procedure. During this whole process, Rahul and I were in constant touch and he was very involved in learning more about the financing, the long process of getting approval from the co-op board for the architect's design and then the six-month wait to get approval from New York City's Department of Buildings and Department of Landmarks before we could start our renovations. Rahul continually showed interest until we moved in. In the end we had a wonderful apartment, and Rahul, who was shown photos of it, was very happy too. Unfortunately, in early 2019, Rahul's doctors wanted him to limit his travels.

Other remembrances: I had also developed a close relationship with Sanjiv and Shefali. They decided to take Siddhant and Sanjali to Disney World when Sanjali was four or five years old. We had a wonderful time there. We bought Sanjali a princess dress, and she loved it and looked beautiful in it. Since then, Sanjiv and I have a very good relationship, and whenever he is in the New York area we get together for a meal or just a quick visit. When his entire family was in New York, we spent time with all of them and went to dinner and a Ranger playoff hockey game. Siddhant loved the action of the game and compared it with soccer. I remember a typical email from Rahul to me: 'Congratulations on the BMW. You kept it a secret from me. However, I have ways to find out things about you.'

My mother, who had just turned eighty, married for a second time. My dad had passed away in 1982. It was so nice to see the happy newly-weds. They decided they wanted to take a trip to the Orient and see Hong Kong, Japan and other destinations. I told them that if they were going that far, they needed to visit Rahul in India. My mom knew Rahul and didn't want to be a distraction to him. I told her that the Bajajs are family and that I had already spoken to Rahul, who had arranged a ten-day itinerary in India for them with three or four days at his home. Their friends thought they were crazy to go to India, but with a little persuasion from me, they included India in their trip. The bottom line – they loved their India trip, and especially their stay with Rahul and Rupa. After they left Akurdi (Pune), Rahul called my mom every night to make sure they were taken care of. When they got back to the US and their friends asked them about the highlight of their trip, and they said it was India. The hospitality and love the Bajajs showed my mom and Barney was extraordinary and shows the wonderful warmth and soft side of Rahul.

Baseball: Rahul could never understand how someone as old as me could play competitive baseball, especially in the seventy-five-plus age bracket. When we were together and I showed him one of the championship rings I had won, he was surprised. A typical email I received from Rahul said, 'Though it appears tough, I send you my very best wishes for the playoffs and, very difficult as it may seem, for the Championship rounds on Saturday.'

FORB (Friends of Rahul Bajaj): During May–June, Rahul typically flew to the New York or Boston area to participate in the board meetings of the international New York Stock Exchange as well as in meetings with the Brookings Institution. At these times, a group of us would get together and spend some time with Rahul. It became a regular tradition. Initially, our group would go with Rahul to domestic locations such as the Greenbrier Resort and The Sanctuary at Kiawah Island Golf Resort. Finally, Rahul suggested that we use his plane to visit places in Europe.

This group included Sandy and me; Tom and Suzy Beach; Drs Dilip and Smita Kittur, and Satish and Kinna Shah. In June 2017, Satish named the group Friends of Rahul Bajaj (FORB). Satish then started a private chat group on WhatsApp with the eight of us, plus Rahul. It took some of the older members of our group, like Tom and me, some time to get used to this. But I just looked at the FORB chats on WhatsApp and couldn't believe the interactions we all had from 2017 through to the present day. All of us had our own special time with Rahul, but it was our love for Rahul that had brought us together. Satish had shirts and caps made for all of us with FORB monograms. We all regarded Rahul as our leader, but Rahul in one of his emails said, 'I am a friend, not a leader.'

On one of our international trips, we visited Positano in Italy and stayed at the beautiful San Pietro hotel there. We used this as our base while we toured many beautiful sites on the curvy Amalfi Drive from Sorrento to Positano. We also explored Amalfi and Ravello as well as other interesting cities, whose names I forget.

In 2016, Rahul also arranged for a trip for our group to Lugano in Switzerland. We stayed at a beautiful hotel, the Villa Castagnola, overlooking Lake Lugano. We took a sightseeing trip on the lake, and the next day Rahul arranged for a magnificent trip near Lugano. I have no idea of the names of the places we visited, but we took a car up a mountain trail passing some magnificent scenery, including the gorge where a scene from a James Bond movie had been shot. Over the gorge, the daredevil in the movie had bungee-jumped off the bridge. After this stop, Rahul took us further up the mountain to a beautiful stop with a view of a waterfall. There was a restaurant there, where we all had a delicious lunch. Then we headed back. Please note that Rahul had been there before, as well as at our next stop, Lake Como. Again, this was the person that Rahul was – enjoying being with friends and sharing experiences with them. There is no one like Rahul!

At Lake Como, a magnificent spot near Milan, Rahul knew the manager of the hotel, Villa d'Este. It was one of the best hotels we have ever stayed at. We had a great lunch at the hotel, explored other towns around Como and went to the city square. I found out that La Bohème was playing at La Scala in Milan, one of the most famous opera houses in the world.

I tried my best to convince Rahul and the rest of the FORB to join us. I told Rahul he needed culture and would like it. Unfortunately, when Rahul said he did not want to go, the rest decided to stay with him. Sandy and I then went ahead and had a wonderful time in Milan. We had dinner at a restaurant near the opera house and we saw a magnificent performance of La Bohème. It had been on our bucket list, and we loved the ambience of La Scala, and the music and singing in the opera. We went back to Villa d'Este, caught up with Rahul, and the nine of us had a great last day together.

Unfortunately, Rahul's health was failing, and he had a stroke on 15 January 2019. At that time his doctors advised him that at least for a year or so he should not travel abroad and that he should restrict his travels only to Mumbai and Pune. This was the last time I saw him in person, but we always stayed in touch by email and phone.

The twilight era

We missed Rahul at our fifty-fifth reunion at HBS. Sandy and I, John and Caroline Trask, sent Rahul an email telling him that it wasn't the same without him. His response was, 'So am I very much.' In March of 2021, Rahul wrote to me saying, 'I am trying to do my best to do some exercise and walk for a few minutes. I can only hope that I can increase the duration of my walk.' Rahul told me that the tricuspid valve in his heart was leaking. I tried to convince him to at least talk to an expert about it and even gave him the number of a doctor I reached at the Cleveland Clinic who was very well known and knowledgeable about such a situation, but Rahul, as he could be, was very stubborn. I sent him additional information. In March 2021, I told him to at least get a second opinion. He said he had already got one and that all the doctors available to him were outstanding and that some of them were his friends and were fully aware of what was happening in the US, including the Cleveland Clinic.

I knew then that Rahul had made up his mind. I never brought it up again. I spoke to Rahul on his birthday, 10 June 2021, and we also exchanged emails. We were constantly in touch via telephone until the very end. When he could not talk, I spoke with Sanjiv, who gave me constant updates and relayed my messages to Rahul.

My best friend, my brother, passed away on 12 February 2022. His life was extraordinary, given all his accomplishments. To me, having had a friend like him for sixty years was a blessing. We loved each other, and his family was mine and my family his. He introduced me to India, a country I love, but more important to me was the way the Bajaj family embraced Sandy and me as part of their family. Further, when their travels took them to New York and their schedules allowed, they always tried to visit us or call us.

I miss Rahul very much, but he will always be in my heart. As a result of our friendship, I am proud to regard myself as 'half Indian' and a member of the Bajaj family.

MICHAEL ALPERT, *friend of Rahul Bajaj and classmate from Harvard Business School*

Mukesh Ambani

Rahul Bajaj was a phenomenal person in India's public life. He was, of course, a legendary business leader. But his reputation was much larger than his position at the company he built and led to great heights of success. For several decades, he was the voice – indeed, the conscience – of Indian industry. When he spoke, the nation listened. Rahul-ji was a man of many shades, a multifaceted personality – each shade, each layer, as unique and as fascinating as the other.

He was a medley of diverse and apparently contrasting qualities. He was poised yet passionate; quiet yet adventurous; humble yet outspoken; principled yet pragmatic; and assertive yet affable. And most importantly, he had the mind of an *udyogi* and the spirit of a *yogi*.

The yogi in him took root quite early in life and was shaped by his noble family heritage, steeped as it was in Gandhian values. The Bajaj family is a proud and worthy inheritor of the legacy of India's freedom movement. Mahatma Gandhi often described Jamnalal Bajaj, his close and trusted associate, as his 'fifth son'. Thanks to this inheritance, Rahul-ji became one of the foremost votaries of the 'nation first' principle in Indian business. It also taught him to live life with honesty and integrity, to think with focus and clarity, and to act with compassion and empathy. All his life he abided by his conscience, led by example and never compromised on his principles.

He displayed all these qualities soon after he took over the reins of the Bajaj Group from his illustrious father, Kamalnayan-ji, in 1965. And what a remarkable legacy he went on to create! Since his taking over, the turnover of Bajaj Auto increased 1,600 times in five decades.

A man with a vision, he led with a mission – to make India a strong and self-reliant nation and help it reclaim its rightful place in the league of global powers. Such was his determination to realize his mission that when the chains of the licence raj shackled him, he boldly declared that he would rather go to jail for excess production than slow down.

This statement by Rahul-ji, made when I was just a teenager, left a deep imprint on my mind. It showed that, like my father Dhirubhai Ambani, he too strongly believed in the philosophy of liberalization much before economic reforms were unveiled. To me, it symbolized his love for the nation, as well as his faith in the power of private enterprise to create prosperity for India and drive social transformation. His belief that a strong and empowered private sector is critical for realizing the ideal of 'AatmaNirbhar Bharat' has been proved right.

This belief, coupled with the stellar performance of his Bajaj Auto, encouraged the younger generation of Indian businessmen to set more ambitious goals. But Rahul-ji also constantly reminded them that it takes more than just ambition to attain success. You must pursue your goals with all your heart, nurture your vision with passion, build teams that share and surpass your commitment, defend your vision against all odds and persevere relentlessly till it sees the light of day.

Another quality I admired in Rahul-ji was his passion for self-reliance and technology-led innovation. He demonstrated that India could manufacture global-quality two-wheelers that were sturdy enough to suit Indian conditions and affordable enough for

India's aspirational middle class. His sons Rajiv and Sanjiv have made the name and fame of Bajaj brighter by growing diversified businesses in the era of heightened competition.

I consider myself fortunate to have known Rahul-ji personally for almost three decades. I have benefited from his wise counsel on several occasions. To the nation, he will always remain a hero, a reformist and a patriot. To the youth, he will remain a timeless icon and an inspiration. To industry, he will remain an enduring legend. And to his family, a loving memory and an eternal guiding force. And to me, he will forever be *hamare pyaare* Bajaj-ji.

MUKESH AMBANI, *Chairman and Managing Director, Reliance Industries Ltd*

Chandrajit Banerjee

I remember one evening, around thirty-five years back, when I was a young executive trainee at the Confederation of Indian Industry (CII). I was standing in a corner of an auditorium in Calcutta filled with giants – leaders of Indian industry. An icon of industry, a role model, a leader whose name was a household word in the country, was delivering a talk on leadership, and the audience was enthralled by his inspirational words. I also heard him, learnt, admired and got bowled over by him!

In the years to come, I would meet many a tall leader, but few, or rather nobody, would ever match the stature Rahul Bajaj held in the pantheon of Indian industry.

That evening remains entrenched in my memory to this day. Not only did I listen with rapt attention to one of the most commanding speeches of the day, I also contrived to get hold of the 'cassette' tape of the recording and went over the talk many times over the years.

In a way, that passionate speech, full of what a CEO should be as a leader, what Indian businesses should be and could be, became my lodestone for what industry should stand for and how it can catalyse change. Rahul Bajaj led by example in all that he advocated, and spoke forcefully to one and all, irrespective of their position, to persuade them to drive change. It is not important to get into the nitty-gritty of the speech because everything Rahul Bajaj ever said is in the public domain. I have narrated this anecdote to make a short point – that he shaped my faith in the ability of businesses to forge transformative change. It is a belief that has only grown stronger over the years.

As I moved forward in my career with the CII, I had many more opportunities to hear his thoughts. He was an effervescent and hearty personality who used his persuasive skills to become an evangelist for corporate ethics and fair competition. I saw how he managed to change the mindset of many people and shape a better industrial sector in the country.

The likes of Rahul Bajaj were instrumental in shaping the CII's clarion call, 'India before Industry', and in bringing about a significant change in the way India approached business. Generation of profits and creation of employment are the basic outcomes of any business that is run efficiently.

What men like Rahul Bajaj held to be far more important was how one earned that profit and what they did with it. During his tenures as president of the CII (he was elected twice to that post), Rahul Bajaj played a crucial role in the codification of corporate governance norms in India, contributing to good business practices even before they were regulated by law. He also worked hard to increase the competitiveness and visibility of Indian industry on the global stage.

Let me try and reflect on a few of the many facets of his leadership and how he worked with others in a wide range of areas.

First, he was able to interact at any level, be it with the highest personages in government or with the most junior officers of the CII. Whether he spoke in Parliament as a member of the Rajya Sabha or sat with the CII secretariat, he dealt with all in the same manner. In fact, he made little or no distinction between his family and the CII family; he would reach out to the youngest team members, showing great interest in their personal lives.

His affection, care and compassion for those he held dear, be they his family or friends, were his special characteristics. He liked to remain connected. He had so much fondness and attachment for the CII that many presidents of the confederation most affectionately referred to him as the 'owner' president! He always took it as a joke, but never failed to show his love and attachment to the CII or to contribute to it. His empathy for it was well reflected in the many dinners and lunches that he hosted. Despite being a strict vegetarian, he had excellent knowledge of a wide range of cuisines and dishes, and ensured that the tastes of all the guests were well considered and catered to.

He was one of the very few, very special people who would typically call on Sundays on my home landline to discuss some issue, to share his ideas or just to even have a nice chat. I miss his calls on policy matters, where his gentle but provocative questioning showed the way ahead and helped me come to a decision on a policy strategy or a CII matter. Sometimes, when he called without any agenda simply to say that he hadn't heard from me for a while, I felt his warm affection for me.

Rahul Bajaj was always a good source of wise guidance and insight for those around him. He was always accessible to the CII to assist and guide it in making vital decisions for the country and industry. I was lucky to have discovered a guide in him through my many interactions with him, both private and public.

First, Rahul Bajaj was a great friend and made time for his cherished friendships despite his busy schedule. He had a charming habit of randomly calling his friends and colleagues for a 'quick' (but never was it less than forty-five minutes) chat to stay connected. Through his infectious smile and open-hearted approach, he always created lasting bonds with those he interacted with. He taught me the value of genuine connections and the importance of investing in relationships.

Second, I learned hugely from his insistence on delving deep into any policy option to understand all its dimensions. I was always astounded by the amount of reading he did on any subject he was supposed to speak on, and he would closely question the person who had drafted his notes at the CII. Any CII team member tasked to do this had to go fully prepared, and yet Rahul Bajaj always managed to know more about the issue than they did. I often wondered how on earth he could find the time to go into issues in such depth as he did and know so much.

Rahul Bajaj's breadth of knowledge spanned a wide spectrum of subjects, allowing him to provide expert advice on policies, niche subjects and critical issues. This deep knowledge came from his diverse experiences and his determination to learn something every day.

In tough situations, his words of encouragement were frequently, 'Don't be concerned; if you do the right thing, nothing will happen. You do what you believe is right, and we're all here to support you.' Those statements gave you a lot of courage to speak up for something you believed in. For him, it was always 'country first'.

Third, the first codification of corporate governance norms under his stewardship was one of the many firsts that he brought to Indian industry. In 1998, well before any regulation had been introduced in this important space, he conceptualized this code. He set an example through leadership for the CII and Indian industry. This set of norms is still referred to whenever corporate governance is talked about in India.

For me, this leadership-by-example was a great illustration of how he pushed through his ideas for an ethical industry, in tune with the needs of society. I am sure this mindset and moral compass came down to him from the ideals of Mahatma Gandhi as well as of his father, who was considered a 'fifth son' of the Father of the Nation.

Over the decades, Rahul spearheaded many such firsts in the

CII, in areas such as competitiveness, technology, engineering and international engagement. He continued to guide us till the last, leaving behind a legacy that is defined by his commitment to promoting entrepreneurship, encouraging competition and supporting the growth of small- and medium-sized firms.

Fourth, Rahul Bajaj set a social vision for companies, encouraging the trend of public trust in corporates. A believer in ethics and integrity in business, he was one of the earliest flag-bearers and drivers for maintaining the highest standards of corporate governance and corporate social responsibility (CSR). He was one of the first industrialists to realize that corporations in India should have a larger purpose – that is, the purpose of giving back to the community – than mere profit making.

His interventions in CSR showed the world that Indian industry was ahead of many others when it came to societal interaction, community development and inclusive growth, setting new paradigms of engagement with national development through involvement in areas like rural development, education and healthcare. He was a true leader who inspired and motivated others to strive for excellence and to always put the needs of the community first.

Fifth, as an architect with a grand vision, he laid the foundations and supported the formation and growth of organizations that would stand the test of time, and ensured that they were steered to success. The Bharatiya Yuva Shakti Trust (BYST) for micro-entrepreneurship and mentoring, the Ananta Aspen Centre for thought leadership on strategic foreign policy, the CII Foundation and many others benefited from his presence on their governing bodies. His range of interests can be seen in the fact that all of these organizations belonged to different fields of activity. In all his endeavours, he maintained the philosophy that businesses should not only be successful but also be meaningful and add value to society.

An institution builder par excellence, Rahul Bajaj made immense contributions to the progress of Indian economy and industry during his leadership of the CII, Indian Airlines, the World Economic Forum, the Indian Institute of Technology Bombay, the Brookings Institution and Harvard Business School.

Sixth, Rahul Bajaj's commitment to promoting entrepreneurship, encouraging fair competition and supporting the growth of small- and medium-sized businesses are hallmarks of his legacy. His unbiased approach earned him unmatched respect and trust in the industry. He had the ability to remain calm, maintain neutrality and make impartial judgements even in critical situations.

Seventh, Rahul Bajaj had unshakable trust in Indian industry, firmly believing that its unique blend of traditional values, diverse talent and unwavering resilience would make it stand out on the global stage. He expressed these sentiments numerous times, emphasizing that India's rich talent pool, entrepreneurial spirit and dedication to innovation would ultimately propel Indian industry to become the best in the world. He recognized the importance of a skilled workforce and was a vocal advocate of improvement in education and training opportunities in the country. He also advocated making Indian industry a key part of the global economy and was instrumental in promoting trade and investment between India and other countries.

Always uncompromising in his beliefs, Rahul Bajaj spoke truth to power and remained the voice of reason in any room. Due to his staunch ideals, the CII was able to emerge as an independent body charting its own views without being subject to influence, either from powerful corporates or from the government and its institutions. He also championed sustainable development and eco-friendly practices, promoting technical education, training, research and development, and industrial engineering at the CII. This has served us well over the years, and we owe our progress to his far-sightedness.

Many years after my first encounter with him in that Calcutta hall, I had another experience with him which I shall always cherish deeply. I was the southern region head of the CII in 1998 and Rahul Bajaj, in his second term as president, came to attend the annual regional meeting and applauded our work, which was as a balm to all of us who were eager to hear his words of praise. On the dais, he repeated that the southern region's annual day celebrations were the best among all the CII regions. I went up to him and gathered the courage to ask him how he could say this in public. Lo and behold, a few weeks later, at the annual session of the CII in New Delhi, while complimenting all the regions, he singled out the southern region again for praise! His praise always meant a great deal to me.

When I last saw him he was in the hospital. He was upbeat and cheerful. It left me hopeful that we would continue to have him with us. But that was not to be. All good things must come to an end. My phone calls with him (mostly in the late evenings or on Sundays) lasted around an hour (I am sure everyone else's experience has been similar). But his last phone call to me lasted less than five minutes. It touched me immensely. That day too was a Sunday. I was answering many calls and this one was from an unknown Pune landline. The person on the other side said it was from a hospital in Pune and connected me to Rahul Bajaj. His voice was unlike him – it sounded feeble. He wished me on my birthday. That was the last phone call I had from him.

Rahul Bajaj may have gone. But his legacy lives on and I hope that it will grow even stronger in the years to come. I miss him deeply and I will always strive to be true to the ideals he fostered in me for a compassionate way of doing business and, above all, to be a great human being.

CHANDRAJIT BANERJEE, *Director General, Confederation of Indian Industry*

Thomas Beach

I arrived at Harvard Business School (HBS) straight out of the University of Michigan in the fall of 1962. I was in my early twenties. As I began to organize my belongings, a tall, dark Indian entered the room from our adjoining bathroom (the dorms were organized with four double-occupancy suites around a 'head', as bathrooms are referred to in nautical jargon). We chatted a few minutes, and my initial impression was what a friendly, articulate yet proud and commanding person it was that stood before me.

This was, of course, Rahul. We walked around our dormitory building, and soon our friendship was kindled by a funny incident. Somehow, it came out that I had played tournament ping-pong. Rahul suggested that as a poor Indian he had no time or money to indulge in trivial games, but that – since we had nothing better to do at the moment – he would play me for $10 if I would sport him 15 points (of the 21 needed to win a game). Naively I accepted, feeling secure that I could easily dispatch this poor fellow. Of course, he beat me badly. When I produced the $10, he revealed that he had been a ping-pong champion at his high school and that I was a stupid American! With this disarming prank, a friendship began, which continued for sixty years. I learned a business lesson that day, as valuable as any I received in the classroom.

Before long, his new room-mate came along, a wonderful Yale

graduate by the name of Howie Whitmore. They shared fun-loving personalities and made for most enjoyable 'headmates'. Howie called Rahul, 'Hul', which seemed fine with Rahul, but he could not capture Howie's pronunciation of his own name and proceeded to refer to him as Harvey for the entire first semester.

Rahul and Rupa together

After Rahul's dear wife, Rupa, followed him to Boston, they took a small apartment in Cambridge. When asked to join them for dinner, I of course accepted. It was a great opportunity to spend some time getting to know Rupa. She was just perfect. Intelligent, perceptive and insightful, yet firm and composed, she complemented Rahul, and whenever appropriate, her retorts, interjections and good humour served as a light-hearted foil to Rahul's carrying on about whatever subject surfaced.

On one occasion, when we were in Istanbul together, my wife was purchasing a bracelet, and a long bargaining process ensued, with Rahul taking the lead from our side. As the deal was about to be struck, Rupa interjected from the back of the room, where she had been quietly observing us, that the price must go lower because the negotiation had stopped on a number which she said was most unlucky in her family. A lower price was soon agreed on.

Late that afternoon, we were purchasing a rug, but this time Rupa was unable to intervene as the conversation became heated between Rahul and the shopkeeper. The shopkeeper became so exasperated by Rahul's speech on the superiority of Indian carpets over those made in Turkey (better dyes, more threads per inch, etc.) that he rolled up all his offerings, gave up completely and concluded that we were impossible to deal with. Rupa, my wife and I could barely contain our laughter. Rahul took satisfaction in the outcome and indicated that when we got to India we could find a superior rug at a sensible price. Lesson: A Turkish rug salesman was no match for Rahul.

A visit to Squam Lake in New Hampshire

Rahul was awarded the Alumni Achievement Award at HBS in 2005. This is given to the graduate who represents the best traditions and highest aspirations of the school. Few receive this honour, and so a large contingent of the Bajaj family made the trip from India to attend the award ceremony. The speeches at that ceremony beautifully captured Rahul's contributions to Bajaj Auto and the Indian business community.

Following the event, Rahul suggested we take his family to visit our New Hampshire home. Rahul and Rupa had previously visited, and they decided it would be worth the two-hour drive from Boston for other family members to see the New England countryside and hopefully take a brief 'cruise' on the lake.

We rented three or four cars, and our caravan headed north out of Boston, with Rahul and I in the lead vehicle. He and I were assigned the task of stopping to procure snacks. Upon arriving at the supermarket, I pointed Rahul towards the vegetable display, since many of the family members were vegetarian. He was aghast, gave me a tongue lashing and redirected our efforts towards cheese, donuts, bread, rolls, butter, potato chips and then, finally, all the cakes and related sweets we could lay our hands on. We moved on to our camp and Rahul triumphantly displayed our purchases and then described them in detail to anyone who would pay attention.

At that point the Bajaj ladies took over. They organized a lovely high-carb spread and took it down to our 'barge', a rustic swim float with a 10-horsepower engine. As we made our way to open water and the party got well underway, the wind picked up and I realized that we could soon find ourselves in a precarious situation and possibly be in serious trouble as the waves came over the side.

By that time Rahul had taken over the helm and captaincy. I intervened and struggled to get our ungainly craft to come around. Despite being overcrowded and old, the 'barge' eventually made it to land, where the party continued on our patio in the lovely environs of the Squam Range and Red Hill. Later, the Bajaj women showed the versatility of their talents by cleaning up and insisting on returning all the serving dishes to their proper storage locations. We headed back to Boston and then on to our far-flung homes. Most of us carried back pleasant memories, but I remain haunted to this day by the thought of how terribly things might have gone wrong if the old barge had floundered 50 yards from shore.

Perhaps a few additional, very brief stories might be revealing and help illustrate the character and range of traits and capabilities that define who Rahul Bajaj really was. My dear room-mate and friend Mickey Alpert is preparing material on our several cruises with Rahul, his family and friends, so I will relate a few other experiences.

There is one cruise story that deserves brief mention. Dr Dilip Kittur was a close friend of Rahul's and was involved in all our outings over the years. Educated in India and then at Johns Hopkins, he became a renowned transplant surgeon and then even more well known for other, more complex surgeries.

Dilip and I decided to take Rahul to the ship's doctor/trainer for an examination and then ask him to design an exercise routine for him. Our initiative failed completely as Rahul lectured the trainer regarding his physical prowess and what incompetent and presumptuous fools Dilip and I were. Clad only in a bathrobe and slippers, he then proceeded to walk on a treadmill for three minutes to demonstrate his endurance. Eventually, the doctor/trainer declared Rahul was an unusual but, in some ways, remarkable physical specimen. Dilip and I were summarily dismissed, and the doctor/trainer and Rahul became fast friends!

One Saturday during a visit by us to Paris, Rahul and I took a train out to Fontainebleau to the well-known French business school, INSEAD, to meet two Indian professors. They came prepared to lecture Rahul, aggressively and relentlessly, about his managing Bajaj Auto too conservatively, carrying too much cash, etc. Knowing the success the company had enjoyed over the years, I was quite taken aback. What was even more surprising was Rahul's equanimity throughout the whole harangue. He only responded to say that he had his reasons and plans for the situation his company was in, and that time would tell if he was correct.

Rahul was perhaps more well known and famous in India than those of us in the West realized. One evening, we visited a night club in Pune where a party was held for a business friend who, that day, had received an important award. There were some twenty of us inside for the celebration, but outside in the front courtyard there were hundreds of what appeared to be young professionals enjoying a night out after work. As we were preparing to leave, Rahul indicated that we best go by a side door and that a car would be waiting there for us. Word had already spread that he was there and the young professionals swarmed our small group – one young man exclaimed to Rahul that this was a life-changing moment for him, and Rahul told him briefly that if he worked hard he would have a successful life. Eventually, the throng parted and a path was opened up so we could make our way through to the car. Many reached out and indicated their respect for him as we passed.

I must confess that I ate a delicacy at the party which Rahul said I should avoid at all costs but which our hostess insisted was absolutely safe. Rahul was right, and on the way to his house I yelled, with great urgency, to have the car stopped immediately. I ran behind some paving equipment in what looked like a dangerous location and returned possibly 10 pounds lighter. At that point, and seeing I was okay, Rahul erupted in laughter and told me I was foolish to disregard his warnings. The episode was complicated by the military jeeps in front and behind our vehicle containing troops with machine guns, including one soldier standing with an enormous gun on a swivel. This was during a troubled period between India and Pakistan, when threats were made to the lives of Rahul and four other leading Indian businessmen. One thing I came to observe about Rahul over time was that he was fearless.

Once, when Rahul visited Naples in Florida, we organized a dinner party in his honour. He charmed all the guests, putting everyone at ease as only he could. But when he realized we had located a chef who was in the kitchen attempting to prepare an Indian dinner, he decided that his culinary skills (ha! ha!) were indispensable and he stepped in to support her efforts. He lectured her and many of the others on the choice of spices, how they had to be properly blended together, on cooking techniques and in which order the dishes should be served. In the end, the meal actually turned out fine and everyone had a great time.

During another visit to our home in Florida, Rahul asked to see a copy of the letter my firm sent to clients annually. He read it on the way to the Miami airport and immediately called to ask if he could show it to a few people in India for the list of characteristics that we looked for in prospective investments. I think to some extent they reminded him of the principles he had developed with respect to Bajaj Auto. As such, they are worth listing here.

- A history of stable earnings growth under the present management

- A degree of insulation from competition
- Accounting transparency and integrity with respect to pensions, revenue recognition, restructuring charges, stock options and the like
- An uncomplicated business that is easily understood and unlikely to change substantially in the foreseeable future
- High inherent profitability, measured by returns on assets and equity
- Management that is honest in the fullest sense of the word and that views shareholders as partners
- A revenue stream generated by recurring purchases by present customers
- A transparent and conservative balance sheet, along with strong fixed charge coverage for the type of business in which it operates
- Generation of free cash flow based on high returns and limited capital spending requirements
- A management having most of their net worth in their company's stock and intending to stay with the company and maintain ownership of its stock

A few concluding words

Mickey Alpert and I were extremely fortunate to be assigned rooms next to Rahul's in our first year at HBS, and thus we enjoyed an extraordinary lifelong friendship with him. What a great man he was! He embodied a unique combination of caring love for family, friends and country. These pillars of his life were combined with his unique ability to muster his intellect and judgement to deal with issues and situations fearlessly and in an appropriate, clear and compelling manner. He approached the powerful and the lowly with the same disarming humour and honesty. He directly addressed whatever matter came along . . . from the needs of a friend to the overreach of a minister.

I am not current on the political landscape of India today, but my sense is that Rahul's voice will be sorely missed in the years ahead. Few are able to speak truth to power with the moral authority that he embodied.

THOMAS E. BEACH, *Managing Director, Beach Investment Counsel, Inc.*

Arun Bharat Ram

I first met Rahul when I was sixteen years old and he had joined St. Stephen's College in Delhi. His father, Kamalnayan Bajaj-ji, used to call on my grandfather, and sometimes Rahul would accompany him. My initial impression of him was of a strapping, good-looking young man who would steal the hearts of many a damsel. And that turned out to be true!

Rahul was junior to my brother at St. Stephen's, and I remember my brother telling me that they often lunched together at the canteen and shared a common passion for motorcycles.

After that, Rahul and I established contact once again in the late 1980s, when he asked me to join a contingent of Indian businessmen at the World Economic Forum in Davos. Davos was still in its infancy and much more informal than it is today. Rahul showed me the ropes, telling me which lectures and interactions to attend, since he had already become a veteran of Davos.

As one may recall, India in the 1980s was still a controlled economy. Hence, we were looked at with a certain degree of disdain and suspicion in the western world. It was largely through Rahul's personal charisma that the Indian contingent played above its weight. Of course, after 1991 things began to change rapidly at international events, and Rahul was often at the helm as we started projecting India as a newborn industrial destination.

I had joined the Confederation of Indian Industry (CII) in the mid-1990s, and while being a regular at Davos, I continued my friendship and relationship with Rahul. In 1998, I was invited by the CII to become the president the following year. At the last moment I had to withdraw my nomination as at that time my family was going through a messy separation of businesses. I did not want media attention to be focused on the president of the CII for the wrong reasons. Rahul was persuaded to take up the presidency of the CII; it was the first and only time that a past president had stepped into the position again. He gracefully agreed to do so, and I had the privilege of being his vice president in 1999.

By this time Rahul and I had become very close friends, and he suggested a match for my daughter with Amit, who is the son of the Pune-based industrialist Baba Kalyani. Things worked out well and the marriage took place in 2001. So, Rahul turned out not only to be a happy matchmaker but also a guide for my daughter, who moved to Pune after her marriage.

In 2002, Rahul, Baba, some other friends and I went on a cruise to the Nordic countries. Rahul and Baba cornered me one day and bluntly asked me if I was planning on losing control of my company to my CEO. I was flabbergasted that they even had any inkling of the situation in my organization. My CEO had been trying to convince me that business families should just remain investors and let the companies be run by professionals. Both my sons, who had earned a very good education from abroad and had had the opportunity of working in other companies, had joined SRF in junior roles. The CEO was preventing them from taking on more responsibility. The message from Rahul was very clear, and on my return I took charge of my company as the CEO for a second term, while my sons grew into leadership positions and proved themselves to be future leaders of the organization.

I happened to be in Pune with my daughter a couple of months before Rahul passed away. While I was there I called on Rahul, and that was the last time we met. I feel fortunate that I was able to have a conversation with him even though he was failing in health.

I will always cherish my memories of our interactions over six decades.

ARUN BHARAT RAM, *Chairman Emeritus, SRF Ltd, and past President, Confederation of Indian Industry*

R.C. Bhargava

Rahul was a person who, after Independence, contributed in a big way to the industrial development of India. Despite the very difficult regime for private industry, he enabled millions of citizens to own a low-cost means of transportation. Who can ever forget '*Hamara Bajaj*'? That India became the largest two-wheeler manufacturer in the world is because of his vision and understanding of what the country wanted and because of his enormous managerial capabilities.

Bajaj Auto became by far the leading two-wheeler and three-wheeler company in India, and in many ways Rahul Bajaj's success was a benchmark for other entrepreneurs. He could achieve low costs of production and high profitability because of his ethical and frugal management style. He was not one who generated black money from the company or evaded taxes.

This was not easy to do in the environment that prevailed at that time. He looked after his workers and respected them. They in turn loved him. He did lose his number-one position to Hero Honda in the two-wheeler segment, and that was probably because he was reluctant to give equity to a foreign partner in his company, this being against his principles as a nationalist. He always ribbed me about Suzuki's presence in Maruti, and we had good-natured arguments about the value of getting technology and capital from outside to increase manufacturing competitiveness and growth.

Rahul came from a family that was in the forefront of the freedom struggle, inheriting the now rarely found value system of the stalwarts of that time. He was never afraid to forcefully speak the truth, and his actions always reflected his thinking. There was not a shred of hypocrisy in him, and possibly this very quality kept him away from playing a bigger part in the governance of the country.

He was a person who had strong family feelings, and as the patriarch discharged his role very ably. He was always concerned about other members of his extended family. His two sons have proven to be extremely capable successors, no doubt because of the value system they inherited from Rahul.

I really got to know Rahul only after I joined Maruti. We had no business dealings with each other, but he persuaded me to take a more active interest in Confederation of Indian Industry (CII) activities. In many ways, he and the organization went together. His active involvement in it and his clear views undoubtedly helped the CII gain stature. We got to know each other much better during the several CII missions we made to different parts of the world. He was one of the individuals who made India a very influential member of the World Economic Forum. My one visit to Davos is memorable largely because of the time I spent with Rahul.

Our families got to know each other. My wife and I would often meet him for dinner at his suite in the Taj Palace. Some of our mutual friends, like the late Naresh Chandra, would be there, and these were very pleasant evenings. Now only the memories remain.

Rahul enjoyed the good things life offered. At the same time, he did not indulge in ostentatious living and competing in that respect with his peers. I believe he took pride in showing that he was not wasteful or unconcerned about what he spent. I have attended the wedding receptions of his sons and daughter and was impressed by the simplicity and grace of the functions.

He was always a wonderful host, and I can never forget a lunch he served when a CII committee meeting was held in the Bajaj Auto premises. He had brought in cooks from Rajasthan, and the Marwari food was to die for. My regret is that I could never get a repeat!

In 1997, I was diagnosed with prostate cancer. One of the persons with whom I shared this information was Rahul. He spent time with me and talked about the disease, its various facets and his own experience with it. He gave me a great deal of confidence and good advice on how to proceed with its treatment.

Rahul was criticized when he was identified as a member of the Bombay Club and seen as a person who was against competition. My understanding is that Rahul recognized that the prevailing government policies made doing business very hard and greatly reduced manufacturing industry's ability to compete with imports. Opening up imports, with no changes in the ability of Indian industry to compete on level terms, was not correct, according to him, and being Rahul he gave voice to what he thought was right. That competitive manufacturing in India was not possible was recognized in 2014, and the government has been correcting the situation over the last nine years.

Rahul has left behind a void that cannot be filled. His energy, strong views and insights will be missed by me and all who knew him. His memory will never fade.

R.C. BHARGAVA, *Chairman, Maruti Suzuki Ltd*

Subodh Bhargava

An inspirational entrepreneur, iconic role model, leader, mentor, gracious friend and, above all, a great human being, Rahul Bajaj was all this and more. Indeed the one and only '*Hamara Bajaj*', his warmth and charm lives on.

Rahul-bhai, as I called him, lived life king-size. A man of substance with diverse interests, he was a people person who believed in nurturing solid relationships. Apart from his family, friends and Bajaj Auto, the Confederation of Indian Industry (CII) was an entity he was firmly committed to. He was the only CII president to be elected twice, which earned him the tag of 'The Owner', a term that was used affectionately.

He also carried his legacy of extraordinary leadership to several other organizations, including the Association of Indian Automobile Manufacturers (AIAM), later called the Society of Indian Automobile Manufacturers (SIAM), the World Economic Forum (WEF), Bharatiya Yuva Shakti Trust (BYST) and many more.

Rahul-bhai was a man of principle and never hesitated to put forth his views strongly. He was known for calling a spade a spade, but he was flexible too. He always listened to and respected the views expressed by others.

My association with Rahul-bhai dates back to the mid-1980s, to the first-ever Auto Expo in India, the flagship automobile show jointly organized by the CII and the AIAM. Held in Delhi in 1986, it was a fantastic event for the new auto and auto-component sector entrants. However, it failed to deliver value to the old, established Indian auto manufacturers. Hence the 'big guns' resisted the holding of the ensuing bi-annual shows. Perhaps they needed a strategic 'pause' to introduce new models for display at the next expo.

Abhay Firodia was the president and I the vice president of SIAM in 1989–90. It took us much persuasion and effort to get the nod to organize the next show.

The second Auto Expo was held in 1991 with excellent participation from the old, established manufacturers too. At the show's conclusion, Rahul-bhai acknowledged publicly that it was a mistake not to have held the exhibition in 1988 and 1990.

The 1991 liberalization of the Indian economy was welcomed by Indian industry, with the CII at the forefront. The CII marketed 'India' overseas to multinational corporations (MNCs) and other global stakeholders for investments and trade. And then there was the 'Bombay Club', ostensibly initiated and chaired by CII's 'owner' Rahul Bajaj, who was admired and applauded for his quote, 'Competition is the greatest guru.' The media played it up to convey that all the members of the Bombay Club, including Bajaj, were 'afraid of competition'.

Charismatic and forceful, Bajaj was always ready to oblige the media with spicy sound bytes. He was equally comfortable with the TV programmes 'Walk the Talk' and 'Big Fight' and was known to be the darling of the media. He, however, paid the price for his popularity by being projected as anti-liberalization and anti-competition. The Bombay Club had only talked about the sequencing and timing of the liberalization and was not against the entry of competition for Indian industry. In fact, the concerns sounded by the Club came true, and Tarun Das had to articulate the same in his famous article in the *Economic Times*, about foreign partners behaving like 'cowboys'.

BYST also owes its gratitude to Rahul for bringing stature, credibility and total commitment to the youth entrepreneurship movement. As its chairman, he guided and led the mission to help disadvantaged Indian youth develop their business ideas into viable enterprises. He believed in the power of youth and in turning job seekers into job creators.

Rahul-bhai chaired the CII centenary committee in 1995, when I was the president. He was generous in his support and guidance to me, which was most valuable in enabling smooth and successful celebrations at various locations throughout the year while keeping a tight control over costs and the purse strings. It was the same at the WEF in Davos, where he was a veteran and extended all support and advice regarding everything, from the venue of the sessions to the food, entertainment and even the dance floor. He ensured he made all Indian newcomers to the forum comfortable, in his signature style. He leaves behind a legacy of corporate and political leadership that spelt transparency, clarity and simplicity.

Besides the several hats he donned, Rahul-bhai was also a gracious host. (And a gracious guest too! He always enjoyed the simple vegetarian meals at our home.) And he carried on with his hospitality even on our overseas travels as part of the Indian industry delegations to the WEF or the Horasis meetings. He would often invite all group members for drinks and dinner at the best restaurants in town.

In fact, a particular incident remains etched in my memory. During one such occasion, I requested him to allow me to be the host to celebrate the award I had received earlier in the day. After dinner, when I asked for the cheque, I was informed that Mr Bajaj had given his credit card in advance to settle the bill. But, as luck would have it for me, the transaction did not go through due to some technical glitch. The same thing happened with another card he gave. I once again requested him to let me pay, but he called his secretary in Pune instead to get the credit card glitch sorted out immediately. Finally, I managed to pay as the issue couldn't get resolved until the next morning. But the gracious host that he was, Rahul-bhai insisted on taking the group out the next day for another evening of good food and company.

A Gandhian who made immense contributions to India, Rahul Bajaj was an institution in his own right. He has given the young generation a blueprint for India's future economic development and has paved the path for New India. But for me he will always be a great mentor, leader and a fabulous human being.

SUBODH BHARGAVA, *Chairman, Eicher Group, Tata Communications Ltd, Wartsila India, and past President, Confederation of Indian Industry*

A.K. Bhattacharya

Three episodes involving Rahul Bajaj are vividly etched in my memory as I attempt to present a portrayal of one of India's bold industrialists with a fiercely independent mind and sound business sense.

In the early 1980s, Rahul Bajaj was riding high on Bajaj Auto's successful entry into the American market with its scooters. In 1971, it had terminated its technical collaboration with Italian scooter-maker Piaggio. About a decade later, Bajaj had entered the American market, slowly and steadily, but Bajaj was expanding its numbers at a pace that began rattling Piaggio. After all, Piaggio had a decent share in the scooters market in America and it did not want competition from a former technical partner.

Piaggio filed court cases against Bajaj in the US and in many other countries, including even in India. It was a long-drawn court battle and Bajaj employed some of the finest lawyers to fight Piaggio. The court battle ended in an out-of-court settlement in the US, without any payment of the compensation that Piaggio had demanded from Bajaj.

The court battle with Piaggio undoubtedly made Bajaj a little bitter about the Italian company. But what irked him more was the way the Indian government in the 1980s decided to give a licence to Piaggio to produce scooters in collaboration with other partners. Bajaj made it into a battle over how an Italian company, which had prevented an Indian company from exporting its scooters abroad, was being given a licence in India. He even used the media to project his view point quite effectively.

Eventually, he lost that battle as the government went ahead with the grant of licences to a couple of Indian companies to produce scooters in collaboration with Piaggio. But where Bajaj stood out was in expressing his belief that what he was doing was nothing more than what any business rival ought to have done. 'It was a serious business fight and in their (Piaggio) position, I might have done the same thing,' Bajaj was reported to have explained. That was Rahul Bajaj.

The second episode pertained to the way the Rajiv Gandhi government decided to sell a state-owned scooter manufacturing company, Scooters India Limited, to Bajaj Auto. Those were the pre-reform days, even though industrial policy liberalization had begun in 1985 in small doses and the idea of a long-term fiscal policy had been mooted. Almost like a bolt from the blue, the Rajiv Gandhi government decided to try out privatization of the company and Rahul Bajaj was in the eye of a political storm.

The winds of change, however, had begun to blow a little earlier. In 1986, the then Prime Minister Rajiv Gandhi had invited Rahul Bajaj and Ratan Tata to become the chairpersons of the state-owned entities Indian Airlines and Air India, respectively, for a three-year term. This was part of the young prime minister's experiment with using private managers to beef up the running of state-owned enterprises.

Clearly, the experiment did not stop there. Gandhi got the Cabinet to clear the sale of Scooters India to Bajaj Auto, subject to finalization of the terms of the privatization and the sale of surplus land with the public sector unit. It was one of those decisions that made everyone in the industry and the government sit up in awe as well as in surprise.

A major hue and cry, fuelled by the left political parties and trade unions, erupted over the sale. How was the choice of Bajaj Auto to take over Scooters India made? Was there any competitive bidding process? What financial package or other support plan was formulated for the thousands of surplus workers? There were no easy answers. It seemed a good idea was being implemented, but with poor planning, which gave it a bad name and led to it being abandoned.

The privatization deal was finally given a quiet burial. I had an opportunity to ask Rahul Bajaj how he intended to revive Scooters India after its sale to Bajaj Auto. Bajaj looked at me and said, with one of his disarming smiles: 'Please ask the government.' Nobody heard anything about the privatization deal after that.

The third episode took place several years later, in 2019. The Narendra Modi government had completed its first term and had got re-elected with a bigger majority than in 2014. But the government had also begun to be seen as a little intolerant of any criticism from any quarter. Rahul Bajaj was believed to be close to the Modi regime. Few expected Bajaj to risk incurring the displeasure of the Modi government by advising it that it needed to be more sensitive to criticism. But Rahul Bajaj was different.

In December that year, during a media event, Rahul Bajaj decided to call a spade a spade. He told Home Minister Amit Shah in a public meeting that people were afraid of criticizing Prime Minister Modi and his government for fear of reprisal. Bajaj said the Modi government was doing good work, 'but if we criticize you, there is no confidence that you will appreciate that'. Bajaj didn't mince words when he said that during the Manmohan Singh government of the United Progressive Alliance, people could criticize the administration without any fear.

The home minister had no option other than to respond. After all, it was Rahul Bajaj who had raised the issue at a public meeting.

He told Bajaj that industry need not fear the Modi government, which in any case was being criticized by the media. But if Bajaj believed that there was an environment where industry was afraid to speak out, then 'we need to work to improve this'. In the subsequent days, Prime Minister Modi did hold a few meetings with industry leaders where they were encouraged to share their views candidly.

Whether this helped improve the relationship between industry and the Modi government was debatable. But it was significant that Indian industry's first big move to speak out was initiated by none other than Rahul Bajaj.

A.K. BHATTACHARYA, *Editorial Director and former Editor,* Business Standard

Sugata Bose

During the climactic phase of India's freedom struggle during the late 1930s and 1940s, a small village named Sevagram close to Wardha served as the home base of Mahatma Gandhi. Towering leaders of the Indian National Congress, such as Jawaharlal Nehru and Subhas Chandra Bose, went there frequently to see the Mahatma. Key meetings of the Congress Working Committee were convened at Wardha for Gandhi's convenience.

The man who had persuaded Gandhi to set up an ashram in this rural setting was Jamnalal Bajaj, Rahul Bajaj's grandfather. That was the proud legacy of the Bajaj family's service to the Indian nation, which Rahul Bajaj nurtured with care. I got to know Mr Rahul Bajaj during the last two decades of his distinguished life and interacted with him in two very different settings. Between 2001 and 2010, as I was building the institutional foundation for India and South Asia studies at Harvard, I spoke to him about my intellectual vision and plans. He listened carefully.

Mr Bajaj was an alumnus of Harvard Business School. Yet, he agreed with my view that the scholarly core giving India and South Asia a higher profile at Harvard had to consist of both the faculties of arts and sciences while forging links with the professional schools. He believed in a holistic approach towards understanding the history, culture, economics and politics of the subcontinent.

The other institutional space we shared was none other than

Parliament of India, where we came from the very different worlds of industry and academia. My term in Parliament did not overlap with his in the Rajya Sabha, as his term there had already ended by the time I was elected to the sixteenth Lok Sabha in 2014. But I met him on a couple of occasions in the Central Hall of Parliament. His gregarious nature drew a large number of his friends to gather around him, and his candid expression of his views could be easily overheard by those sitting some distance away. At a time when I was seeking ways to best express my principled opposition to the government of the day, Rahul Bajaj's rare boldness in speaking truth to power won my admiration. I could see that the positions he took were not shaped by the kind of political partisanship of the present, but rather principles that he held dear from the spirit of national service of yesteryears.

When I was invited to be a trustee of the Ananta Centre once, I had the opportunity to appreciate his philanthropy and his commitment to training young leaders. He spoke with passion and authority. At a time when our national life is mired in the controversial imbrication of the domains of business and politics, the memory of Rahul Bajaj's statements and actions should remind us of the possibility of that relationship being guided by an ethical sensibility.

SUGATA BOSE, *Gardiner Professor of Oceanic History and Affairs, Harvard University*

Roger Bullard

(With Jody Bellows, Jacqueline and Jean-Robert Bugnion, Ralph Cuomo, Ed Hajim, Eula Hoff, Tony Mayer, Malcolm Salter, Cedric Suzman and George Zwerdling, who were at Harvard Business School (HBS) with Rahul Bajaj)

Rahul Bajaj lives large in the hearts and memories of his classmates at HBS. Our HBS Class of 1964 came together, 650 of us, in August 1962. Everyone was a high-potential applicant, destined for leadership.

Yet there was something special about Rahul. His intellect, sense of humour and personal charm were huge assets. We all knew that Rahul would go on to greatness. That is confirmed as we reflect on his obituary in the *Telegraph* from India, which read: 'It is a measure of the high standing enjoyed by Bajaj that the Maharashtra government immediately announced they would give him a state funeral – an unheard-of honour for an industrialist.'

Greatness aside, it was his indomitable sense of humour that lives on in the memories of his classmates. All of us miss his sense of humour, his jokes about offering to take a bet with us, slyly noting he would cover his losses in rupees, not dollars.

The story of Rahul, more accurately the legend of Rahul, has been presented in detail in the notice of his death in *Forbes* magazine. Nevertheless, for his classmates, the real story of Rahul lives on in the deep care he expressed for each of us and for HBS across the years. His support of our school was 'legendary', reports classmate Tony Mayer.

Rahul attended each of our every-five-year class reunions. Rahul seemed to be everywhere, yet never missed the chance to be with us, with a smile or a joke, at reunions. My wife Joso Bullard and Rahul often exchanged jokes. Invited to the wedding of our eldest daughter, he begged off at the last minute. His excuse was that he was called to join Prince Charles on *HMS Britannia.* To which my wife, no respecter of social hierarchy, responded: 'So . . . ?'

Each of us has their own individual fond memories of Rahul, either of enjoying his hospitality in Pune or of his visiting us at our own homes. His first-year room-mate, Ralph Cuomo, has many fond memories of him. Ralph and his wife Regina invited Rahul and Rupa to join them at home for dinner several years after their graduation. Ralph does not remember what Regina prepared, but remembers that it was blazing hot. Rupa asked whether the dinner was especially hot and spicy solely for their benefit. Regina fibbed, saying, 'We love hot food!' 'Trust me,' says Ralph, 'that dinner was super-hot, the heat was entirely in honour of the Bajajs.'

Rahul's good friend and classmate, George Zwerdling, recalls the day of President Kennedy's assassination, 22 November 1963: 'Immediately after Kennedy's assassination, Rahul, Rupa, my then wife Beverlee and I drove around for hours, pretty much aimlessly. We wound up in Rockport, Massachusetts, eating lobster. Well, Rupa sure did, perhaps not Rahul, who was a vegetarian! It was a strange moment in time, seeking comfort with friends. Rahul and Rupa were our warm friends and good people.'

Classmates Jacqueline and Jean-Robert Bugnion were also close to Rahul: 'We entertained Rahul at our home in Geneva each time he passed through for the World Economic Forum. We attended the Bajajs' fiftieth wedding anniversary in Pune with classmate

John Trask and his wife. It was the biggest party we had ever witnessed. There were more than 500 guests in the park adjoining the Bajaj Auto campus. A "phantastic" party, as you have never seen and will not see soon again! Rahul then returned to join our fiftieth wedding anniversary celebration in Switzerland. He was truly a giant, a leader and the universal man. It was a privilege and joy to know Rahul and Rupa.'

Many of Rahul's classmates responded to news of his death with their own memories of him. Classmate Cedric Suzman in South Africa commented: 'Rahul was a good friend to so many of us in the class of '64. We remember him with fond memories and condolences to his family.' Classmate Rodolfo Granados offered prayers for the repose of his soul.

Classmate Paul Hoff and his widow Eula Hoff were close friends of Rahul and Rupa. Following Rahul's death, Eula recalls: 'When Paul arrived at HBS, he had travelled to Delhi during the summer before his final year at university. This led to his close friendship with Rahul. We visited him and Rupa twice in Mumbai and Pune. After Paul died twenty-one years ago, the Bajaj friendship continued. Rahul invited me to his family wedding, where I was treated like royalty.'

Jody Bellows, widow of Rahul's classmate Arthur Bellows, also entertained Rahul and Rupa at their home in Connecticut. My wife, Joso and I were guests that evening. It was a splendid meal, totally vegetarian; so well prepared that none realized it was meatless! Jody and Arthur met with Rahul on each of his travels to the USA and were also Bajaj guests in Pune.

Rahul's classmate Malcolm Salter, now a professor at HBS, offers his remembrance of him: 'Rahul and I had many, many study meetings and dinners together at HBS. Indeed, many more get-togethers afterwards as well. My most memorable moment with Rahul takes place at Zurich airport in 1990. I have just disembarked from my overnight flight from Boston, I am staggering, heavily sleep-deprived, across the crowded terminal seeking the train connection to Davos. Deep down in my subconscious I hear a booming voice yelling "Mal . . . Mal".

'"Wow," I think, "those Tylenol sleeping tablets I took are strong, with serious after-effects!" As the booming voice rises out of my subconscious to near-consciousness, the vision of Rahul appears ahead, charging towards me across the terminal. Directly behind him follows a large delegation of serious-looking compatriots, also heading for Davos. I'm sure they think their leader has suddenly gone bonkers. Sprinting towards me, Rahul gives me a great bear hug, greets me with great gusto, then turns to introduce me to the surprised and bewildered delegation. Rahul makes introductions that only he can make – full of impromptu irony, wit and tease – which, of course, signals to everyone standing around that he is, indeed, himself once again! That's Rahul – to which I dearly need to add "uncommon common sense". A great friend, whose life and work has made a big difference near and far.'

I close with this observation from our class leader, Ed Hajim: 'Rahul Bajaj was a giant of our age. He occupied every role to which one could aspire: statesman, businessman, philanthropist, parent, friend. He was someone it was important to spend time with. On our several trips to India, the invitations from Rahul and Rupa were always the highlight. Visiting his company's factories, his homes and rising to the challenges of many long evening events with Rahul were experiences of a lifetime. His regular travels to New York live in my memory as examples of much talking, too much drinking and eating. Never a dull moment. With Rahul, it was always a great learning experience. He made life better just being with us. So many remembrances, but here is one special moment. While we are in India on my daughter's birthday, Rahul presents an elephant decorated with a headdress displaying "Happy

Birthday". A spiritual gift. What living memories we have received from Rahul!'

Includes contributors who were at Harvard Business School with Rahul:

JODY BELLOWS, *friend of Rahul Bajaj*
JACQUELINE *and* JEAN-ROBERT BUGNION, *friend of Rahul Bajaj and classmate from HBS*
ROGER C. BULLARD, *friend of Rahul Bajaj and classmate from HBS*
RALPH A. CUOMO, *friend of Rahul Bajaj and classmate from HBS*
ED HAJIM, *friend of Rahul Bajaj and classmate from HBS. A Wall Street executive, philanthropist and recent author*
EULA HOFF, *friend of Rahul Bajaj*
TONY MAYER, *friend of Rahul Bajaj and classmate from HBS*
MALCOLM SALTER, *Professor Emeritus, Harvard Business School, and classmate of Rahul Bajaj from HBS*
CEDRIC SUZMAN, *friend of Rahul Bajaj and classmate from HBS*
GEORGE ZWERDLING, *friend of Rahul Bajaj and classmate from HBS*

Raj Chengappa

Rahul Bajaj was courteous to the last. I had put him on my WhatsApp mailing list, and every week I would send him a PDF of the latest issue of India Today *magazine. He would never fail to acknowledge that he had received it. At times he would send me a cryptic comment about some article from it that he had read. There was an openness about him, an honesty of thought that was both engaging and endearing. Rahul Bajaj may have grown his business empire that he inherited multifold, but he always draped his achievements in a cloak of humility. He spoke with a rare candour and at times could be brutally frank.*

In 2008, I had the privilege of getting him to narrate his life story to me for India Today Aspire, *a magazine for the young. We spoke over the phone for over an hour – he was in Pune and I in Delhi. As he took me down memory lane, he would guffaw, recalling the advice his father gave him when he was in college and how he courted his wife, Rupa. Rahul Bajaj was seventy years old then and was still chairman of the Bajaj Group, though he had delegated most of the day-to-day responsibilities to his son Rajiv. From a turnover of ₹3 crore in 1965, he had created a revolution in the two- and three-wheeler business, growing it into a ₹10,000-crore empire. Most importantly, in that interview he outlined the values that had guided him throughout his remarkable life, including honesty, ethicality in one's dealings, courage, hard work, preparation for any task much in advance, and the skill to conceptualize a vision and see it through. Here is a reproduction of the first-person account of what he told me, which appeared in the* India Today Aspire *issue of April 2008:*

To a large extent, my life, especially my business life, has been moulded by the fact that I happened to have been born the grandson of late Jamnalal Bajaj, who was like a son to Mahatma Gandhi. Because of this, I remember that till I finished my schooling, I always wore khadi. Our family members had burnt all their imported clothes and textiles as part of the freedom movement. Although we hail from Rajasthan, for the past 100 years or so, my family has settled in a small town called Wardha near Nagpur. My father, Kamalnayan, was Jamnalal-ji's elder son. He was a member of the Lok Sabha from Wardha from the Congress party.

In 1946, we shifted for business purposes from Wardha to Mumbai. From then, till I passed out my senior Cambridge, I was in Cathedral School. I did very well at school and passed out in 1954 with a distinction securing 9th rank in the whole of the then-Bombay state. I learnt a great deal at Cathedral. The teaching methods were very good and there was a lot of personal touch. I became a prefect in standard 10 and a prefect and house captain in standard 11 and my classmates always wondered how I could be so good at studying and yet fulfil all these responsibilities. I was also the school captain in table tennis and boxing. I also debated.

I wanted to study economics and chose St. Stephen's in Delhi because then in Mumbai it used to take four years to graduate after senior Cambridge, while in Delhi it took three years. Also, the hostel experience was an attraction. In college, I had a scooter, mine being one of only two in the entire St. Stephen's complex! The Vespa scooter I had was later to become the Bajaj Chetak. But my father made it a condition that I would not carry a pillion rider so it did detract from the fun. In college, I enjoyed myself thoroughly. My father always said, 'Do what you want to do but once you decide what to do, try to be the best in the world in that.' He said, 'I don't even mind you becoming a playboy, but then you must become like Prince Ali Khan (then a well-known playboy who married Hollywood star Rita Hayworth).'

I was very clear that I wanted to be in business. Bajaj Group, whatever it is, was really created and consolidated by my father. Jamnalal-ji's legacy was invaluable but that was not money or assets but goodwill. So when I passed out of St. Stephen's, I worked for four years in Bajaj Electricals and Mukand Ltd (we started making scooters only in the early '60s). On the job, I learnt marketing, finance, accounts, production and about the shop floor. While working, during my spare time I got a diploma in accounts and a law degree. All this knowledge proved to be valuable when I got into Harvard Business School (HBS) for my MBA. There were hardly any Indians studying at HBS then. I learnt a great deal at the business school and rarely missed a class.

HBS opened up my horizons from Mumbai to Boston. I learnt the rudiments of business, finance, accounts, marketing and production in a very cosmopolitan environment. I learnt that in the case study method the stress was on the ability to think and analyse, unlike the lecture method where the stress was on memory. Once in an exam paper, a question was posed as to whether one had to buy or sell a particular company. I said buy and my friend wanted to sell [This is Michael Alpert who also narrates his version of the same incident] but both of us got a distinction. That's what I learnt at HBS, it's how you analyse things.

Meanwhile, I got married to Rupa in December 1961, and we took a small apartment close to the school. Rupa was staying near my house in Mumbai and I had gone out with her often. One day my mother asked me to my surprise: 'Young man, are your intentions honourable to Rupa? Of all your girlfriends, she is the only one I have seen you go out with often.' I mumbled something then. But a year later I told my mother that I did want to marry her. My family didn't believe in castes or communities. So my father invited her to dinner and later after making some enquiries, he agreed but with the condition that we wait for a year and not go out with each other. Both Rupa and I were upset but we did wait for a year and then got married.

When I returned to India in 1964 we decided to shift to Pune to manage Bajaj Auto that my father had started earlier. We were then making Vespa scooters and three-wheelers but no motorcycles. I worked on the shop floor familiarising myself with the work and getting to know the people and the industry. Only after that did I become CEO of the company in April 1968.

By 1979, a decade later, though we were producing more than our licenced capacity, Bajaj scooters had a 10-year waiting period. I concentrated on cost and volume. They are inter-related. I wanted size, and to have size, you must have high quality and low cost, and to get low cost you need volume to get economies of scale. So they are linked to each other.

It was not easy to do business then. You had to get licences to import things like steel and components. We were even hauled up under the Monopolistic and Restrictive Trade Practices Act

– a case that I argued myself and won. After 1991, of course, all restrictions were lifted. Till 2000, we were clearly the No.1 two-wheeler manufacturer in the country. By then the market had begun switching to motorcycles and we had started making the Kawasaki.

Last year (2007) we made a total of 2.7 million vehicles making us number two in the country. (Hero Honda is the leading two-wheeler manufacturer.) When I joined in 1965, the turnover was ₹3 crore and the profit after tax was about ₹20 lakh. Last year, the turnover was about ₹10,000 crore and after-tax profit was ₹1,200 crore. Since 2000, I have handed over the running of the business to my son Rajiv because he has proved his competence on the job. The days are gone where the owner can sit and do what he likes and others manage the company. In today's competitive world, top people don't join you if they have to work for an idiot or somebody less competent. In a competitive environment, it is in your enlightened self-interest that the best guy manages. The owner need not be the best guy. He can do what he wants, enjoy himself, go to the south of France, but don't spoil the company.

You may ask what are the values I uphold the most which helped me grow the business. I have always believed in ethical dealings. I challenge any bureaucrat or politician to get up and say I gave him cash under the table for anything. We have given donations by cheque to political parties and that is mentioned in the annual reports. But I didn't believe in giving cash for a favour to anybody. I believe in ethical dealings not just with respect to corruption and tax payments but also to my customers. I bring in elements of philanthropy, corporate social responsibility and good corporative governance in whatever I do. The other quality I believe in is courage. You must have the courage to say no. We all like to say yes. But if there are wrong requests being made, like people asking for someone to be given a job even if he doesn't deserve it, giving a dealership or making someone a vendor as part of a favour, then you have to say no. You must have the courage to take the right decision.

I believe you must be fair to all your stakeholders – shareholders, customers, employees and the society in which you operate. Not to let go of your principles and not to compromise on them either but at the same time, not become too idealistic or sentimental. It's good to be a level-headed and a pragmatic businessman. The other thing which is not very easy in life is to maintain a balance. People tend to go to the extremes one way or the other and I find that very often this leads to wrong decisions. For example, in business, you are very busy and find it difficult to spare time to meet people.

On the other hand, you need to be accessible too. But if you only keep meeting people, you won't be able to do your work. You will only keep becoming a chief guest at functions. So you have to have the right balance. In everyday life too, you need to maintain that balance. Things like hard work goes without saying. You may have an IQ of 180 but without hard work you will not go far. For example, whenever I have gone to any meetings, whether it is within my company or on other boards that I serve on, I never go without adequate preparation. Even if it means staying up till 3 a.m. to finish it, I never go unprepared. Common sense, of course, is extremely important but I count that as part of your balance. These are linked to what HBS taught me – the ability to analyse and then take a decision because ultimately you are also training for bigger responsibilities. Last, but not the least, is the ability to conceptualise with a long-term vision.

Rahul Bajaj's CEO TIPS

Ethics: I have always believed in ethical dealings. I challenge any official or politician to say that I had paid him under the table for a quid pro quo.

Courage: You must have the courage to take the right decision without compromising on your values.

Vision: This is important because you should have the ability to conceptualise your vision and then, through long-term thinking and planning, execute it.

Hard work: This is a prerequisite to all success stories. Even if you have an IQ of 180, you won't go far if you don't put in the right kind of hard work.

Balance: This is essential at all times. Let common sense be your guide to how to maintain this fine balance.

India Today Aspire ***article reproduced courtesy the India Today Group***

RAJ CHENGAPPA, *Group Editorial Director (Publishing), India Today Group*

Farrokh N. Cooper

On 17 January 2023, I received an e-mail from a gentleman I don't know personally. But I knew of him. His name is Tarun Das, former head of the Confederation of Indian Industry (CII), a prominent personality himself, a leader and a man of high reputation. He told me that they were writing a book on Rahul Bajaj and they wanted me to say something. Well, that really put me in a spot. I asked him why me, because I'm too small a man to write about such a big man.

So he said, 'Look, Mr Cooper, your name has been mentioned in several of his notes and we'd like you to say something about him.' When I heard that I took courage and I said, 'Well, I did know the grand old man and I did think very highly of him.'

I really started thinking about why it was that people loved Rahul Bajaj so much.

Was it because of his money, was it because of his industry? Or was it because he had something within him that was unique? And was it because he loved people; he reached out to people, and he was someone who was committed to succeed and do something that created happiness for India and for the world?

As I pondered these questions, I said to myself, 'Okay, now let me see how I can contribute.' It is said that as you grow older you start remembering more vividly things that have never happened in your younger days, but fortunately I have not reached that stage yet!

So what I'm going to say will have a great deal of accuracy, and it should be a little amusing, in part, for people who don't know all about Rahul Bajaj (or about me, I suppose).

My earliest recollections of Rahul Bajaj are of his always standing at the airport wearing a safari suit with a boarding pass in hand, waiting to board a flight from Bombay to Pune; and he'd be accompanied by one Mr Shah, I think. They would be busy talking about the problems they were facing with the government and in getting sanctions and approvals from Delhi, and so on and so forth. Those were the days of licences and permits under the Congress regime. Apart from that, we never talked at the airport because we didn't know each other that well.

We really came to know each other better when he used to visit Maharashtra Scooters and there would be the odd party or two. We actually started our connection in a very funny way. Once there was an enormous strike in my factory and the union leader who was trying to muscle into our company was a very strong union leader at Maharashtra Scooters. So we were very adamant about the strike, and being stubborn is what Parsees are all about. So we stuck to our guns, which may have been strong but a bit stupid.

We didn't give in and the union leader didn't give in either, because he had might on his side. We said, 'We don't care about might, we talk about right.' So the strike went on and on and on, and this gentleman started tightening the noose. He decided to slow down production at Maharashtra Scooters, and things like that went on. Then, out of the blue, there came along a gentleman who was vice president of Kirloskar Cummins, J.B. Patil. He was a socialist at heart; he had been to jail once or twice but he decided to spend his life advising capitalists on how to deal with labour-related social reforms and how to create empathy for labour.

So Patil went to see this gentleman who was on a hunger strike. He said, 'I'm talking to the protesters and let us see how we can sort things out.' The Cummins assembly line was also drying up and things were in a tight spot. Eventually, J.B. Patil succeeded in getting us what we wanted and the union leader went away. We learned a lot, and we've never had any trouble since then.

This was about thirty years ago. When Rahul Bajaj heard about this, he called me to see him and he said, 'What on earth have you been up to – you are disrupting the environment, you're disrupting the society, you are an angry young man.' I said, 'Yes, I'm very sorry, I'm an angry young man but I can't help it.'

So we two had a few exchange of views and I immediately got attracted to this person because I had a small-scale unit and there he was, like an emperor sitting on the throne of one of India's largest industries. He was spending the day talking to me. Well, we got on and he gave us lunch and we departed. Then, as we got on to the street, we heard that Rajiv Gandhi had been assassinated, and that left a little hollow in our hearts.

Anyway, I can't say that I was very close to Rahul Bajaj or that I used to go to his house or we used to meet a lot. But one day I was reading his shareholders' report, which had a lot of information, not only about the profits made by his company but also about the technologies used, about his vision, about the way he managed things, and I learned a lot. I tried to emulate his example and copy some of the things that he had done to improve his factory. In one of his reports there was a photograph of Rahul Bajaj with his two sons, Rajiv and Sanjiv, and the rest of the board. They were posing with folded hands and had big scowls on their faces. So I wrote Rahul Bajaj a letter saying that this was the type of photograph one needed to put up in the union's office with the caption, 'BEWARE AND BE AWARE WE ARE THE MANAGEMENT'. That photograph did not need to be sent to the shareholders because they knew him as a very loving, caring person and had nostalgic memories of his Vespa scooter and his Priya scooter. He instantly phoned me and had a good laugh, and at the end of that conversation

I did say that the only one who was smiling a little bit was Sanjiv – was he any relative of his (of course I knew who Sanjiv was)!

During the course of that conversation, I said, 'Look, I'm writing a book about my grandfather Sir Dhanjishah B. Cooper, would you like to come and attend the function, inaugurate the function. Mrs Kirloskar is coming, Baba Kalyani is coming, so we'd be grateful if you came.' Without hesitation he said yes. And I said I would like to go over to Pune and give him the invitation personally. He said, 'Don't stand on formalities – I'm coming.' And he came and he enjoyed himself, and the crowd was very interested in meeting him because he always reached out to people.

After that we would meet once in a while, but then time passed by and three or four years ago, when I had made some donations to Ruby Hall, Dr Purvez Grant said to me, 'The chairman of Ruby Hall is Rahul Bajaj, so why don't you invite him to the function and celebrate your seventy-fifth birthday in a grand way and hand over the donation for Ruby Hall?'

So, once again, we asked Rahul Bajaj to our function and he instantly said, 'Yes, I'm coming.' Well, he arrived in his helicopter and gave me a bottle of champagne though I'm a teetotaller. He wasn't keeping too well, but he still came, and he asked me to give him a promise, 'Please don't ask me to talk.' So I said, 'Okay, otherwise you won't talk to me again.'

It was a good function and a small group came to attend, and then we had dinner. After that the COVID pandemic began, so there was a gap again in our meetings. But he would contact me once in a while on the telephone and we'd have a chat with a laugh and a joke or two.

But now that I'm being asked to look back, I think about one thing that he's done that has left an indelible mark in Pune. Apart from his industry and his fame, he will live on in Pune's memory as the man who not only donated a lot of money to Ruby Hall but also became its chairman. He laid out his principles, his ethics and his morals, and made Ruby Hall a great success. Everybody donates money, but along with his donation, he donated his time and mind share too, and that made it a success.

Ruby Hall was a unique amalgam of cultures, because on the one hand you had Rahul, who was a committed Gandhian, and on the other you had Dr Purvez Grant, who was far from a Gandhian. Dr Grant too was totally committed to the hospital and to treating and healing successfully both the rich and the poor with the same dedication. But after that, in his free time, he loved to move around in the company of the rich and famous.

Rahul Bajaj made many investments in a number of fields, but not believing in the flesh trade he didn't buy any horses, nor was he visible at the race course, hobnobbing with high society.

Rahul Bajaj will also be remembered for his fierce, open, independent and honest outspokenness, and where there was injustice he would never mince words to tell the authorities where they had gone wrong. Annually, the Bajaj Foundation honours outstanding people for their achievements.

It will be in the fitness of things if something like that is done in his memory so that its fragrance lingers on and on. He has left behind the next generation, which continues his legacy with the same streak of determination. He was always very fond of all his children, and he would remark that Rajiv was a very good mimic – though I have not had the pleasure of seeing him in action.

FARROKH N. COOPER, *Chairman & Managing Director, Cooper Corporation Pvt. Ltd*

Dara Damania

Rahul Bajaj was an extraordinary man.

When I first heard of Rahul Bajaj, he was known as the entrepreneur and visionary leading the two-wheeler industry, revolutionizing private transportation in India, from a small startup at Akurdi in Pune. As his company grew, so did his reputation. A staunch follower of Gandhian principles, Rahul was not shy about voicing his opinions, believing that you should give more than you receive.

A sharp mind, Rahul led Ruby Hall in Pune and turned it into a fine healthcare institute, with the reputation it enjoys today.

As I interacted more and more with Rahul at business meetings, I got to appreciate Rahul Bajaj, the man. He was a dedicated family man. We got to meet his family, especially his beloved wife Rupa, often. He seemed to prefer intimate encounters with his friends to large gatherings. When we met socially, I always felt valued because he spent time with each of us. It was always a pleasure and a learning opportunity, listening to him talk about his experiences. He was widely knowledgeable, and his ability to talk on any subject without hesitation was admirable. He was a fascinating raconteur, captivating us with his ability to tell a story, drawing everyone in, leaving us feeling fortunate to know him.

Over the years, I got to call him my friend, for which I am deeply grateful.

DARA DAMANIA, *Chairman, RIECO Industries Ltd*

Tarun Das

1976. A tall, young (thirty-eight-year-old) business leader emerged out of the 'woodwork' and into the firmament of what was then the Association of Indian Engineering Industry, or AIEI (now the Confederation of Indian Industry, or CII). He was an immediate box-office hit. Charismatic. Articulate. Straight-talking. Intelligent. Capable. And more.

His name was Rahul Bajaj, and he was the managing director (and CEO) of Bajaj Auto Ltd, the two-wheeler manufacturing pioneer of India.

He made an impact immediately.

Within months he became the leader of an industrial mission from the AIEI to South Korea, where we visited the Hyundai plant and its legendary chairman. We also signed a memorandum of understanding with the Federation of Korean Industries (FKI), and much else. This was the first time I was to be at close quarters with Rahul Bajaj. The relationship was easy from the start. He was likeable. Fun. Serious. All in one.

Several influential members of the AIEI council were members of the mission, and Rahul was immediately drafted to chair the national industrial relations committee dealing with trade unions and workforce issues.

By April 1978, he was elected vice president, and one year later president. He was put, literally, on the fast track. He was the second exception to the convention that to be president you needed to have been a regional chairman.

And so, this nascent organization, the AIEI, formed by the merger of two engineering associations in 1974, acquired a new, high-profile young leader. He was talkative. His phone calls went on forever. But he was also dedicated, serious and sincere. At that time, Morarji Desai was the prime minister, a man well known to the Bajaj family, and so for the first time ever, AIEI got the prime minister to address its annual meeting. Referring to the merger of two associations to form the AIEI in 1974, the Prime Minister said it was nice to be at a forum where people had come together at a time when the trend was the opposite.

Rahul Bajaj, a member of the Marwari community, came from a family involved with the Federation of Indian Chambers of Commerce and Industry (FICCI).

His uncle, Ramkrishna Bajaj, was a highly respected and popular FICCI president. But Rahul joined the AIEI, which was not connected to FICCI or to the Associated Chambers of Commerce and Industry (ASSOCHAM). That was a coup for the AIEI.

And he became a magnet for other young business leaders, especially from Marwari business families (who were influential and resourceful!) to join the AIEI.

This was another turning point for the AIEI.

The elders of these families stayed in FICCI, but the younger generation, full of energy and new ideas, liked the Rahul Bajaj effect at the AIEI.

Though he strode the domestic market like a colossus, he also enjoyed involvement in international affairs. He became an early member of the World Economic Forum in Geneva, renowned for its annual Davos forum, and remained connected to the WEF all his life.

And when the WEF decided to step into India to organize the

annual India Economic Summit, Rahul led their engagement with India from the front.

But he was excessively fair. He did not recommend the AIEI for partnering with the WEF. He recommended the AIEI, ASSOCHAM and FICCI to the forum and asked it to make its own choice after working with all three in the first year. This was a real surprise, considering he had been AIEI president. This presented a real challenge for the AIEI, since it was much smaller than the other two apex bodies.

After the first year's meeting, the WEF chose AIEI, and that relationship has endured to this day, for forty years – nurtured by Rahul, shepherded by Rahul, monitored by Rahul.

The relationship has gone through its ups and downs as some personalities on the WEF side changed, but Rahul always intervened to set the 'marriage' back on the right track and engaged Klaus Schwab, chairman of the WEF, directly when required.

On the international work front, this was a very significant ongoing, lifelong contribution of Rahul Bajaj's to the CII/AIEI. It gave the association a special platform and entry to the world stage. And, more than that, Indian industry benefited from this connect and exposure. The partnership also served as a strong platform from which to project India, and later even specific states, as a potential investment destination.

Rahul Bajaj's involvement with the AIEI, therefore, did not end with his presidency in March/April 1980. In keeping with the association's tradition, former presidents continued their engagement with it 'for life', some to a larger and some to a lesser extent. But for Rahul, his involvement became larger and larger and larger. He trusted the institution. He trusted the staff team. He believed in its future potential.

One other specific, significant contribution by Rahul Bajaj came in the late 1980s/early 1990s.

Prince Charles, then Prince of Wales in the UK, had set up an organization to promote and support micro-entrepreneurship amongst the underprivileged and the disadvantaged. It was The Prince's Trust, and its beneficiaries were disadvantaged youth.

Lakshmi Venkatesan, daughter of the then president of India, R. Venkataraman, had connected with the Prince of Wales on an official visit to Britain with her father and had initiated the work to set up a similar institution in India. She reached out to business leaders for support.

Entirely thanks to Rahul, the newborn Bharatiya Yuva Shakti Trust (BYST) tied up with the CII, and that partnership continues to this day, in spite of many challenges. This partnership gave BYST a strong institutional partner with national reach, and it gave to the CII a role in supporting micro-entrepreneurship across the country.

1995 was the centenary year of the CII. Five companies in what was then Calcutta had set up this organization. The automatic choice for chairmanship of the CII centenary committee was Rahul Bajaj, and he played a major part in planning, participating in and leading the celebrations.

The inaugural ceremony was held at a stadium in Calcutta, with Prime Minister P.V. Narasimha Rao as the chief guest. The valedictory had Goh Chok Tong, prime minister of Singapore, as the chief guest.

Those three days, 4–6 January 1995, were truly incredible and left a mark on Calcutta, on Indian industry, on international connections made by the institution, and on the institution itself. Rahul Bajaj led from the front, as always, fifteen years after completing his presidency.

It was at the centenary function that the CII pledged to set up Centres of Excellence (CoEs) to build knowledge and capacity in Indian industry. Today there are ten CoEs.

A third unique happening involving Rahul Bajaj was in the late

1990s, when Vijay Kirloskar, incoming president at the CII, was unable to assume the post and the organization was faced with a leadership crisis. This was just a few weeks before Kirloskar was to take over.

Multiple names that had not served as vice president were considered to step in as president, but eventually the choice was Rahul Bajaj for the post the second time around. It was unprecedented then, and remains unprecedented to this day.

When the choice was veering towards Rahul, it became very important to consult his wife, Rupa. She was a person of great character and strength. I called her up, and she supported and welcomed the choice. She had another reason, as she told me, to approve the proposal. She wanted Rajiv, their elder son, to get space to lead the company.

So, this man, who had stuck with the AIEI /CII since 1976, returned to don the mantle of president once again, and did so with his usual flair, distinction and quality. He truly enjoyed his second term and made no secret of it. He never forgot to mention it!

There were some special qualities that this person had which set him aside.

The first was his *loyalty* – to his friends, his family and the CII. His was a deep loyalty, never weakening, never faltering. Loyalty was his middle name. Even when some disagreed with him, his loyalty would not allow him to speak against them. Even when some people let him down, the loyalty factor stayed.

The second was his *trustworthiness.* You could trust him because he was just amazingly straightforward. His trustworthiness was unwavering, constant and solid – to individuals he connected with, to his company and to the institution he cared for.

The third was his *frankness.* He was frank to the point of bluntness. Sometimes this hurt. But he was no diplomat. If he had to say something that was on his mind and heart, he said it. And we had to lump it, whether we liked it or not. Once, at a council meeting of the CII, we had differences on industrial strategy and he was rough, very rough, on me on a difference over policy. But that was Rahul. Our friendship endured.

The fourth was his large *vision* and his fantastic eye for detail. He would read everything, notice every word, point out every flaw. He was just incredible when it came to eye for detail. Every comma, every full stop, every semi-colon . . . would be captured by his eye. What an eye he had! There was just no one like him.

The fifth was his talent when it came to *finance* – anything to do with money and finance. He was obviously born with a superhuman ability to understand, analyse, dissect and comment on finance. He may not have been CII's finance chair, but he was one person who read the accounts and balance sheet each year and raised questions, always relevant.

No one was ever a match for him in finance. He used to joke saying that he was all for empowerment but that if anyone wanted to spend ₹5, he needed to know what it was for.

The sixth was his *nationalism*. How many times I have heard him say 'I am a proud Indian', even when things were going downhill for the country!

He felt for India deeply. He never gave up his deep feelings for India. He was an amazing spokesman for the country – always, everywhere, externally, internally. But he spoke up when he had concerns, even if he was nobody's favourite when he did that.

Seventh, he was deeply misunderstood as a Protectionist.

He wanted a strong India, economically and otherwise. He cringed when India was seen to be weak and indecisive. This went with his 'nationalism' and his constant refrain of 'I am a proud Indian'.

These qualities were deeply ingrained in him.

He cared for India. He felt for India. He revelled in India's successes. He cried at India's failures.

The imaginary 'Bombay Club' of the 1990s, supposedly headed by Rahul Bajaj, was all about building a strong, competitive Indian industry before it was swamped by foreign competition. That is what we are doing now with the production-linked incentive (PLI) and AatmaNirbhar programmes and policies (and the world is calling India protectionist!) Which country, other than India itself, would want India to be strong? Even in India there are many who do not understand the importance of the country's being strong. Rahul did.

There were other facets to this man.

His generosity and heart were reflected in the wide-ranging philanthropy and support to causes he believed in and supported.

Kailash Satyarthi's work with children was such a cause. Also, healthcare, be it the eye hospitals he supported, or others, like Ruby Hall in Pune.

Leprosy-related work is a much-neglected area in the country. India has 60 per cent of the world's leprosy patients. When the Sasakawa-India Leprosy Foundation first approached him, he was uncertain. Like many others, he thought leprosy was not a current concern. When a proposal and a presentation were made to him, he readily agreed that Bajaj Group would fund livelihood development, skills programmes and other activities in a large number of leprosy colonies in Maharashtra. He thus became a pathfinder; his was the first corporation to put money into addressing the challenges faced by persons living in leprosy colonies. That programme still continues.

Another example relates to the Ananta Aspen Centre, of which he was a founder-trustee. Ananta organizes a highly effective 'leadership with values' programme called, initially, the India Leadership Initiative. Ananta ran into a resource crunch, and at a board of trustees meeting it was mentioned that this really worthwhile programme would need to be closed.

Rahul, who was present and listening, suddenly started asking questions about the programme, and within minutes had confirmed funding for the programme to continue. He had to be convinced that it was worthwhile and, once convinced, his support was assured.

Rahul's path-breaking, pioneering work and contribution was his leadership in the 1990s of the CII task force on corporate governance, which led to the framing of guidelines for industry. This happened before the government or the Securities and Exchange Board of India (SEBI) had taken any such initiative. These guidelines were widely acclaimed and voluntarily followed by several major companies. It was only later that the government and SEBI followed the CII example and set guidelines of their own.

I can go on and on. For me it was nearly fifty years of friendship, agreements and disagreements with Rahul. But always, there was mutual respect and mutual Trust with a capital T.

Rahul's life took a different turn when he entered Parliament, the upper house, the Rajya Sabha. There was so much pride, so much joy in him when he did so, almost like a child. He revelled in the few years he spent in Parliament, made it a point to attend the sessions religiously and spend maximum time there. He was in the 'seventh heaven' there. He spent a great deal of time with parliamentarians and built friendships across political parties. There was no question that he was sad when his term ended.

In case all this gives the impression that he was 'perfect', let it be recorded here that he was a man of strengths and a man of weaknesses, as we all are in different ways. The rock in his life was Rupa, his wife, and her passing hit him like a bullet in his heart. She was truly a great lady, and some of my most precious moments during the two years that I used to attend the Bajaj Auto board meetings as a member consisted of my visit to their residence and the time I spent with her. I was privileged to enjoy her trust.

My eternal memory of Rahul's is of him as a 'giver'. And this began when I first got to know him and continued to the end of his days.

I have described elsewhere that he was in 'life imprisonment' in the CII, but throughout he added value and served as a conscience keeper to keep the organization on the straight and narrow.

Our personal friendship, which started in 1976, lasted till the end of his life. I could confide in him, and he in me. We kept each other up to date on what was happening in our respective families. And we also gossiped about a variety of people, again because of our complete trust in each other; and respect, as always. Our differences in views never impacted that trust and respect – and we did have differences. Our forty-five-minute phone calls were frequent and helped us enormously in overcoming any issues we had. Communication, both ways, was a constant.

TARUN DAS, *former Director General, Confederation of Indian Industry*

Srikant Datar

I knew of Rahul-bhai long before I met him. His cousin Niraj and I were very good friends, and Niraj spoke of his oldest cousin with wide-eyed reverence. Rahul Bajaj was already something of a legend at the time, but through the eyes of Niraj I conjured up a larger-than-life image of this famous and much-talked-about figure.

I didn't meet Rahul-bhai until many years later, at a seminar at Harvard. I was as awestruck as I was thrilled. When I saw him, it was as if he had stepped out of my mind and into the room. And in real life he appeared even more of a titan. He stood head and shoulders above the others, literally and figuratively, with his extraordinary brilliance and superb intellect. I, on the other hand, was tongue-tied. When we finally spoke, I blurted out that Niraj and I were close friends. That awkward introduction and initial meeting set the stage for a long and very special relationship.

Over the years, Rahul-bhai became like an elder brother to me. I will always cherish the wonderfully close and warm personal relationship I had with him for the last twenty-five years. I benefited greatly from his wisdom about leadership and life. I always felt that he cared deeply about me. In fact, he created this impression quite naturally among everyone he met, no matter their background or accomplishments. He exemplified the very definition of leadership that we teach at Harvard Business School (HBS): the ability to make those around you better and help them to be their better selves.

Rahul-bhai gave everyone the dignity of an equal conversation and always listened intently. I experienced this as both a gift and a responsibility. As we all know, Rahul-bhai had little patience for sloppy thinking, and I knew I had to be sure of what I was saying. In all our conversations, it was clear that he had a keen and curious mind that was always searching for deeper insights. He was a learner and a teacher without claiming to be either, and I always felt there was much to learn just from being with him.

I miss our talks. We could have long and intense conversations on practically any topic in the world. He especially loved talking about entrepreneurship and business and what it could do for society. Whenever Rahul-bhai came to Boston, we would meet, and usually I would volunteer to drive him back to his hotel afterwards. Our conversations were so engrossing that when we arrived at the hotel, I would park the car and we would keep talking animatedly till late into the night. The first few times my wife got quite worried, but she quickly came to expect it as being par for the course when Rahul and I met.

I recount an incident that happened during one of those conversations. I had a few shares in Bajaj Auto. The company had declared a dividend, which I had not received because we had moved. The company contacted me about the problem and asked me how I would like to proceed.

To my mind, Bajaj Auto had gone beyond the call of duty in trying to trace a shareholder, and I said as much to Rahul-bhai. To my surprise, he was not satisfied with this and promptly picked up the phone. He said to the employee on the other end of the line, 'Whose money is it after we declare the dividend? It is not ours any more. It is the shareholders' money. It is your responsibility to do even more to make sure they get it quickly.'

To cut a long story short, I soon got my cheque. I also got a unique view of leadership – which is to hold an organization to the highest of standards and to do what is right, however challenging and difficult it may be. The *how* of doing business trumped every other consideration. I was fortunate to have access to Rahul-bhai, but he wanted to make sure that all shareholders were treated with the same respect.

Rahul-bhai greatly valued management education and its role in developing ethical managers and leaders. He was very close to HBS. He was instrumental in helping us launch our India Research Centre and served on its advisory board, as well as on the school's board of dean's advisors, for many years. He realized the importance of deepening the school's understanding of business in India and recognized that the cases we wrote about Indian companies would be helpful not only to students in the United States but also to students in India and around the world.

The mission of HBS is to educate leaders who make a difference in the world. Rahul-bhai epitomized what it means to be such a leader. In 2005, HBS gave Rahul-bhai its highest award – the Alumni Achievement Award. We reached out to ask him how many guests would accompany him to the ceremony so we could coordinate the logistics. He replied, 'I am afraid I will have to bring a larger-than-usual contingent. You see, many members of my family want to come and see for themselves because they do not believe I am receiving this award.' He had a disarming sense of humour. It was always, always, great fun to be with him.

When it came to being an ambassador for Indian business, there was no one quite like him. He was a giant and a titan of Indian industry. The most hallowed business leaders would stop to hear him speak. It stemmed from his uncanny grasp of international affairs, global business and politics, and his ability to articulate the most complex issues in an engaging fashion. He was a voracious reader and researcher and a natural orator – in many ways, he was an academic. Engaging with him was akin to being in a master class.

Rahul-bhai was a proud Indian with a deep love for his country. He was never afraid to speak his mind, or truth to power. He had both the courage and the character to say what he thought was in the country's best interests. I am sure this came from his upbringing. He would often talk about how being brought up in a Gandhian value system had shaped him as a person and as a professional. He and I shared a tremendous admiration for Gandhi-ji.

I have many fond memories of him, but one stands out especially for me. When I had the honour and privilege of being appointed the eleventh dean of HBS in October 2020, a note went out by email simultaneously to 90,000-plus alumni and well-wishers. Within a minute of the message going out, my phone rang. It was Rahul-bhai, calling to congratulate me.

In November 2021, I travelled to India to receive the Padma Shri award. Meeting Rahul-bhai was an important priority; his health was failing, and I was worried. I travelled from Delhi to Pune to spend time with him. It was a poignant moment for both of us. He was touched that I had travelled to see him; for me, the award would have meant less without his blessings.

Life tires the strongest among us. The colossus appeared frail at that last meeting. Despite his illness, he insisted on joining Sanjiv, Shefali, Skip Nordoff and me for lunch. It was touching to see how much he wanted to be with us, despite his tiredness. Sadly, that was the last time I saw him, but I will always remember him for his scintillating brilliance, deep humanity, sharp wit and incredible generosity.

Rahul-bhai was like a brother that life sent to walk with me for a while. His friendship was a gift I will always treasure.

SRIKANT DATAR, *noted academic and eleventh Dean of Harvard Business School*

Michael Diekmann

A lot has been written about Rahul Bajaj, last but not least, the book *An Extraordinary Life,* by Gita Piramal. It is hard to imagine how one can add anything new or of interest to this biography . . .

I met Rahul Bajaj for the first time at a business conference of Indian and German business leaders in the Bavarian Alps, and my first impression of him was – dominant, intense and uncompromising. When we talked over dinner, I said that I could not imagine becoming business partners. This was a comment from out of the blue, as there had never been any intention to talk about partnering.

Somehow, that triggered a reaction, and during the course of that year I received a call from Rahul Bajaj with an invitation to talk about a potential insurance joint venture in India. And after some exchange on the mutual benefits of such a joint venture – not surprisingly, he was well prepared and convincing – we soon started discussing terms and conditions. Very soon, that developed into a very intensive negotiation and I had to hire an Indian PhD in mathematics to stay ahead of the discussion on modelling future valuations.

Rahul's personal involvement in the contractual debate and the setting-up of the businesses was as intensive as his involvement in the running of our two insurance joint ventures in life and property and casualty (P+C).

He insisted from the very beginning on moving out of the comfort zone of Mumbai, on sending all expats home and avoiding competition in the major cities. So we started in Pune with an Indian management and marketed our products in the second-tier cities and the countryside. And the success of the venture proved him right.

Rahul Bajaj was not a man to compromise on anything. He was direct in a way that I have rarely experienced in others before. But he could also be most charming and warm-hearted when it came to personal topics, family and hospitality at his home.

It makes me proud that we managed to go through that process of challenging each other, spending time to understand each other better and laying the ground for a very successful business on Rahul Bajaj's home turf in India – mostly on his terms, and mostly for good reasons.

Rahul Bajaj has left a remarkable footprint and will be remembered.

MICHAEL DIEKMANN, *Chairman and former CEO, Allianz Group*

Naushad Forbes

Great men and women generally fall in one of two groups: there are the helicopter people, those who see the whole landscape and make sense of the big picture for us lesser mortals; and there are those who delve into the details, who make sure that each piece is deeply and richly understood in all its nuance. (God, we know, lies in the details.) The philosopher Isaiah Berlin called people who knew something in great detail hedgehogs. The others were foxes: they knew many things, if more superficially.

Rahul Bajaj was unique in his mastery of both the 30,000-foot view and the small details. His ability to see the big picture was legendary, as he connected the success of Indian industry with his knowledge of Indian history and his connections around the world. But he was equally at home dealing with the minutest detail. As the Bajaj Group chairman running our board meetings, he constantly amazed us with his ability to spot the misplaced comma that changed the meaning of a board minute. I've personally experienced the detail with which we planned a dinner we jointly hosted for the Confederation of Indian Industry (CII) national council in Pune, down to every last bit of the menu and the variety and brands of the alcoholic beverages.

Many in this volume have written about Rahul's amazing success in creating some of our most valuable companies, his essential contributions in building the CII and other institutions, his deep integrity, his fearlessness, his being the articulate voice of and for Indian industry and India in forums around the world. In my book *The Struggle and the Promise*, my belief in India's potential for great achievement is front and centre. No one lived this belief more visibly and articulately than Rahul Bajaj. My book argues for much change in government policy and our institutions. But I especially demand much more from Indian industry. To achieve its potential, Indian industry must look a lot more like Rahul Bajaj and his companies.

Indian industry must, in the future, be more of four I's: inclusive, international, innovative and independent. The Bajaj Group illustrates these I's. We must be more inclusive by investing our corporate social responsibility (CSR) funding in education and skilling, thus building human capital. The Bajaj Group consistently ranks among the top ten CSR spenders in the country. CSR was a personal passion for Rahul; he chaired the CSR committees of his companies, knowing in detail which project was being funded and, why and how it was performing. Bajaj Group CSR funding is increasingly focused on skilling, so hundreds of thousands more can get good-quality jobs. But *inclusive* also applies to markets for the products and services of the Group. A Bajaj Auto motorcycle is often the first consumer durable the aspiring Indian youngster buys. Bajaj Finance has over 60 million consumers who live a better life because of their ability to immediately access goods they otherwise would need to save for.

We must be more international. Bajaj Auto gets half its sales from exports, selling motorcycles and three-wheelers in over 100 countries around the world, and it is the lead brand in markets ranging from Nigeria to Bangladesh and Iran to Egypt. Rahul Bajaj spoke commandingly and effectively for Indian industry and India in forums around the world – at the World Economic Forum, the Harvard Business School, Brookings, the Commonwealth Business

Council and others. His motive was always to be fiercely competitive – to outcompete the best firms worldwide.

We must be more innovative. Bajaj Auto is known for its research and development. Its product designs support several leading international brands. Bajaj Finance may officially be a consumer finance company, but it is really a fintech company that innovates constantly. And new ventures in the Bajaj Finserv stable are defining new business models in exciting fields.

We must be more independent. Decades of the licence raj bred a private sector that looked to the government for protection and favours. A private sector dependent on the government cannot speak with an independent voice. When Rahul Bajaj made his famous comment in late 2019 about industrialists fearing the government to three Union ministers at an awards function in Mumbai, he ended with the line, 'I may be wrong but everyone feels that.' True enough, and while everyone felt that, only Rahul had the courage to say it. His comments made headlines across media, with our talk shows organizing their usual shouting matches several evenings running. An industrialist criticizing the government should not make the headlines. That must be a basic feature of an independent private sector. To get there, we all need to follow Rahul's example, praising when it is due but criticizing equally when that is due – until criticism stops being newsworthy.

There is much more for us to learn from Rahul. He always exuded confidence – in himself and in his group, yes, but equally in India and Indian industry's ability to compete with the best worldwide. He was completely authentic. Both government and close friends heard the same words in the same voice. Rahul was a highly secular individual and was also highly secular in his criticism of the Indian government – whichever government happened to be in power at that point in time. In short, he inspired trust. He was institutional, wanting the institution to prosper and thrive.

He took tremendous pride in both his sons as they built businesses that achieved even greater success than under him. He took pride, too, in those of us who succeeded him in various roles; I do not think he ever realized how much his support meant to us. I remember when I was at my first CII annual general meeting as vice president, with the finance minister on the dais, looking out at thousands of faces and wondering why I was doing this. I saw Rahul (and some others) in the first row. A small nod, a brief smile, somehow conveyed an abundance of support and confidence. I knew I had a legacy I must do my best to live up to. He generally had the last word in meetings, sometimes because it was the loudest, but always because it was the 'rightest'. Whether at the CII or the many other institutions that Rahul was involved with, he engaged completely. He studied the papers, was questioning, demanding, humorous and hugely supportive all at once.

Underlying this life of amazing achievement was a warm, generous, forthright and principled human being. I know of no one else who could warm up a room as quickly by walking into it as he. His entry brought zing to a board meeting, sparkle to a dinner party, interest to a conversation and depth to an exchange of letters. His forthright nature made some fear him, but he was one of the most open people I've met. If you pushed back and argued with him, he would listen and respect you. If you rolled over with your paws in the air of the prevailing political winds, he – quite correctly – ignored you. The only area where we differed was on the role of protection for Indian industry. When I wrote one of my articles criticizing tariff increases, he wrote to me saying he disagreed, but also saying that he liked the article and was glad I'd written it.

His forthrightness showed in the expression of his principles. This was his most publicly appealing quality. His principles showed in the way he operated – using a Skoda as his car in Delhi as he did not want to show off when he went to Parliament. Refusing a personal attendant till health left him no choice. Not being surrounded by the flunkies who carry the papers and bags of lesser industrialists.

Rahul's principles and forthrightness show in the many stories in this book, and in Gita Piramal's biography of him. He stepped in as chairman of Mukand Iron and Steel when Viren Shah went to jail during the Emergency and, later, when Shah became governor of West Bengal; and then stepped down as soon as Shah was back. Stepping in is not uncommon among Indian industrialists; but stepping out is less so.

He went and saw the insurance regulator to approve a payment to a joint-venture partner and pointed out that the alternative was to do it illegally offshore (the regulator approved it). He spoke out after the post-Godhra riots in Gujarat. He was the most articulate spokesman of the Bombay Club, which he did not convene but where he ended up being the only member willing to say what the government of the day (the Congress, in the first phase) did not wish to hear. He repeated this act of courage any number of times, last when he told three ministers (from the BJP) in December 2019 that industrialists were scared to speak up under the current government. He also ensured a smooth succession to his sons so the Bajaj Group could continue to thrive.

For me, and for all those who knew Rahul well, his most endearing attribute was his sense of fun. Whether at dinners, meetings, parties or a one-on-one conversation, you came away stimulated, engaged, inspired, amused. He was among the last to leave a party. The last to leave the dance floor – at seventy-five. He loved telling stories. Telling a story, he would be diverted by an aside, then by an aside to the aside. This was not unusual. But Rahul would loop back from the aside-to-the-aside to the aside, and then back again to the main story. This takes a very powerful mind and concentration of unique proportions.

I have dozens of fond memories of this sense of fun and engagement of his, but my warmest was of the CII presidents' retreat in 2017 in Bhutan. We were a small group, which included Rahul Bajaj and P.K. 'Bodie' Nanda, whom many referred to as CII's founder-president. Rahul and Bodie were colleagues in the CII for fifty years. The long weekend was one long tennis match of playful insults flying back and forth between these two wonderful human beings.

If Bodie was CII's founder-president, Rahul was its 'Owner', a title he disliked. He was considered the 'Owner', not only because he was the only person ever to have been president of the CII twice and was its most generous and engaged past-president, but also because he was the owner of the soul of CII, the one who ensured that we as office-bearers stayed true to our principles of speaking for India first, then for Indian industry, then for the CII, and never for our own firms. And that all the work we did within the institution as members and in the secretariat reflected that purpose.

My year (2016–17) as president of the CII provided an abundance of great memories. Among the most pleasurable was presenting Rahul with the CII president's award, the highest award given by the CII to one of its own. I tried to come up with words or phrases that described Rahul to me – warm, kind, forthright, principled, and a lot of fun. President Pranab Mukherjee, who presented Rahul with the award, leaned over after I spoke and said he agreed fully with all five of those descriptions.

Thinking back on the life of this warm, generous, forthright and principled human being, on this life of amazing achievement, what is Rahul's legacy? Certainly it is the Bajaj Group, the wealth it has created and the wealth it will continue to create. It is all the institutions that owe their existence, or are today stronger, thanks to his contributions of time, money and leadership. It is a much stronger and more independent CII.

Rahul inspired Indian industry with an ethos – an ethos of greater confidence and independence, greater thoroughness, competitiveness, generosity, more public-spiritedness, and one that is national and more international, all at once. Rahul's leadership inspired society to trust business. He made the world a better place for all of us who were fortunate enough to know him.

NAUSHAD FORBES, *Co-Chairman, Forbes Marshall; past President, Confederation of Indian Industry, and Chair, Ananta Aspen Centre*

Rajmohan Gandhi

In the 1950s, Rahul was in college with me in Delhi (at St. Stephen's), but during those years I did not interact much with him. Seniors are notoriously aloof towards younger college mates, and I, three years older than Rahul, was no exception. But I had known Rahul before he joined college, for his parents, uncles, aunts, grandmother, siblings and cousins were very close to our family.

This familiarity lasted until old age, although our meetings were infrequent. It descended, of course, from the incredible association between my grandfather, the Mahatma, and Rahul's grandfather, Jamnalal Bajaj. Twenty years younger than Gandhi, Jamnalal Bajaj died in 1942 at the young age of fifty-two, but not before playing a critical role in the freedom movement. Had he lived on, Jamnalal, looked upon as a son by Gandhi, would surely have become a forceful and large-hearted leader of free India, either in its politics or in its economy, or more likely both.

When Rahul's sister Suman married Naresh, who was my classmate and close friend in school and also in college, our relationship was further cemented.

Rahul's parents, Kamalnayan and Savitri Bajaj, as also his uncle Ramkrishna (Kamalnayan's younger brother) and Ramkrishna's wife Vimla, were remarkable individuals whom I was fortunate to get to know quite well in the decades that followed. Let me assert with confidence that the candour that people admired in Rahul was inherited from Kamalnayan, who was blunt with everyone and never saw himself as subordinate to *anyone* in India or the world.

Rahul's uninhibited tongue was matched with an amazing capacity for detailed involvement in the situations of his friends. This was underscored to me in December 2014 when, in his Chinchwad home, Rahul quizzed me on the prostate cancer with which I had been diagnosed a year earlier in the US. Rahul's precise questions on the stage and intensity of my cancer were joined by a sharp admonition: Why was I delaying treatment? The surgery that I underwent subsequently, which has given me remission thus far, owed not a little to Rahul's frank words to me.

Also strongly imprinted on my mind is Rahul's close and warm relationship with Ramkrishna Bajaj's three sons, Shekhar, Madhur and Niraj. We know that such trust and teamwork among cousins is both rare and wonderfully productive. The path to this had been paved in 1972, when Kamalnayan died at the young age of fifty-seven, and by Ramkrishna Bajaj's graceful and wholehearted acceptance of young Rahul's succession at the head of the Bajaj empire. That empire grew and grew.

Suggestions to Rahul for supporting initiatives to foster reconciliation, partnership and honesty in India's society almost always found a favourable response. I know, too, that in the final years of his life Rahul was wrestling with a difficult yet crucial question: How to reignite in the twenty-first century the proud values of India's freedom movement that he had imbibed from his forebears.

Rahul was a star and a fine human being. His outstanding life merits study. It will not fail to inspire.

RAJMOHAN GANDHI, *biographer and historian*

Kumar Gera

Rahul was undisputedly an outspoken leader who always said what needed to be said without any fear and no matter to whom. This was a trait that industry and business greatly respected and admired, as they knew what courage this required and the risks associated with being outspoken.

I also saw that while being strongly opinionated, Rahul was not dismissive of differing views. In fact, he respected dissent.

The level of respect that Rahul attained was painstakingly earned.

An unforgettable incident took place over a decade ago involving Rahul and another dear friend, Ram Jethmalani, both of whom, sadly, are not in our midst any more.

Whenever Ram used to come to Pune and had a free evening, he would be at our home and we would invite some friends to join us. If Rahul was free and in town, he was always happy to drop in. Both these giants, in their respective fields, always displayed respect and admiration for one another.

We also did the Mediterranean cruise from Turkey to Spain together, which was marked by a great deal of camaraderie amongst the eighteen in the group.

Now, about the incident I referred to: One evening, Rahul, Ram and two other couples were at my home. We had not started dinner and were chatting and enjoying the pre-dinner mood over drinks. Nalini, my wife, had just stepped into the kitchen.

It was after a few drinks that the topic turned to politics and the 'state of affairs', or rather, the affairs of the state. Ram, in his devil-may-care attitude, made an unacceptable remark against Gandhi-ji. This was instantaneously challenged by Rahul, who hailed from a strong Gandhian family influence. Rahul's hackles were up and Ram stuck to his ground, which further infuriated Rahul, who pointed out his family's closeness to the Father of the Nation. I had never seen Rahul as mad, as angry and raising his voice as he did that day, to the extent that we felt tremors in the room. Ram of course was not one to back down, initially. So, salvos were fired back and forth. Nalini heard the commotion and came running in. We tried our best to get them to calm down, which happened fairly soon – in two or three minutes, though it felt like two hours. At first I was quite shocked to see Rahul lose his cool, but upon reflection I understood his passion and respect for Gandhi-ji and the family legacy that had triggered his responses.

Soon thereafter, both gentleman showed their greatness in an attitude of forgive and forget. The moment Ram initiated the cool off, Rahul reciprocated, though gingerly at first. I think before dinner was served, or maybe before we had dessert, things were heading back to normal.

We were together on several occasions after that incident and I watched carefully to see if there were any undercurrents on either side. I could see none. Genuinely there seemed to be no hard feelings; it was as if that incident had never happened. This reconciliation was something that only great people are capable of.

KUMAR GERA, *Chairman, Gera Developments Ltd*

Nalini Gera

In the mid-1980s, I was editor of a city magazine, *Poona Digest*. Rahul was an eminent personality of national stature, and naturally we wanted to feature him in the magazine. However, at the time Rahul was somewhat reserved about meeting the media. My colleagues tried, repeatedly, to get an interview with him but to no avail.

Frustrated at their inability to get access to him, they designed a card, which they asked me to send him. The Bajaj tag line for its ads read, 'You just can't beat a Bajaj'. Our altered version read, 'You just can't meet a Bajaj'.

Somewhat apprehensively, I signed and sent the card, not knowing how Rahul might react. Although I had met him several times, I would not have gone go so far as to call him a friend at the time. In fact, the few times we had met socially until then, I have to admit I was a little in awe of him.

To my great relief, when he received it he called and had a good laugh. That was my first glimpse of Rahul Bajaj, the person, a man who was able to laugh at himself. Needless to say, he did give us an appointment for an interview, and our staff were delighted.

While I was the editor-in-chief of the daily newspaper *Maharashtra Herald*, I approached him for an ad campaign. Again, with some trepidation, as ours was a local daily, unlikely to be an obvious choice for Bajaj Auto. However, we needed their support, and as I now knew him a little, I decided to reach out to him. It wasn't an easy sell, but he did appreciate the importance of a local daily. He finally agreed, but bargained hard and made sure that his money was well spent!

In time, Rupa and I became good friends and we would meet regularly for lunch. And when Rahul was in town we would have dinner together. Both were unassuming and surprisingly down-to-earth and friendly.

We all have preconceived notions about people, and especially famous people . . . And it is not always easy to be friends when there is an imbalance of wealth and power between you. But with Rahul and Rupa that was never an issue.

The first time they suggested that our families travel together, my husband Kumar and I hesitated a little. But Rahul very quickly addressed the elephant in the room by stating clearly that we would not need to try to match up to them on the trip . . . Rahul had the uncanny ability to make others comfortable. He never made one feel that he was in a different league.

Rahul, as everyone knows, was not afraid of speaking truth to power. However, what may be less known was the fact that he was also not afraid of hearing opinions he didn't necessarily like. Many of my friends berate me for speaking my mind and being too forthright. But I think it is possible that Rahul and I were able to become good friends precisely because he didn't need to be surrounded only by people who agreed with him. One of the things we regularly argued about was the role and rights of women, especially in the context of family and family businesses.

Rahul was frequently interviewed on TV and my husband Kumar and I usually watched the interviews, appreciating his candour and his ability to always hold his own.

However, I think it was in 2006, in an interview with Karan Thapar for his show, the *Devil's Advocate*, that he surprised us.

Of course, Karan is known for his abrasive manner and style and for getting a rise out of his guests. For some reason, he got under Rahul's skin and the interview did not end on a good note. The next time we met, I mentioned to Rahul that I was surprised and disappointed to hear his responses in that interview. There were others who were around and heard our discussion. They jumped in and said they thought it was a great interview!

Rahul's response was unexpected. He did not justify his responses. Instead he said, 'I have the recording. Let's watch it and discuss it in detail another time.'

I can think of few people, if any, who would respond that way instead of being defensive!

In 2006, Rahul became a member of the Rajya Sabha. Although he refused to be called a politician, he plunged wholeheartedly into his role. He was very engaged and committed to his responsibility as a parliamentarian. In small groups, he would discuss the parliamentary debates and share his insights.

I'm sure much has been said about his sense of integrity. He stood out because he spoke his mind and because he was an Indian for whom the country came ahead of profits.

The last few years he avoided large parties and was happy to meet up only with a few close couples. Although they lived an hour away, Rahul was happy to come across town for a dinner of cheese raclette with us. We all spent many evenings together being regaled by his anecdotes.

We have lost a wonderful friend and the country has lost a great personality.

NALINI GERA, *Editor-in-Chief,* Maharashtra Herald

Jamshyd Godrej

Over the years, Rahul Bajaj came to be described by a sum of clichéd adjectives – aggressive, blunt, competitive, forthright.

Only those who knew him well were privy to a different side – one that thrived on friendship and camaraderie. He was a friend for all seasons, the kind who stood by you through thick and thin and offered to walk with you even when your family did not. Rahul made friends easily. He was genuinely interested in people, had a phenomenal memory and loved to talk. A 'five-minute conversation' with Rahul would inevitably run into fifty minutes. He was also the life and soul of any party.

Since he was the stuff of headlines in India, you seldom saw him letting his hair down. But during our business trips abroad, an evening with Rahul was the kind of experience you frequently recalled to common friends. There was a lively air about him that rubbed off on everyone and led to a natural bonhomie. If we were out having a meal at a restaurant, he would banter with the waitresses and include them in the mirth and merriment. That was Rahul – he made every person feel visible and counted.

Rahul liked people. But equally he liked recognition.

When he accepted the Rajya Sabha seat, some of us were sceptical about the move. We asked him why he was setting himself up to be a lone voice with little power to affect change. I think he took up the Rajya Sabha seat less to engage with the legislative process and more because he saw it as a contribution to society. But he did leverage the friendships he forged during this stint to help the larger cause of business in India.

During that period he spent a lot of time in Delhi. If he and I were in the city at the same time, we would have dinner together. He would often invite political friends over; he had a few in every party. At these dinners everyone was extremely cordial, relaxed and unguarded. Nobody felt like it was an imposition – gossip, rumours and interesting anecdotes flowed freely. Even though many of us felt he was wasting his time in Delhi, he enjoyed every bit of his stay there. Mingling with power appealed to him.

Proximity to power and politics was not alien to Rahul. The Bajajs' close association with Gandhi and the Indian freedom struggle is well documented. Rahul was aware of this legacy and interpreted Gandhian values not as the philosophy of frugality but of self-reliance and honest work. He believed in working hard and playing fair, and was unapologetic about enjoying the hard-earned fruits of his labour.

Rahul enjoyed the good things in life – but that in no way meant that he was flashy or extravagant. Rupa and Rahul relocated to Akurdi in the mid-1960s, when the place was little more than a jungle. He took Bajaj Auto to dizzying heights by staying within the gated factory colony for forty years. His children grew up there; they went to the same school that the children of Bajaj Auto employees did. I am sure he led a comfortable life, but not one with the bells and whistles that he could so easily buy. It takes conviction and a certain disdain for convention to do what he did.

I have seen that disdain extended to people who did not have a strong moral compass. Lack of ethics in business irked him, because the entire Indian business community then ended up being tarred by the same brush. He would often say – how can India move if we behave like this? But he never called them out in public.

People often misconstrued Rahul's nationalism. When Dr Manmohan Singh and Prime Minister Rao came up with the reforms in 1991, everyone in the Confederation of Indian Industry (CII), including Rahul and I, welcomed them. The CII had been pushing hard for these reforms for a long time because we all felt that the Indian business landscape needed to change. However, while we supported the need for reforms, we were not entirely in agreement with what was being proposed. The economy needed opening up, but Indian industry also needed a level playing ground to compete in. However, no one wanted to speak up because the government had finally done what industry had been asking for for years.

No one but Rahul Bajaj.

Rahul was a skilled communicator who believed strongly that India needed industrialization. He argued that while imports were good for consumers, big foreign players with their muscle power and global operations would sound the death knell for Indian industry unless the country provided the right environment for fair competition. Given equitable reforms, Indian industry could more than just compete, it could give people the best run for their money. The press termed this world view as that of the Bombay Club and presented it as anti-reforms.

Rahul was a powerful voice, but he always took the middle course and spoke for Indian industry. We did not always agree, but he stood his ground and conceded that others had the right to do the same. He and I differed on the pace of change. I felt that we needed reforms sooner rather than later because competition was good for Indian business. Rahul, on the other hand, was in favour of a more conservative pace. He would often tell me, 'You can speed it up for your industry but I don't want it in mine.'

The government took his views into consideration, and they were validated in the long run. When the economy opened up, all the strong Indian industries did well and thrived. Rahul was very proud of the fact that Bajaj Auto did not just stand up to established global brands like Honda, Suzuki and Yamaha in India, but also took the fight overseas.

There was little that could keep Rahul down.

He was extremely combative even when his brother wanted to separate from him. He fought spiritedly and made no concessions because he felt he was in the right. The only time he looked vulnerable was when his wife fell ill. He immersed himself in researching the illness, the treatment and the procedures and meeting all the doctors personally. The amount of time and effort he put into ensuring his wife would get the right treatment was incredible. Despite all his efforts, Rupa did not make it. I think it was a bit downhill from there for him, with his health failing gradually too. As the years rolled by, his body did not keep pace with his unflagging spirit and intellect. But he never lost his zest for life – to the end he remained what we always remember him for. A man for all seasons – *Sabka Bajaj*.

JAMSHYD N. GODREJ, *Chairman and Managing Director, Godrej & Boyce Manufacturing Co. Ltd, and past President, Confederation of Indian Industry*

Nadir Godrej

In the good old days of the licence raj,
Rahul led the two-wheeler charge
In three-wheelers his role was large,
And they were often called Bajaj!
Before India went everywhere,
Bajaj already had been there!
In the days when government was deaf,
Rahul had joined WEF.
And thanks to Rahul's early stand
Other Indians joined the band.
This year at Davos, Rahul wasn't there
But India could be seen everywhere.
With company and state pavilions,
The presence seemed to be in the millions!
And Rahul was a visionary seer
In many things a pioneer.
With his entry in the Upper House,
He had a forum for every grouse.
I doubt that you can ever find,
Someone else who speaks his mind,
So freely without any fears,
For this he does deserve our cheers.
What he said had to be stated

No matter who was alienated.
Now honest feedback is the need
For anyone to succeed.
Shame on those who resent
Good advice that is well meant.
Most businesssmen were far too scared
To say the things that Rahul shared.
He was a builder of the nation.
He had a spotless reputation.
Everywhere we can now see
His everlasting legacy!

NADIR GODREJ, *Chairman and Managing Director, Godrej Industries Ltd*

Pheroza Godrej

Rahul Bajaj, our intimate and long-standing family friend, was by any standards an exceptional and multidimensional human being. He was a great visionary who always insisted on honesty, hard work, dedication and perfection. He symbolized the human face of Indian industry and was an architect of industrial development in India.

He felt a great responsibility for Bajaj's legacy and he carried it within him with pride and grace. Rahul assumed the onus of running the Bajaj Group after the untimely death of his father. Although he assumed the position at a fairly young age, he never seemed unprepared for the challenges that he had to reckon with. A robust man who was bold in thought and action, he never looked away from the consequences that his decisions triggered. After becoming the patriarch of the family and the business, he worked towards developing the conglomerate and reached the apogee of success with the iconic Bajaj scooter.

I remember my first nodding yet warm acquaintance with Rahul in 1989 during a meeting organized by the Confederation of Indian Industry (CII) in Vikhroli, Mumbai. He always greeted me with twinkling eyes and a mischievous smile. I didn't know about his sense of humour when we first met, but I eventually realized that he approached everyone with a sense of curiosity.

My joy knew no bounds when I learnt that Rahul had attended the Cathedral and John Connon School in Mumbai, which also happens to be Jamshyd's and my alma mater. Although we were apart in age, we bonded over our fondness for our alma mater and our shared interests in social welfare. I was in admiration of the person that Rahul was.

Rahul and Rupa Bajaj were as two peas in a pod. They complemented each other in every possible way. Our rendezvous with Rahul and his wife Rupa were always warm and enjoyable. He described his beloved wife Rupa as his best friend with whom he would share every nitty-gritty of his life. Away from the bustle of the city of Mumbai, they had built their dream abode in Akurdi, which was decorated with the help of my dear friend Pinakin Patel. I was fortunate to visit their house for several social gatherings and parties organized by the couple for CII members and close friends.

Above all, I developed a deep friendship and sisterhood with Rupa, which continued until her last days. At every party or gathering, Rupa would assume a peaceful corner of the room and welcome everyone. Always cheerful and graceful, her infectious smile touched my soul and heart. Her presence was so magnanimous that everyone greeted her and paid their respects to her. Whenever she saw me she would call out my name while pointing to an empty seat adjacent to her and say, 'Pheroza, come and sit with me!' and I would ardently comply. We would sit and talk endlessly about the earth, the sky and everything in between. As I got to know her more, I realized that Rupa once had a successful modelling career. I was also great friends with her late brother Nanoo Pamnani and sister-in-law Chitra.

Some of my fondest memories of Rahul are from our travels to Davos, where members of the CII participated annually at the World Economic Forum. Rahul always advocated for an enriching representation of Indian industry at Davos. After spending all day at the board meetings, he would still be left with enough enthusiasm to attend social events in the evening. He was a vegetarian by choice, and he made sure that he was only served vegetarian meals on every trip. We had to hunt for places where he could enjoy vegetarian food, and I recollect vividly a Chinese restaurant, Zauberberg, at Hotel Europe, on a promenade opposite the Central Hotel where we all stayed, which was a must during the World Economic Forum (WEF) week. After his business at Davos, he would travel to the slopes of the Alps to ski to enjoy the scenery. Another significant travel memory that I share with Rahul was of our trip to Salzburg, where he showed us around the KTM factory, which has a collaboration with Bajaj.

As we often met the Bajaj couple, we grew closer to the family too. I remember travelling with Jamshyd to Aurangabad for one of CII's board meetings. There, Rahul insisted we meet his sister and her family. Our bond with his sister's family has developed deeply over the years. I have also built a strong bond with his children, Rajiv and Deepa (with whom I share a passion for dogs), and Sanjiv and Shefali (with whom I share a passion for community welfare), and especially with Sunaina and Manish, who reside in Mumbai now.

Rahul's powers of persuasion, fortified by an analytical mind and dispassionate reasoning, brought public attention to several issues. Apart from taking his own industrial house to great heights, he acted as a catalyst for several important causes, one of them being the Jamnalal Bajaj Foundation (JBF) and Jamnalal Bajaj Awards, in which he was passionately involved. As a trustee and chairman, his contribution to the growth and development of the foundation was enormous. He rarely missed a meeting and he was deeply committed to the success of the foundation. He was a person truly driven by Gandhian values.

I became associated with the JBF through Rahul, who insisted that I join him in this noble cause. His solemn approach towards welfare and social accountability inspired everyone on the team.

His work ethic was unmatchable, and he emphasized the need to be meticulous and thorough. Whenever we met as a group to discuss the activities of the JBF, he required articulate statistics and facts to be presented in front of him. He demanded reasoning and deliberation on every decision that we made to benefit the recipients of the JBF, and rightfully so! Every year he would organize a gala to honour the recipients of the Jamnalal Bajaj Awards and made sure to exchange his thoughts and good wishes with each recipient candidly.

Within the JBF, I was appointed a member of the committee for development and welfare of women and children for selection of the Jamnalal Bajaj Awards. I have enjoyed my interactions with my team, and especially with Minal Bajaj and secretary Shubhangi Karkannavar. I am privileged to still hold this position.

Rahul had a penchant for straight and truthful talk, and his hands-on approach to diverse important national issues was well-received and respected. His indomitable spirit will continue to inspire me throughout my life.

DR PHEROZA J. GODREJ is an art historian, a PhD in ancient Indian culture, and Founder, Cymroza Art Gallery

Omkar Goswami

It was July 1978. I was a twenty-two-year old flunkey, an executive assistant at the Association of Indian Engineering Industry (AIEI), then located at 172 Jor Bagh. Tarun Das, who ran AIEI, had asked me to prepare a note, which was delivered to Ram Shahaney, then the president of AIEI, and to Rahul Bajaj, who was the vice president. I sat while they read the note carefully, with the southpaw Rahul making minor changes and correcting typos in his copy of the draft. After their approval, I took my leave of them ... only to meet Rahul at the AIEI loo. There, while peeing together, he said to me, 'Good job, young man!' It was like an approval from the Almighty.

Even then, Rahul was very much a God-like creature. Tall, handsome, then with a mane of black hair, he used to wear safari suits in summer (which he subsequently substituted for Aligarhi pyjamas and kurtas), smoked 555s (which he gave up), always had a smile and, most importantly, treated everyone around him as equals – be they his peers in industry and government, or a minor executive such as me, or the man serving tea and biscuits.

He loved to laugh and joke, often talking nineteen to the dozen on various topics, all backed by facts, and encouraging everyone around to argue or debate with him. Equally, as I noticed from my very first encounter with him, he was a stickler for detail. No document sent to him would be approved unread, and nothing would pass his keen eye without underlined comments, suggestions and a myriad corrections of typos, all squiggled in his tiny handwriting.

In 1979, I left AIEI for my DPhil at Oxford, and over the next decade and a half I didn't interact with Rahul. He was immersed in Bajaj Auto and his various corporate responsibilities, and I was an economist firmly rooted in academia. Then suddenly, in 1996, when I was at the Indian Statistical Institute (Delhi), I got a call from Tarun Das, then the director general of the Confederation of Indian Industry (CII), which was what it had transformed into from AIEI.

Tarun wanted me to draft a detailed note on what should be the most desirable practices of corporate governance for listed companies in India. He had put together a high-level committee of past presidents and senior members of the CII and had persuaded Rahul to be the chairman. I agreed, and prepared a fairly long and detailed draft, which I had to present to the committee at a CII meeting at the Taj Bengal in Kolkata. I remember the meeting well. While presenting my draft in a concise PowerPoint form, I was getting increasingly frustrated to find many committee members talking to one another, cracking jokes and bon mots across the table, and seemingly occupied with everything else but the item under discussion. After the presentation, I shared my not-so-pleasant thoughts with Tarun. To which he replied, 'Do you trust Rahul?' I said I did. Tarun said, 'Rahul will fix it with you, and then he will sell it to the committee. Leave it to Rahul.'

Soon enough, I got a call from Rahul. When could I spare three clear days to finalize the draft with him? We fixed the dates, and I travelled to the Bajaj Auto campus in Akurdi, Pune, for the meeting. Rahul was a late riser, so my first meeting with him was around noon. Over three consecutive days and evenings, running right up to 10 p.m., he fixed one draft after another. He questioned everything. He never assented to anything until he was fully satisfied, and always cross-checked everything with other pieces of data. He copiously corrected every line and checked each word. He suggested innumerable syntactical and grammatical changes. All in his tiny squiggles. Finally, at around 9 p.m. of the third day, thanks entirely to Rahul, we had a draft that was far superior to what I had first written.

Then, as we were having a pre-dinner drink at his home at Akurdi, I asked him, 'So, how do you propose to get this fundamentally important and far-reaching document passed by your fellow disinterested committee members?' Rahul's reply was classic: 'Leave that to me, young man. And don't you open your mouth at that meeting, unless I ask you to do so.' True to form, Rahul took complete charge at the next committee meeting. In an hour and a half the draft was passed, with only a few minor changes. It became the *CII Voluntary Code of Corporate Governance*, India's very first on the topic.

I was invited to attend the occasion when the *Code* was formally released at a CII annual general meeting at the Taj Palace hotel in New Delhi. Characteristically of Rahul, he invited me to the stage and announced that while he was just the chairman of the committee that begat the *Code*, the writing had been done by me. I remember saying that this was an uncharacteristic falsehood of Rahul's and that he was as involved in the framing of every sentence and word in that *Code* as I was. Which was utterly and entirely true.

In September 1998, I joined the CII as its chief economist. Then came a major CII annual event in Jaipur in January 1999, where we discovered that the president-elect who was to take over for 1999–2000 was unwell and reluctant to take up the responsibility. What could have been a potential succession crisis was averted by all the past presidents unanimously deciding that Rahul should step in. He agreed. So, Rahul Bajaj became the one and only person who became president twice: first of the AIEI in 1979–80, and then of the CII for 1999–2000.

It was then that I began my continual professional interactions with Rahul, which started with a longish PowerPoint presentation for his first presidential interaction with the press. Unlike most other presidents and committee chairmen of the CII, Rahul went through every slide, suggesting a large number of changes – typically for the better – before he agreed to the final draft that he used for the presentation. Many, many others followed as I accompanied him to various CII meetings in India and abroad. By then we had got used to one another's working ways: I knew what he wanted from me and what to deliver for him.

Somewhere along that time, I approached Rahul with an idea. I said, 'You are the CII president who also chaired the committee that prepared the *Code*. Will you consider incorporating each element of that *Code* in the annual report of Bajaj Auto?' Rahul immediately agreed, and Bajaj Auto became the first listed company in India to have a truly modern annual report with a chairman's letter, a detailed chapter on management discussion and analysis, a directors' report that was more comprehensive than ever before, a chapter on corporate governance and another on additional shareholder information. These are par for the course today. But one must never forget that, thanks to Rahul, Bajaj Auto was the pioneer.

I helped in preparing some fifteen such annual reports, for which I would spend four to five days every year at Akurdi, help prepare the drafts with the then CFO Kevin D'Sa; send these to Rahul's office for vetting; get called there and spend hours together doing the corrections with him; invariably have dinner with him at his house, sometimes with his younger son Sanjiv; chat and argue about everything under the sun; and leave only after the final drafts were okayed by Rahul. This task gave me the chance to spend quality time with Rahul and observe how he went about his business.

Then there were the World Economic Forum's annual meetings at Davos, for which Rahul was probably the first Indian industrialist to sign up. He soon got the CII involved in it, and between him and Tarun Das they increased the size of the Indian delegation from a motley dozen to well over fifty, and occasionally as high as 100. Rahul was the prince of India at Davos, and his temporary capital was always the Central Sporthotel, which more or less housed the entire Indian delegation. There is nobody of consequence that Rahul did not know at Davos, and each of them was a friend. I remember a gesture of his very well. He had someone who was always his driver at Davos. On one occasion – probably on his second-last visit to Davos – he got this person on his private plane, and he came as Rahul's guest to Akurdi. Most people don't do things like this. Rahul did.

He had a particular idiosyncrasy. Whenever he took you out to dinner at a restaurant, he would super-carefully scrutinize every line of the bill to ensure that it was correct and properly added up. On one occasion in London, I asked him, 'Why do you do this? What can be wrong with the bill?' His answer was classic Rahul: '*Tera baap ka paisa hai kya*?' Never again did I dare ask him that question!

Over time, he became increasingly familiar with my work and asked me to join the board of Bajaj Finance Limited, followed some years later by him asking me to join Bajaj Auto. There I saw him closely as the chairman of the board. While he controlled the meetings, Rahul always allowed board members to air their views, though he could come down fairly hard on them if their questioning went on for too long. I got blasted by him once for this. He was right; I wrong; and I immediately apologized.

Another thing was the detail to which he wanted the minutes to be perfect – in their wording, grammar and sequencing. Perhaps most important to him was truthful minuting, which he was consciously determined to ensure. Occasionally, on a tricky topic, I would suggest some seemingly clever word smithing options, and his invariable response was, 'No. That's not really the way it is. Put it down exactly as it should be.'

Let me share a few vignettes of my observations about Rahul. First, as I briefly alluded to earlier, the speed and meticulousness with which he read and corrected drafts was second to none. Having interacted with Rahul on hundreds of such drafts covering various topics, I concluded that he must have been a truly great copy editor in his previous life. With neither spectacles nor reading glasses, he is the only man I know who would speed-read any page typed in 10-point single space and unerringly mark all the typos as well as grammatical and syntactical errors in a trice. Occasionally, for the sheer fun of it, I would insert the odd grammatical error and tiny spelling mistake in a draft just to see if he could spot them. Never once did he fail to. Reading a typescript super-fast, almost diagonally as it were, his Cross ball pen would invariably circle the errors; changes would be made and I would inwardly grin to see that the Master had caught them yet again.

Once, he and I decided that too much form had replaced the substance of corporate governance in India. So we chose to write a joint article for the *Economic Times*. It was a revealing exercise for me. I usually write a draft quickly, check the text and typos and send it in. Not Rahul. We went through six iterations until he finally okayed the draft and then insisted with the newspaper that not a word be changed, which wasn't either.

Second, there was his large stack of daily correspondence to be attended to. That was always parked on the left side of his desk. Even amidst work, Rahul would fiddle with these, constantly arranging and rearranging the order in which he would reply to them. He would then call his long-standing secretary, Mohan Keyyath, dictate a few replies, put those in another stack, and again fiddle with the order of the un-replied-to stack, and continue this process until he finished responding to all of them. Never did I see

Rahul not fiddle with the stack; and never did I see him leave his office for the day without having dictated and signed every reply.

Third, all who knew Rahul can vouch for his unquenchable curiosity and love for facts and debate. There was nothing he loved more than an argument – the longer and more detailed the better. Yet, if the debate went against him, he would be first to acknowledge it with grace.

Fourth, a joke that he and I often shared was that he must have failed the précis-writing test in class seven. Remember the one where you had to rewrite 250 words down into 100 or fifty? With great gusto, Rahul could dictate something which, with all the various qualifiers that went through his mind, could turn 250 words to 500. Without even trying!

Fifth, Rahul spoke without fear or favour. I have never seen any Indian businessman stand up and say things to politicians – from prime ministers and home ministers to chief ministers – in the manner he did. Sometimes it was worrying, especially when he wore the CII hat. But his position on this was simple and non-negotiable: 'I seek no favours. I have never done anything that is either morally or ethically wrong. I pay my taxes. So why should I not speak my mind, especially when I have something important to say that the other side should hear?' It was as simple as that. It never changed.

Sixth, for all his peripatetic ways, Rahul had a North Star. That was his wife Rupa, the mother of their three children and the magnet that kept the wider Bajaj family together. Theirs was a love marriage, and I dare say not a day passed without the two spending quiet, quality time together. To the outside world, Rupa was almost invisible. To Rahul and the family, Rupa was the lodestone. Indeed, Rahul took a turn for the worse after Rupa passed away. Though he never publicly displayed his grief, I can imagine how terribly lonely his evenings were at Akurdi without her by his side.

Seventh, Rahul never carried an iota of malice towards anyone. In the last thirty-odd years of his life, I never heard him speak spitefully about any person, though he was observant enough to be uproariously catty in private company. Rahul also had friends across society, not just business persons. His treatment of fellow employees, household staff and other people he met was exemplary. He was always fair, always solicitous and always ready to help.

I will forever remember Rahul's broad smile; his open laugh; his embarrassing inability to go on any diet worth the name; and his knack of being able to take a joke on himself. He was loath to praise his family. But, in the privacy of his living room in Akurdi, he was incredibly proud of his two boys – Rajiv with Bajaj Auto and Sanjiv with Bajaj Finance and the insurance companies.

And what a dancer he was! I have not seen anyone doing a close dance as well as Rahul used to. With a style and swing that were, and are, lacking in most Indians.

Rahul Bajaj. My mentor. Friend. And the trusted elder brother that I never had. There won't be another like him.

OMKAR GOSWAMI, *Chairman of CERG Advisory, economist, corporate consultant and Independent Director on the boards of listed companies*

Purvez Grant

I first met Rahul in 1986 when I had just returned after my training in cardiology from the United Kingdom where I had spent nine years. The first few times we met, he really did not know me very well. But one day my father, Dr K.B. Grant, felt we needed to inject some new blood into Ruby Hall, so he made an appointment to see Rahul at his house and proceeded to take me with him. My dad suggested to Rahul that he would like him to be a trustee of Ruby Hall. Rahul, in his polite way, told us that he was sorry but he had too many commitments and did not have the time for it.

My father and I just waited outside his office for half an hour, and as Rahul was leaving he saw us and said, 'Doctor, you are still here?' I pleaded with Rahul to reconsider our request. Much to my surprise, he agreed to our request to join the board, but on one condition: to make the hospital the best in western India. I was overjoyed. After he joined the board, he did not miss even one board meeting, and he considered Ruby Hall Clinic as his little baby. When my father passed away fifteen years ago, the board decided to elect Rahul as the chairman of Ruby Hall Clinic, a post he retained on unanimous agreement until his demise.

As the chairman, he guided Ruby Hall Clinic in many ways and always listened to everyone. However, he always had the final say, which fortunately always turned out to be correct. I remember when the Manikchand group wanted to make a big donation to us and change the name of Ruby Hall Clinic to Ruby Hall Manikchand Clinic. Rahul opposed it with all his might, and even today the name remains Ruby Hall Clinic.

I remember when my former CEO Bomi Bhote wanted to close our nursing college, Rahul opposed it, and the college remains open to this day and is flourishing. Rahul regularly also made many donations to Ruby Hall Clinic, which have, over the years, amounted to more than ₹28 crore for our institution.

Rahul had a very sharp memory and never forgot a single detail. One day I asked him, 'Rahul do you remember when you first donated to Ruby Hall Clinic?' He immediately replied, 'It was in 1979; I gave ₹10 lakh for the cancer machine.' Obtaining funding was never easy.

One day I met Madhur, his brother, who had come back from the USA after prostate surgery. He wanted to set up a robotic machine that cost ₹20 crore. He said he would fund half the cost of the machine and intended to ask Rahul to pick up the rest. But when he went to Rahul to ask for the money, Rahul said, 'No way I'll pay!'

It was Kumud, Madhur's wife, who then rang Rahul and told him that her husband was very upset that he had refused him. The next day I got a call from Rahul saying he had changed his mind and that we should go ahead and buy the robotic machine as Pune needed it and it was for cancer treatment. We installed the robotic machine, and over the last few years we have used it to treat over 300 patients successfully.

In the later stage of his life, Rahul and I became very close. Some days he would call me daily and wanted to give me advice, not only about the hospital but also about my family. He always wanted the best and never compromised on anything.

In the last few years of his life, Rahul's health was slowly deteriorating. This brought him closer and closer to Ruby Hall Clinic.

We used to meet every three months with Dr M.S. Hiremath, Dr Huprikar and Dr Nirmala to help him and to keep his morale high. He had atrial fibrillation, which troubled him, and a tricuspid valve that was unfortunately leaking. We procured opinions on these, but finally we always decided mutually what was best for him. Rahul was admitted many times in Ruby Hall and always bounced back.

I remember that even during his last admission he was not well, but his first question was about how the hospital was doing, since as its chairman he felt responsible for it. Rahul suffered in his last few days and unfortunately left us. I miss him greatly and very often look back to the great times we had together and the love he gave us all.

DR PURVEZ GRANT, *Chief Cardiologist and Chairman and Managing Trustee, Ruby Hall Clinic*

Naresh Gujral

I vividly recall the day when I passed out of school in 1965 and got admitted to St. Stephen's in Delhi. Since public transportation was a challenge, it was my dream, like many college students, to somehow acquire a scooter.

In those days of licence quota raj, there were only two brands available – Vespa and Lambretta. The waiting period was eighteen to twenty years for the former and seven to eight years for the latter. The black market premium for a Vespa was almost the same as the official price of the scooter – a princely ₹3,200. Consequently, the dapper, savvy and Harvard-educated Rahul Bajaj (managing director of the company that manufactured the Vespa) was an icon for our generation.

Three things stood out about him. First, his emphasis on delivering a superior-quality product – a rare feat in the days of the '*sab chalta hai*' attitude of the industry. Second, it was well known that the Bajaj Group was squeaky clean and did not profit from the black market price of their scooters. Also notable were Rahul's determined refusal to give any out-of-turn allotments to the high and mighty; and finally, his endeavour towards and emphasis on research and development to constantly improve the quality of his product. This helped the visionary young man build a strong brand that has endured the test of time.

I personally got acquainted with Rahul when he chaired the

Confederation of Indian Industry (CII) during his first innings as the president. As chairman, he articulated his views in an extremely forthright manner, always calling a spade a spade. Under his charismatic leadership the CII grew from strength to strength and became the premier trade and industry federation in the country, surpassing the decades-old FICCI and ASSOCHAM.

Rahul and I became good friends once I entered Parliament in early 2007. We would spend endless hours sipping coffee in the Central Hall – since parliamentary proceedings were disrupted routinely due to the various scams that the Opposition wished to highlight and the government was reluctant to discuss. There were only two members there who drew the MPs and journalists to their table like magnets – Arun Jaitley and Rahul Bajaj. They often shared the same table, which would become the centre point of attention and envy of even the ministers.

Many MPs would often walk up to Rahul to ask for favours, like agencies or jobs for their relatives and friends, but Rahul never ever gave them any false promises. His standard reply would be that he had no executive role in his group but would forward the requests to his sons. However, whenever a waiter or a peon approached him, Rahul would hear them out patiently and try and help them as much as he could. I admired that quality most in him. Rahul loved to say in a self-deprecating manner that he was a '*Kanjoos Marwari*', but he actually had a very large heart!

During the COVID pandemic, the gurudwaras in Delhi were serving free 'langar' to the needy. However, at one stage, when fear gripped the city, gurudwara finances came under severe stress. At that stage, the Delhi Sikh Gurudwara Managing Committee, with the help of NDTV, decided to do a fundraiser. I called up Rahul for help, and he responded readily and generously, but only after repeatedly satisfying himself that the money would be used only for the cause that it was being raised for. Such was his attention to detail. Apart from this, I am personally aware of his generosity in supporting many other causes that he thought would help the weaker sections of society.

Rahul Bajaj was an exceptional parliamentarian. He conscientiously represented Maharashtra in the Rajya Sabha from 2006 to 2010. It was a momentous time to be in Parliament. Significant national events, like the dastardly Mumbai terror attacks and events with international implications, like the Indo–US nuclear deal and the 2008 global financial crisis, all occurred during this time, and Rahul was in the thick of debating and questioning the government about them. His parliamentary responsibility was also towards the state of Maharashtra, and he made Vidarbha's cotton farmers the focus of his maiden speech in August 2006.

He intervened on the critical issue of suicide by farmers across the country and the demand to increase the minimum support price for food grains. He marshalled statistics and drew upon his experience to champion the cause of cotton farmers. He said:

> I believe that the relationship between agriculture and industry is symbiotic. A prosperous agriculture develops industry and a prosperous industry develops agriculture incomes. I strongly believe that India can't move forward, unless its farmers move forward; and the growth is only of value when it is inclusive.

His maiden speech was a master class in parliamentary intervention. He deftly threaded the farmers' issue with the economy and geopolitics. He said:

> In the world, India is not just a flavour of the week or the month or the year. We are the flavour of the times. Previously, it was only China. Now it is China and India. Both in the services and manufacturing sector, we are poised to gain from the developments in the world economy.

He believed in the potential of our youth and said:

> . . . we will remain a country of the young even in 2025. We have to ensure that we encash this demographic dividend by investing in their education and their skills. With education and skill, India will become a great country; capture the world in the next 25 years. But if our youth are not educated, are not skilled, instead of becoming a great asset, they will become a great liability.

He was also of the opinion that having simultaneous state and general elections allowed for hard policy decisions. Rahul said,

> Democracy is not just elections. Democracy is active participation by every citizen in the affairs of the state, and the state exists essentially to provide public goods and services to its citizens.

Rahul's maiden speech also had lessons on leadership. Towards the end of his speech, he laid down what it meant to be a leader and said:

> Quality of leadership is crucial in determining outcomes. Leadership is not just a matter of charisma or showmanship or public relations. But it is of understanding today, it is of envisioning a better tomorrow and having the confidence in oneself and of one's team to make our future happen. Leaders are those that deliver better outcomes. Occupying a chair does not make us a leader.

True to the high standards he set for himself in every aspect of his life, he set a high standard for his parliamentary tenure. Towards the end of his speech, he set out the roadmap for his time in the Rajya Sabha:

> In this august House, I will endeavour in all humility to play the role that the Constitution envisaged each Member to play. That is, on behalf of the people of India, hold the Government accountable. No more, no less. We have enough good laws. What we lack is speed and justice in their implementation . . . I will try to be even-handed as an independent, with right and wrong for the country being the sole yardstick for holding an opinion, though I may be mistaken sometimes.

I have quoted extensively from Rahul's maiden speech to demonstrate how diligent he was as a parliamentarian. He utilized every parliamentary intervention to fulfil his constitutional responsibilities. His association with Parliament continued even after he finished his term. He would regularly drop in at the Central Hall during parliament sessions to meet old friends and colleagues, who would receive him like a 'rock star'.

Finally, while there is no doubt that the lovable and charismatic Rahul Bajaj became an institution by himself during his lifetime, what stood out about him were his vision, his fearlessness, his courage of conviction, his generosity of spirit and his total honesty, both in his personal and business dealings. RIP my friend!

NARESH GUJRAL, *former Member of Parliament of India*

Shekhar Gupta

If there ever was a man who could look a crowd in the eye, it was Rahul Bajaj. In fact, the first time I saw him was at a public event where he was a speaker. We did not know each other, but I felt that he was talking especially to me. It wasn't oratory; he just had that rare ability to instantly connect with those around him.

You could put him in a conference for geneticists and bet your last penny that at the end of the day, people would be talking about the evolution of the two-wheeler market. And for all the right reasons, too! His wit, spontaneity and intelligence made him a natural conversationalist.

We were part of many panel discussions. I always found him totally unselfconscious and unrehearsed. What he said seemed to come from a space of deep conviction. When he spoke, and he never spoke briefly, people listened intently. In fact, he was such an engaging speaker that once, when I was moderating a panel discussion where he was a panelist, the conversation ended up being a dialogue between the two of us. Of course, when I realized what was happening, I apologized to the others for not steering the discussion appropriately.

Rahul Bajaj was a media favourite. But there's no denying that he loved the media equally, especially the camera. The minute he saw one, he'd say something that would make great copy. He enjoyed bantering with journalists, especially young ladies. There are enough interviews on business channels where he can be seen teasing them. I think we all looked forward to interviewing him because there was little likelihood of a dull moment.

The fact that he put people at ease was also why journalists did not fear throwing curveballs at him. I remember throwing him a particularly tricky one when Hero overtook Bajaj two-wheelers. I asked him how it was that an established fourth-generation Marwari business family could be made to eat dirt by a first-generation Punjabi entrepreneur. He took the question on the chin and answered it at face value. He did not stew over it or hold it against me. You had to give it to him – he never shied away from tough situations.

That said, he was anything but a walkover. Anyone planning to get the better of him was barking up the wrong tree. He was not just articulate but also logical, and he backed everything he said with proof. You wouldn't find him anything but decorous and dignified, even in the face of deep disagreement. I disagreed strongly with him on laissez-faire and never bought into his conservative world view on reforms. Several of the listed companies of the 1990s had faded into oblivion, while some of the older ones had become better and more competitive, Bajaj Auto included. I called him out several times on this, but he never conceded that he was wrong. In fact, he was wily enough to turn every good or bad event that happened in the business world into a reflection of his world view. We just agreed to disagree. He never let it affect our relationship, and I know of several others who will share similar experiences.

There's a popular perception that people shot from Rahul's shoulders because he was outspoken and could be relied on to start tough conversations. That was not true. Rahul was too shrewd to be played. He would often say, with self-deprecating humour, that his sons scolded him for perpetually shooting his mouth off at the instigation of others. But everyone, including him, knew that nothing could be further from the truth. No one could ever get him to say something he did not believe in. He spoke when he wanted to, which was often, and did not care a dime about what others thought about it.

I cannot help but touch on the *Economic Times* awards 2019 episode here. His company was among those being felicitated for corporate excellence. Yet, for no rhyme or reason, he stood up and told three of the most powerful figures in the government that people were not willing to hold a mirror to the government for fear of reprisal.

In all fairness, this was hardly the forum for this kind of conversation. While what he said was what many were saying off the record, no one had asked him to speak the unpleasant truth to the authorities. That was Rahul. He did not say what he did to earn brownie points with his peers or to take a stand against the dispensation. He just said it because he thought it needed to be said and that the ET awards function was as good a forum as any.

As expected, there was a tsunami of negative reactions across the media. But it was water off a duck's back as far as Rahul was concerned. He was nonchalant about it, even though his sons were not. In an interview following the episode, Rajiv Bajaj, while lauding his father's uncommon courage, said that inviting Rahul Bajaj to a durbar or a public audience was like laying a red carpet for a bull. He revelled in such an opportunity. That was so true. Rahul did indeed like to loom large on the radar. The public square was his batting pitch, more so in the last few years of his life. I suspect his sons may have found him quite a handful in his later years.

Over the years, I got to know him very well. Despite being a third-generation industrialist, he wore his legacy lightly. I never knew him to differentiate between the king and the commoner, and that was something unique to him. He was impatient with hierarchies and designations and also disregarded age and gender.

It mattered little to him whether you were the president or the peon, the editor-in-chief or a rookie journalist. He responded to the person, not the label. Rahul Bajaj was just too much of a people person to put much of a distance between himself and others. He was the person you would have liked next to you on an eight-hour flight. Not only would he chat you up, but he would also have you speaking to ten other people in the vicinity. Wherever Rahul Bajaj went, a buzz followed.

With him gone, some of the buzz has gone out of the business beat for us journalists. Love him or hate him, there's no denying that Rahul Bajaj was headline material. With absolutely no fine print.

SHEKHAR GUPTA *is an award-winning journalist, columnist, author and talk show host. He is the Founder-Editor of ThePrint.*

Sudhir Jalan

To say Rahul-ji was a legend or an institution would be a mere cliché. Yet, anyone who had ever been in touch with Rahul-ji, whether intimately or casually, would swear by it.

My personal relationship of twenty-five years with Rahul-ji started on the wrong foot. My cousin, who is very close to me, is married to his estranged brother Shishir Bajaj. Added to this, Rahul ji was a champion of the Confederation of Indian Industry (CII), whereas I was a diehard FICCI person. We were members of two bodies that are so similar and yet so different.

I remember how our paths first crossed in March or April 1999. Rahul-ji was re-elected president of the CII for the second term (perhaps the only time it has been done) and I called him as a matter of courtesy to congratulate him. As soon as he came on the phone, he lambasted me for three or four minutes using several of the choicest four-letter words. Frankly, I did not know what hit me. I did not realize that that was his way of paying a compliment to me.

In conclusion, he said that he always believed the CII was by far the most representative body of business in India, but in the last five months after my taking over as president of FICCI, perhaps for the first time FICCI had nudged ahead of the CII, and it was this act of mine that had forced the think tank at the CII to request Rahul-ji to again take over its presidentship for the second time. Then he laughed in his normal hearty way and said he enjoyed working with good competition.

This first interaction apart, we built a very good relationship during the last six months of my term at FICCI, and it was perhaps a unique gesture on his part to invite me as president of FICCI to many CII programmes as long as I was in office. I of course did the same. We became very close friends.

I would like to relate one more incident that illustrates Rahul-ji's character. The then finance minister Mr P. Chidambaram had called a meeting of all businessmen at Vigyan Bhawan. As president of FICCI, I had the honour to be the first speaker and made my points, particularly regarding the introduction of MAT even for those companies that were supposed to get a ten-year tax holiday.

Immediately after me, it was Rahul-ji's turn to speak. He was his normal eloquent self, and he too supported the point made by me. Mr Chidambaram got up from the seat and said, 'Okay Rahul, I have understood, you please sit down.' Without yielding the floor, Rahul-ji said, *'You sit down, it's my turn to speak'* and believe you me, Mr Chidambaram did sit down. Everyone had a hearty laugh and the point was driven home very well. This of course was a defining quality of Rahul-ji's. He never hesitated to call a spade a spade, without mincing words or caring about who was on the other side. I coined a word for Rahul-ji – *unputdownable* – which I thought truly described him.

The next experience I would like to recall was when we were in a delegation organized by Horasis in Milan. Rahul-ji was a very good host. He booked a yacht for a day and decided to invite a few intimate friends to go with him. I felt deeply honoured when he invited me and said he considered me a worthy competitor and a good friend – coming as it did from Rahul-ji, it meant so much to me!

We had several other experiences travelling together in delegations, whether it was to San Francisco or to Interlaken in Switzerland or elsewhere, and he always went out of his way to befriend me and give me high respect. He would invite me even when he was calling very small groups to lunch and dinner.

This was how Rahul-ji was – loving, affectionate and so sincere.

I miss him.

SUDHIR JALAN, *a serial entrepreneur and former President, FICCI*

Anil Kakodkar

My mother had studied at Mahila Ashram, Wardha. The institution was one among the several institutions connected with Mahatma Gandhi's ashram at Sevagram. It was devoted to addressing the educational needs of daughters from the families of freedom fighters, most of whom had dedicated their lives to the cause of India's freedom, and then of rebuilding the nation based on Gandhian philosophy.

Mahila Ashram, like the other institutions of Mahatma-ji's headquarters at Wardha, had the patronage of Shri Jamnalal Bajaj, Shri Rahul Bajaj's grandfather. I have often heard my mother mention various names from the Bajaj family while narrating stories of her days at Mahila Ashram. Any news about members of Bajaj family, or of their business units, would be supplemented by her narration about her days at Mahila Ashram and the very close and affectionate linkages between Mahila Ashram and the Bajaj family. I have thus been very familiar with the Bajaj family right since my childhood, although I did not have occasion to meet any of them till recently.

I first met Shri Rahul Bajaj when he was appointed as the chairman of the board of governors of the Indian Institute of Technology Bombay. I was also on the IITB board at the time. During that period, IITs were indeed undergoing a major transformation, from being teaching institutes producing BTechs to becoming research and teaching institutes with a significantly larger emphasis on research and output in terms of PhD students. Industry connect has been a consistent feature of IITs. Several industry leaders have made significant contributions to shaping IITs and have provided valuable leadership at the level of the chairman of the board of governors.

Rahul Bajaj was clearly one of the tallest among such leaders. He took great interest in shaping IIT Bombay in the context of its new mission. I have often heard him talk about IIT Bombay. His commitment to and passion for the institution were clearly palpable on such occasions. The Rahul Bajaj Technology Innovation Centre at IIT Bombay that has come up, thanks to his generous donation, is a testimony to his commitment to taking India forward, leveraging institutions like IITs.

When I was entrusted with the responsibility of the Rajiv Gandhi Science and Technology Commission in Maharashtra, one of the initiatives that I wanted to pursue was the establishment of science innovation and activities centres in the different districts of the state. As such, I was keen on looking at similar activities that already existed. The Bajaj Science Centre at Wardha was one such facility that had come up around that time, and so I decided to visit the place. The late Justice Chandrashekhar Dharmadhikari, who had been a close well-wisher of our family, facilitated my visit there. During that time I had the occasion to visit Bajaj Wadi, the ancestral home of the Bajaj family, which was close by. There I met Shri Rahul Bajaj, along with Justice Dharmadhikari and a few other members of the family. It was a great occasion for me to be in a place which was the home of Shri Jamnalal-ji Bajaj and which had hosted several very tall personalities from India's freedom movement. Shri Rahul Bajaj was an excellent host. I enjoyed the lunch there and also loved getting to know more about the historic happenings in the house, which Shri Rahul Bajaj talked about with enthusiasm. We also discussed the functioning of the Bajaj Science Centre and the features necessary to ensure the sustainability of such institutions. The broader aspects of education in the country also came up for discussion. Listening to Rahul Bajaj's views, on both the setting up and running of science centres as well as the state of play with respect to education in the country, was very interesting and useful.

When I became associated with the Jamnalal Bajaj Foundation, in the context of the Jamnalal Bajaj Award for application of science and technology for rural development (I suspect this was at the initiative of late Justice Chandrashekhar Dharmadhikari), our meetings occurred more often. His very lively presence, his readiness to listen to very diverse views, his clarity of thought and frank expression of his views always made these meetings very interesting and productive.

His very successful journey as an industrialist is well known. Since I am from a domain which is not well connected with industry and business, I think I had better refrain from commenting on his career as there are many more knowledgeable people who could certainly discuss this aspect of his life more comprehensively and more competently.

His engagement with and contribution to the CII, as well as his very active role as a member of Parliament in the Rajya Sabha, have also left a very distinctive mark. His independent thinking, fearlessness and very outspoken nature made a significant impact on people at large. As I see it, he was a perfect connect between the generation that spent their lifetime to secure freedom for India and the generation next, aspiring to build a strong, prosperous and non-exploitative welfare society in India.

We all miss him today. My deepest respects to him.

DR ANIL KAKODKAR, *former Chairman, Atomic Energy Commission of India*

Baba Kalyani

Rahul Bajaj saw India go through the Independence movement, which his family was a big part of. He was deeply involved in the industrialization of India. He was an institution builder and gave to innumerable charities through the Bajaj foundations. Rahul was also known for being very outspoken and frank about expressing his opinion on matters that concerned India. These largely related to the fields of business, economy, politics, government and society.

Most people saw him as a big businessman and a towering figure in corporate and social India. But there was another side to him. He was a great friend, mentor and father figure to many of us.

Rahul was a nationalist at heart. He wanted to build a strong and self-reliant India. An India of the values that were fought for in the freedom struggle and were instilled in him by his grandparents and parents. His expression of nationalism came through in his institution building and in his varied businesses providing employment and giving back to society in many ways. His outspokenness was also his expression of what he felt needed to be done to build a great and successful country.

He believed in course correction whenever he agreed or disagreed with anything. Rahul was brutally frank, but always fair. He was able to keep a large multigenerational family together through his values and openness. He smoothly passed on the baton of his businesses to his sons and cousins and became the patriarch who was available for advice and support. This was true for his friends too.

Before Brand India was known in the World Economic Forum, Brand Rahul was already flying the Indian tricolour high. He was one of the first Indians and among the most regular participants at the World Economic Forum (WEF) in Davos. On a personal note, we always looked forward to the third week of January, when we would make our annual pilgrimage to Zurich on a SwissAir flight from Mumbai, and then onwards to Davos, under the leadership of our dear friend Rahul. It was not only a week of intellectual growth and business networking, but also of socializing and building bonds to last a lifetime.

Coming to our lives in Pune, we had a small group of friends who regularly met with Rahul and Rupa for the last thirty years. He was always the life of the party, always jovial, always wanting to share his thoughts and points of view. He was always dependable, a good friend who was always there for his near and dear.

Rahul leaves a huge void in the lives of all whom he touched – family, friends, employees and the countless business associates who grew with Bajaj. India as a whole gained from his clear voice of reason and principle of over four decades.

My family and I have had the privilege of being very close to the Bajaj family for several years, and of having known Rahul personally for close to fifty years.

He will be missed by us and remembered most fondly.

BABA KALYANI, *Chairman and Managing Director, Bharat Forge Ltd*

K.V. Kamath

To me, Rahul Bajaj – Rahul-bhai, as everyone called him – was a tall industry leader. I distinctly remember my first meeting with him in the mid-1970s in his office at Bajaj Auto. I had just started my career at ICICI and was visiting the Bajaj Auto plant in Pune in connection with their loan proposal that we were appraising. I found a tall, handsome jovial person with great wit. In the first few minutes I was charmed. He was taking phone calls as we talked and I saw the same wit as he chatted. He would make jokes and rib people around, all in good humour. That set Rahul-bhai's personality in my mind.

I continued to meet him in the 1990s, when I came back to head ICICI. At that time we would meet at several forums. He was known for being a member of the Bombay Club, though Rahul-bhai was very clear that he was never against the opening up of the Indian economy. In fact, there is ample proof of this in the way both his flagship companies, Bajaj Auto and Bajaj Finance, have faced global competition and thrived. He was never afraid to call a spade a spade and was known for his plain speaking. All wrapped in his charm and wit.

In later years, as he saw both his sons take on business responsibilities at his group, his fondness for them became clear to me. It was overlaid with constant ribbing, designed to make both Rajiv and Sanjiv strive harder to reach higher. Indeed, he would be a very proud father looking down at them today, seeing their success. Of course, I have also seen his fondness for Sunaina and Manish. I also remember his fondness and respect for his sister. He would say that she alone was more than equal to all the brothers put together!

In the late 1990s, as ICICI was embarking on its journey to become a universal bank, he took a leap of faith and made an investment in the bank, which he held on to with great pride for several years. Not once did he question our vision, and in fact he would always encourage me to aim higher.

Of course, we all know of his contribution to the Confederation of Indian Industry (CII) and I will not dwell on it too much here, for there are many others who can speak of it. Rahul-bhai had an important role in getting me to be part of the CII leadership in what happened to be two crucial years – 2008 and 2009 – when it seemed that everything around us was collapsing as the global financial crisis took hold. Thank you, Rahul, for giving me the opportunity to have a look at things from a new perspective and try to settle something very difficult in the economic context. It was a true learning experience.

Rahul-bhai, to conclude, was a visionary. His vision was vast and wrapped in great charm, humour and wit. I'm sure he is now smiling down on all of us as we pen down our thoughts about him.

K.V. KAMATH, *former Chairman, ICICI Bank and, past President, Confederation of Indian Industry*

Shobana Kamineni

I was in my thirties when I was inducted into the Confederation of Indian Industry (CII). It was the late 1990s and the CII was populated by famous business leaders whom I had previously only read about. Among the most iconic of them was Rahul Bajaj.

I first got to interact with him in 2000, when he served as the president of CII for an unprecedented second term. During his presidency, we worked together thrice, since I was the chairperson of the CII in Andhra Pradesh. The most notable of these occasions was President Clinton's visit to Hyderabad. During those days, Rahul Bajaj only saw me as Dr Reddy's daughter (whom he was fond of). I found him decisive, direct and not always very diplomatic.

Over the years, as I spent more time in the CII and started interacting with him more, I realized the truth of all the three D's described above, but as I got to know him better, a new D emerged – depth.

Rahul had character and principles that gave him the confidence to speak his mind. It didn't matter that he was often the sole dissenter if he felt that others were unable to speak their mind and there was something that had to be said. I've always admired this in him; it's a true Gandhian trait. He was so principled in the way he conducted his personal life and his business that he could afford to speak fearlessly. It's another matter that he wasn't always diplomatic. But he always spoke from conviction. When

Rahul was in the room, I think convictions and assertions were always questioned and debated, and due to that more authentic conversations resulted.

I wasn't privy to the conversation among the presidents' council when I was offered a stint as president, but I'm certain Rahul had the conviction that it was time for a woman to take on the responsibility. I would say that while competence for the role was his paramount consideration, he also wanted parity and diversity. As he was a past president, we actually became friends and contemporaries (I was no longer just his friend Dr Reddy's daughter). It was a friendship that didn't last too long, since he became unwell and retired from public life.

The biggest learning that organizations, which had the benefit of Rahul's leadership, internalized, was to develop the ability to question, and sometimes to take hard calls, when it was not the popular thing to do . . . but the right thing to do! To put it the way Robert Frost would have . . . *he took the road less travelled.*

SHOBANA KAMINENI, *Executive Vice Chairperson, Apollo Hospitals Group, and past President, Confederation of Indian Industry*

Nimesh Kampani

As a visionary business leader of India Inc., Rahul Bajaj abundantly demonstrated his ability to think ahead of his time, look at things dispassionately and focus always on the bigger picture during his lifetime. But what made him a truly towering figure was his ability to make things turn out in his favour when the odds were stacked against him and to understand the investor's pulse. He had a fearless and outspoken approach.

I experienced those invaluable leadership traits firsthand while working closely with him on two occasions – during the successful issuance of Bajaj Auto's Global Depository Receipts (GDR) on the London Stock Exchange (LSE) and the corporate restructuring of Bajaj Auto Limited.

During Bajaj Auto's GDR debut in 1994, raising funds from global investors was a challenge, as there was a battle of perception and muted sentiment from the fund managers. Those were the early days of economic liberalization in India and global investors were extremely circumspect about investing in any Indian company. However, Rahul Bajaj's steadfast conviction and his gift for convincing people turned the tables for us during the final road show in London. Bajaj Auto raised US$110 million in the GDR issue by offering 43,42,676 equity shares at an issue price of US$25.33 per share.

It was truly an experience of a lifetime for me to see the demand pouring in from fund managers for allocations after the road show in London. Rahul-bhai made all of us, and above all the country, proud.

I also had the privilege of being associated with Rahul-bhai as his trusted advisor on the momentous decision of restructuring Bajaj Auto Limited during 2007–08. The successful implementation of this highly complicated corporate restructuring was a true testimony to his open-minded approach, exemplary vision and foresightedness. After exploring multiple options, the board approved a demerger scheme, splitting the group into three separate entities with the creation of two new companies.

Under the proposed scheme, Bajaj Auto's various businesses, including auto manufacturing and other strategic businesses such as wind energy, insurance and financial services, were demerged into two newly incorporated subsidiaries, Bajaj Auto Limited and Bajaj Finserv Ltd. The original Bajaj Auto Limited was then renamed Bajaj Holdings and Investments Limited, which continued to hold a 30 per cent equity stake in each of the other two operating companies.

I firmly believe that Rahul-bhai's charm and clarity of thought played a crucial role in winning the approval of all the stakeholders, including his family members, employees, lenders and other shareholders, for this complex transaction. He sensed the true value and opportunity of capitalizing on the Bajaj brand for two diverse business interests – automotives and financial services. The result was the enormous unlocking of shareholder value and the creation of many new possibilities.

The restructuring enabled investors to hold stakes in separate, focused businesses and thus participate in pure-play auto and/or financial services. It also ensured more transparent benchmarking of each of the two companies with their peers in their respective industries. However, there were mixed reactions in the market at that time to this decision. But Rahul-bhai had the prudence and incisive understanding to create the space for two diverse business segments to flourish and grow.

The move paid off brilliantly. Both businesses have grown exponentially, and the combined market capitalization of the three entities now stands at ₹4,02,000 crore, against the market capitalization of ₹25,000 crore of the erstwhile Bajaj Auto Limited in March 2007.

Rahul-bhai had many distinctive traits. He was a passionate and fierce businessman, a doting patriarch to his family and a jovial and trustworthy friend to many. But the traits that will always be dearest to me were the twinkle of optimism in his eyes and his zest for meeting new challenges head on.

NIMESH KAMPANI, *Chairman, JM Financial Group*

Rajive Kaul

Rahul Bajaj was a dear friend and a strong personality who had a deep impact on the way I have thought and acted in my corporate life.

My first impression of Rahul was that of an extremely articulate and dynamic past president of the Association of Indian Engineering Industry, AIEI, (which subsequently became the Confederation of Engineering Industry (CEI) and finally the Confederation of Indian Industry, CII). His many qualities of head and heart ensured that he was the only president to serve two terms in the 125-year history of the organization.

After I assumed charge of the CII eastern region, I got to know Rahul better with each passing year. On one occasion, at a CII dinner in 1984, he suggested that I should attend a meeting along with him at Davos and that he would arrange for me to be invited. In those early days, the World Economic Forum was known as the European Management Forum. He advised me that this conference was great for learning, for intellectual stimulation and for global networking at the highest possible level. The big bonus for me was being with him for five consecutive days in close interaction, amidst the snow-capped mountains of Switzerland. There I got to experience his many-faceted personality, which was always positive, cheerful and candid.

I have a very vivid memory of how, at a plenary session, Rahul came down heavily on the then South African President Willem de Klerk. He expressed his views as to how and why he disagreed with him. It took courage for someone to say what he did in the presence of 1,000 delegates, heads of state, ministers and the global media.

Another instance of Rahul speaking his mind without any fear was at a dinner where the chief minister of a state, who was the guest of honour, said, 'Rahul, you must put up a scooter factory in my state or face the consequences' – to which came a rather combative reply, 'Even the prime minister of India would not speak to me in this fashion and you can take any action you so desire.' That was the end of our dinner!

Being highly intelligent, extremely articulate and a successful captain of Indian Industry, Rahul was fiercely loyal to India and being Indian. He always portrayed our country as a nation that would soon come of age and make all of us proud of being Indian. He was a true visionary!

RAJIVE KAUL, *Non-Executive Chairman, Nicco Corp. Ltd., and past President, Confederation of Indian Industry*

Mohandas Keyyath

I first met Rahul Sir in the early 1980s. It was my first day in his office and I was as nervous as anyone could be. I was told he spoke with an American accent, and I was not looking forward to my first day. However, to my surprise and utter relief, he started speaking with me in Hindi, and in our own Indi-English in between.

He inquired about my family background, interests, etc., which put me at ease. The first couple of days I was asked to just sit in front of him and observe his activities, and when, finally, he started giving me work, I was able to handle it very smoothly. That was my first learning – as to how to be humble and how to make others do what you needed them to.

From then on I never looked back. He never asked us to stay back in office after office hours. Our staying back was spontaneous, and voluntary. There was Rahul Sir, who was regularly working till dinner time when it was not at all necessary for him to do so. With such an example, how could you be any less enthusiastic!

Working with him was such a pleasure, it never occurred to me to note how time flew – more than four decades. It feels like it was just yesterday that I started working with him, and I would have gone on working with him till kingdom come. But that was not to be.

Rahul Sir never imposed anything on anyone. His entire life was full of examples worth emulation by others. He was a man of great integrity and patriotism, and above all he was a man with a big heart. He was accessible equally to everyone, always ready to listen to the problems of others and ready with solutions.

While mostly the outcomes were positive, there were occasions when one had to face a negative decision. However, he was such an artist in saying 'no' that to you it would feel like a 'yes'.

I remember my first visit abroad with him. Right from checking-in, immigration, customs, etc., at the airport, he was there at every point to guide me and teach me the ropes. He would make sure that I put away my passport, foreign exchange, etc., safely. He was also very concerned about what I would eat, where I could get good and reasonably priced food, etc. It was unbelievable. He did not treat me like an assistant but took care of me like an elder brother!

During his tenure as chairman of Indian Airlines and member of the Rajya Sabha, we would go to Bengali Market in Delhi, where we used to have delicious chaat. He was so fond of Delhi chaat that the kind of dingy restaurants we patronized never bothered him.

Rahul Sir was much attached to his family, especially his children, though he never expressed his attachment in front of others. He was very concerned about the *parivar* – his brothers, sister and their families. As a person who has seen him so close, I have witnessed this affection many times.

He was very tight-fisted about one thing: complimenting his family. Somehow, it was difficult for him to show pride in the achievements of his family and close ones, especially in their presence. But when speaking about their achievements to a third person, his words of praise had no boundaries.

What can I say about Rahul Sir's affection for Rupa Madam? Even after fifty years of togetherness, their love still had that freshness, and when Madam passed away, half of his soul went away with her. At times, it was so obvious that her absence was crushing him from inside.

It was like he would continue to live forever. People like him should be immortal – he could have done so much for everyone around him; it was very unfair of God to take him away.

His place can never be filled; he was such a unique person. I shall always miss him, the elder brother I never had.

MOHANDAS KEYYATH, *former Executive Assistant to Rahul Bajaj*

Uday Kotak

As a youngster growing up, the success of Bajaj Auto was the stuff of folklore for me. The battle between the Bajaj and the Firodias over the use of the Bajaj brand name was in the public eye. That was when the persona of Rahul Bajaj as a straight-talking man, not shy of taking on something he believed in, was taking shape.

I finally had the opportunity to get to know the man behind the name when I joined the board of Bajaj Hindusthan. Shishir Bajaj was the managing director and Rahul-bhai the chairperson.

Rahul Bajaj was already synonymous with acumen and courage, having faced off against both the establishment and circumstances to lead Bajaj Auto to great heights. At the board meetings, I came to understand, admire and learn from the man everyone had an opinion on. He had great foresight and the rare ability to keep the big picture in mind without missing the details. I still remember him taking down notes with his left hand, asking incisive questions and easily recalling minutes of previous meetings.

I think he was much ahead of the curve when liberalization came knocking on the door and foreign competition was imminent. He understood that Indian business needed to reimagine and re-engineer itself in order to stay relevant and competitive. But he also saw that in the absence of domestic reforms, foreign competition would overrun the Indian private sector and that would adversely affect local entrepreneurship and employment.

His ask for fair competition for Indian businesses was read as a euphemism for seeking protection, while it was actually rooted in the desire to fight foreign businesses on a level playing ground. Rahul Bajaj was not a man to ever shy away from competition.

The Bombay Club moniker was rather ironic and devoid of context, because it was Rahul-bhai who, through the 1980s, had spoken out in favour of liberalization. He believed that competition made businesses better, and that entrepreneurs needed to look beyond the immediate future.

I had many a discussion with Rahul-bhai when he took Bajaj Finance public; I was the banker for the first issue. He saw Bajaj Auto Finance as being a crucial part of Bajaj Auto's two-wheeler financing strategy. He expected liberalization to bring consumerism in its wake and foresaw that friendly finance would enable people to buy more.

Today, Bajaj Auto and Bajaj Finserv are testimony to the man's vision and his contribution to the Indian business landscape. He made another very important contribution to Indian business – two outstanding professionals and entrepreneurs, Rajiv and Sanjiv Bajaj. Both are chips off the old block, who walk the talk and are not afraid to speak their mind, even to their father. It speaks of great parenting when children respect their parents and yet speak up in their presence.

Rahul Bajaj did not sugar-coat his words. Naturally, this did not endear him to everyone. He may not have been loved universally, but everyone respected him. He stood tall, literally and metaphorically, among his peers because he could speak truth to power. I had a great admiration for this trait. It was not just about courage; he backed what he said with logic and information. Rahul-bhai was deeply involved in the World Economic Forum and therefore well aware of the winds of change that were blowing across the world.

Change is constant and omnipresent.

Over the years, there were differences between Rahul Bajaj and his brother Shishir. I knew both well and hold them in high regard. Rahul-bhai was aware that I was on very good terms with Shishir, but did not let that dilute our relationship. I continue to have a warm relationship with both their families. Pallavi and I are particularly close to Rahul-bhai's daughter Sunaina. During the 26/11 attacks in Mumbai, our families huddled together as the terrorists rained bullets in the vicinity. Manish is an exemplary professional and an entrepreneur in his own right.

Rahul-bhai kept the rest of the family also tightly knit together. Shekhar, Madhur and Niraj continue to be an integral part of this family, under the unique halo of Rahul Bajaj.

It has been a year since the man I consider my mentor has passed – the man who taught me many things, especially how to handle difficult times with courage and grace. The void he has left behind will be difficult to fill. I miss you, Rahul-bhai.

UDAY KOTAK, *Founder and former MD & CEO, Kotak Mahindra Bank, and past President, Confederation of Indian Industry*

Suresh Krishna

When Indian industry was reeling under the licence raj, when most industrial leaders were hamstrung by a plethora of regulations, Rahul, managed to build a company, Bajaj Auto, though he was beset by the same rules. Bajaj Auto products were wait-listed for many years. People used to quip that if you placed an order for a Bajaj scooter today, your grandchild would surely get one. Such was the prestige, quality and value attached to the product.

Rahul was the chief architect of such a sought-after product. He not only led the company ably but also introduced many modern management practices, especially in the field of quality and service, which became bywords for many successful Indian companies.

Rahul was held in such esteem that he was chosen to be the president of the Confederation of Indian Industry (CII) twice, once in 1979-80, when the CII was known as the Association of Indian Engineering Industry, AIEI, and then again in 1999-2000. A rare honour, indeed. It speaks volumes of the goodwill, competence and capability that Rahul possessed and exhibited as a leader of industry. His knowledge and pleasing demeanour were assets to the CII, especially in dealing with the government.

After the liberalization of 1991, Bajaj Auto blossomed under his leadership and became an icon of manufacturing and product excellence. It continues that tradition to this day. Rahul was an inspiring leader of the engineering industry in India, much respected for his views in Indian and international forums.

I remember an old Latin saying, which exemplifies his achievements:

Nemo vir est qui mundum non reddat meliorem.

Roughly translated, it means, 'What man is a man who does not make the world better.'

I cannot think of a better person than Rahul who most aptly fits that old saying.

SURESH KRISHNA, *Chairman, Sundram Fasteners Ltd, and past President, Confederation of Indian Industry*

Narayanan Kumar

Rahul was a personal friend and shared times with my brother N. Sankar (who also passed away last year), when he was in ASSOCHAM, and they travelled together to Latin America and other places in the 1970s.

Fast forward to the 1990s, Rahul became a close friend, notwithstanding the age difference between us. To me and to Bhavani, he was very special. I can recall innumerable occasions of his kindness and special affection to me and to my family. Just to mention one – he travelled all the way to Chennai for my second daughter Mayura's wedding in 2010, which was very special. I was with him and Rupa in Pune for his fiftieth wedding anniversary.

Rahul taught me that when you speak, honesty and conviction are critical. At a Confederation of Indian Industry (CII) meeting in 1997, he stood in front of the prime minister and took on someone who spoke against the CII. Courage is something you attach to Rahul, and he was not afraid to talk critically about governments of any colour or party. He was not afraid to talk against a chief minister or ministers from any party if he thought they were wrong. What carried the day with Rahul was the conviction he had on the subject he was speaking on.

To the CII, he was very special. Though there are many former presidents and members who support the CII, Rahul provided more support than they did, both through his physical presence and, more importantly, by morally standing behind the CII in its every move. I will say that the CII brand has been invigorated by Rahul.

During my presidency, Rahul attended and participated in every important meeting, be it on corporate governance, insurance or industry. His presence was a source of strength to me and to the CII. Tarun Das can vouch for this even more than I can. Rahul was a mentor, not only to me but to successive presidents of the CII, and supported us. That leadership quality comes out clearly today, with both his sons taking the Bajaj Group businesses to greater heights than even when Rahul was at the helm!

My first (real) meeting with Rahul was in 1996 when I went to Pune as vice president of the CII. The respect he showed me even then was special. When we went to the Davos World Economic Forum (WEF), I was a novice, but Rahul ensured that everybody acknowledged who I was and introduced me to everybody, including the president of WEF.

Due to his association with and leadership of not only the CII but also the World Economic Forum, Harvard and other bodies, Rahul always had friends from all over the world. I have travelled with him many times; he was always popular. On my silver jubilee wedding anniversary, he and Rupa invited me to Alaska along with twenty other friends. His cousin Madhur and his wife Kumud were also with us. These friends came from US, Pune and other places in India and all over the world. But Rahul was always inclusive and took all of us into that gang – he made that trip very special.

Rahul – though people may not fully realize this – was a man of heart. On many occasions, I have reached out to him for help to support organizations for charity and causes pertaining to national issues. He always supported them. He was the chairman of the Jamnalal Bajaj Foundation, through which the family does a lot of charitable work quietly, without much fanfare. He always supported good causes, and especially in agriculture the foundation has done commendable work. This side of Rahul is not as well known as some of his other aspects.

At the CII, there is normally a person who gives a vote of thanks for the outgoing president at the annual general meeting (AGM). Mine was on 29 April 1998, and Rahul gave the speech, which was full of wit and humour and was very special to me. If there was a problem with Rahul, it was that he talked a lot. Given a subject to speak on, he would not stop within the time given him and would always exceed it! But everything he said was directly about the subject at hand, which he never diverted from. There was always plenty of wit included in his speeches and talks. Whenever he hit out at something, he made it sound more palatable because he always added a lot of humour.

I recall an incident which was typical of Rahul. A very good friend of his in England was kind enough to invite me, my wife Bhavani, Rahul and the famous film thespian, Dev Anand, to his house for dinner. It was a wonderful dinner, the food was outstanding and the host very warm. But, typical of Rahul, when we entered the venue (Rahul always started with a joke to fix the mood), he mentioned to the gentleman that this was Bhavani, a lawyer from Madras, and she always asked him where the host kept all the money. The host was shocked – Bhavani and I wanted to run away, the floor to open and take us out of sight, but Rahul kept on joking and the host realized too that it was a joke and laughed!!

NARAYANAN KUMAR, *Chairman, Group Corporate Board, The Sanmar Group, and past President, Confederation of Indian Industry*

Raghunath A. Mashelkar

Rahul-bhai Bajaj, to me, was not an individual. He was an institution. Individuals go. Institutions remain forever. And so will Rahul-bhai, through the amazing impact that he has made with his human values, his spirit, his inspiration, his courage, his compassion and his commitment. His commitment to give back to society has been seen by all of us, again and again.

My personal friendship with Rahul-bhai goes back forty-plus years. We became especially close when both of us worked together as members of the Indo-German Consultative Group that was formed by Chancellor Kohl of Germany and Prime Minister Narasimha Rao of India in the mid-1990s.

The group was formed in the wake of the start of economic liberalization in India in 1991, ostensibly to promote bilateral cooperation on a 'non-official' basis, and it was set up for advising on ways to strengthen and diversify mutually beneficial exchanges between the two countries. It had members from diverse walks of life, including thought leaders from industry, trade and commerce, as also social scientists, technologists, policy research specialists, etc. A brief report of every meeting used to go directly to the Chancellor of Germany and the Prime Minister of India.

My respect for Rahul-bhai grew exponentially as I saw his visionary thought leadership at these meetings. I saw him speak freely and frankly. He was known for saying what he meant and for meaning exactly what he said. Later on, as our friendship grew, I realized that it was this hallmark that made Rahul-bhai special.

His inspiring quote given in his amazing biography *Rahul Bajaj: An Extraordinary Life*, by Gita Piramal, sums it up well. He says: 'Integrity and character matter. Without them, no amount of ability can get you anywhere. In addition, you need courage – courage to make difficult decisions, and courage to oppose something if your conscience tells you that you are right.'

And I did witness the exceptional 'courage to differ' in this extraordinary man at the Indo-German Consultative Group meetings.

Rahul-bhai's courage was also accompanied by compassion and commitment to a just cause. His compassionate acts are too many to describe, but I remain grateful to him that he was kind enough to make me participate in some of these. Here are some personal examples.

I remember him asking me to inaugurate the Bajaj Science Education Centre at Wardha in 2007. This was established by Rahul-bhai as a centre for children to learn science through exploration and play. Its goal was to spark curiosity in their minds and to inculcate in them a sense of excitement in studying science. Through this initiative, he strived to nurture creativity and innovation in young minds so that when they grew up they could contribute to science and technology through their innovations.

Then, in 2019, he asked me to inaugurate the Rupa Rahul Bajaj Centre for Environment and Art in Pune. This is a small 'out of the box' experimental building where students are given basic hands-on experience of the environment and their immediate surroundings. Located in the vibrant setting of the Empress Botanical Garden, a green lung of Pune, the centre seamlessly integrates into the natural settings of the century-old British-era botanical garden. The centre has rooms (essentially enclosed spaces) where various facilities, like a library, a laboratory and a gallery, are all linked with strongly grounded curved walls. All this, along with the essential back-up of the house and utility areas, was accomplished in an area under 10,000 square feet.

In 2020, I remember his asking me to inaugurate the Women's Hall of Residence at the Indian Institute of Science Education and Research (IISER) in Pune, which he had set up with a generous donation of ₹50 crore. But there is an interesting and inspiring story behind this.

One day, the director of the IISER in Pune saw me along with some scientists. He said that the entrance examinations for admission to the IISER were as tough as that for IITs. But despite this, girls from rural areas and tier-III cities were passing these tough exams. But their parents would not let them join the IISER as they were worried about their safety in a big city like Pune. The IISER required an exclusive ladies' hostel. But that would cost ₹50 crore, and there was no hope of getting that amount from the government very soon.

The first person I thought I should approach was my dear friend Rahul-bhai.

I called him and explained to him the difference his help would make to the education of girls whose parents were reluctant to send them to the IISER due to concerns about their daughters' safety. It did not take Rahul-bhai even fifty seconds to agree to donate ₹50 crore!

It showed that Rahul-bhai was a man who thought from his heart and not his head. And his compassionate heart helped in the building of a home away from home for these girls. And it was not just the donation. Rahul-bhai personally saw to it that the construction of the hostel was done within the stipulated time and was well within the budget.

It is not out of place to say that in FY2021, the literacy rate among women increased by 8.8 per cent, highlighting the increasing possibilities of Indian women's productive participation in the nation's promising future. India is blessed with a large, capable working-age female population. We can leverage this valuable resource by means of achieving rapid growth over the next few years. Rahul-bhai, through his generosity and commitment towards women's education, gave a big gift towards the upliftment of women in society, and I feel humbled to have been part of this initiative.

In June 2022, the ever-gracious Bajaj family invited me as the chief guest to inaugurate the Rahul Bajaj Technology Innovation Centre (RBTIC) at the Indian Institute of Technology Bombay. I considered it a privilege, the idea of creating such a centre having been proposed by Rahul-bhai himself when he was the chairman of the board of governors of IIT Bombay. Not only had he proposed it, but he had funded it too. The foundation stone for this centre was laid by Rahul-bhai himself in 2018.

Rahul-bhai's generous donation has helped the institute build a centre, a modern building that brings together all innovation, entrepreneurship and research and development activities under one roof. The setting up of this centre is an important milestone that will help in facilitating the conversion of innovative ideas and research activity into new ventures and also support existing industries.

I must especially mention the Jamnalal Bajaj Awards, a very noble initiative, which I have been associated with for close to twenty years. The awards propagate the ideals of Jamnalal Bajaj by felicitating women and men who have been committed to inclusive development and have been involved at the grassroots level, working in line with Mahatma Gandhi's 'constructive programme' and who have taken a vow to selflessly serve the people, their community and the nation at large.

I started my association with these awards by chairing the committee for shortlisting the awardees in the category of science and technology, especially those whose innovations have contributed in the application of science and technology towards rural and tribal development. These potential awardees are the ones who make an impact by transforming the economic, social and ecological conditions of the weaker sections of society.

There are other three categories in which Jamnalal Bajaj Awards are bestowed. One of them recognizes and rewards innovations that contribute to 'constructive work' with a focus on any of the eighteen development areas based on Mahatma Gandhi's constructive programmes for creating a self-reliant and sustainable community in rural India.

Another category of awards is for women and child welfare. The awards are for contributions made by women towards the development and welfare of other women and children and who have focused on their upliftment through education, skills training, healthcare, literacy, livelihood activities, holistic development, advocacy, etc.

The last category consists of the international awards, which honour those individuals who are foreign nationals and have been successfully propagating Gandhian principles and the Mahatma's vision of brotherhood, friendliness, peace, non-violence, harmony, and moral conscience, outside India.

While chairing the science and technology awards committee, I had the privilege of witnessing the deliberations that happened at the main jury committee meeting, where the final decisions were taken. As the chairman of the committee, I had to present and justify the shortlist of candidates in this final jury committee meeting.

The legendary former Chief Justice Chandrashekhar, a great Gandhian himself, used to chair this jury committee. After his passing away in 2019, I was pleasantly surprised as well as greatly honoured when I got a call from Rahul-bhai, saying that there was unanimity amongst the trustees that I should chair the committee.

Incidentally, Rahul-bhai's role had been pivotal in all these awards committee debates and discussions. He never forced any of his personal views on us, leaving the decisions entirely to the jury. Long debates about the relative merits of the awardees by the fiercely independent-minded jury were a norm rather than an exception. Rahul-bhai's light touch, with a well-timed humorous comment, invariably helped to settle the issue on numerous occasions.

Rahul-bhai's pride in and the commitment to the great work done by the foundation came out very strongly when I heard him say at one of the awards functions:

> The light lit by Jamnalal-ji and nursed with care by Ramkrishna-ji will not be allowed to be dimmed and the traditions of constructive work, which are the hallmarks of the Bajaj Group, will be carried on equally vigorously through the Jamnalal Bajaj Foundation, the various Trusts and the Companies belonging to the Group.

In 2022, I had the honour of working in the dual role of not only chairman of the jury for the Jamanalal Bajaj awards but also of giving away the awards as the chief guest. I consider this as one of the greatest honours and privileges that I have received in my life.

I began this essay by describing the human side of Rahul-bhai. But the world has known Rahul-bhai as the man behind Bajaj Group who made it one of the largest conglomerates in India, with a strong presence in both the domestic and international markets. Even at the age of eighty-three, he was an active and influential figure in Indian business and society. He has been and will always be remembered and widely respected for his business acumen.

Rahul-bhai had a clear and unambiguous business strategy. He had said:

> We faced competition head-on and I concentrated on three things. I must have volume, the lowest cost and the best quality. It is very simple; there is nothing intelligent in that. If you don't have these three things, you are in trouble. Others failed to do so, and they could not compete with us on quality or price.

Bajaj Auto always competed with others based on quality, cutting-edge technology and innovation.

Rahul-bhai's business strategy resonated with the concept of MLM (more from less for more) that I and the legendary late C.K. Prahalad had proposed in our *Harvard Business Review* paper (July–August 2010) titled 'Innovation's Holy Grail', which was later ranked among the top ten must-read papers on innovation.

The origin of MLM has to be traced back to my talk in Canberra on 28 April 2008 to the members of the Australian Academy of Technological Sciences and Engineering, when I was inducted as its fellow. The title of my talk was 'Indian Innovation: From Gandhi to Gandhian Engineering'.

The essence of Gandhian engineering was based on the two tenets of Mahatma Gandhi. The first one was, 'Earth provides enough to satisfy every man's need, but not every man's greed.' That meant getting 'more from less' – meaning, using less of our exhaustible resources, and using them more efficiently. The second tenet was, 'I would prize every invention of science made for the benefit of all.' That meant innovating for 'more' people. Combining the two, we have the essence of 'Gandhian Engineering', namely 'more from less for more'.

The objective of the MLM type of innovation would not be just to produce low-performance, cheap knock-off versions of rich-country technologies so that they can be marketed to poor people. Rather, the objective is to harness sophisticated science and technology know-how to invent, design, produce and distribute high-performance technologies at prices affordable to a majority of the people. This would mean the highest quality at lowest cost for the largest number of people.

And that was precisely what Rahul-bhai delivered. He had said, 'I must have volume, the lowest cost and the best quality.' And he achieved this goal with 'speed, scale and sustainability' and by using the power of 'talent, technology and trust'.

Rahul-bhai was not just a great industrialist and businessman but also a great industry and business leader.

As regards leadership, he held the position of the president of the Confederation of Indian Industry (CII) in 1979-80, and again in 1999-2000, the only leader to have held this position twice. Through his long and close association with the CII, he championed initiatives in competitiveness, technology, corporate governance, community development and many other areas.

Indeed, Rahul-bhai was a true and steadfast mentor to the CII since its transformation in 1974. As president of the CII in 1979-80, he presided over landmark initiatives in the competitiveness and international engagement of Indian industry, which guided its future.

I was in Delhi as the director general of the Council of Scientific and Industrial Research during Rahul-bhai's second stint as president of the CII during 1999-2000. I saw how his presidency took forward the IT industry to catapult the country into the digital age. His passion for India's progress illuminated the Indian economy. The CII credits him with building an industry lobby in India with his able leadership and guidance.

There are many specific things that I remember of our interactions at the CII. One of them occurred when I was the chairman of the CII technology committee during Rahul-bhai's presidency. Those were the 'dotcom' days. I was the keynote speaker for the CII annual summit. I remember saying that the only dotcom that India needed was a 'hassle-free dotcom'.

By then everybody was irritated by the hassles and hurdles created by bureaucratic government processes, and there was a huge burst of applause. Rahul-bhai, in later years though, used to remind me of the phrase that I had used and say that despite all the pronouncements about ease of doing business, the country still did not have 'your hassle-free dotcom'!

In the end, I must say that although Rahul-bhai is no more, I am sure that each of us who knew him feels that he is everywhere.

I am grateful to Rahul-bhai and the Bajaj family for giving me an abundance of love, affection and trust in the decades gone by. I am grateful to my dear friend Tarun for giving me this opportunity to express publicly my affection and admiration for the legendary Rahul-bhai.

RAGHUNATH A. MASHELKAR, former Director General, Council of Scientific and Industrial Research

Colette Mathur

Being married to M.G. Mathur, a senior officer of the Indian government, I was a frequent visitor to India. I had discovered a wonderful 'joint family' in the pure local tradition. I had easily adjusted to this new environment and in fact very much enjoyed being part of such a closely-knit group. I also met many very senior civil servants whose intelligence, high education and culture were the backbone of India's government leadership.

Politicians and business leaders were not part of my new world.

This was the situation until 1979, when I joined the World Economic Forum. I wanted to engage India more in the forum's activities. I proposed to Klaus Schwab that I start working on this project. This was also when I was fortunate enough to meet Rahul Bajaj, who agreed to help me identify a partner with whom I could start working.

With no hesitation, he suggested I meet Tarun Das, director general of what is now the Confederation of Indian Industry, the CII.

Thanks to Rahul, this partnership led us to successfully integrate leading members of the Indian business community and also top government members at the yearly India Economic Summit that we had created. We also ensured that Indian contingents went to the annual meeting in Davos. Rahul became a very dear, widely admired and active member of the forum. He was very popular among his peers for his great sense of humour, generosity, business talent and charm.

Goodbye, my dear friend Rahul. We miss you.

COLETTE MATHUR, *former Director (South Asia), World Economic Forum*

Vikram Mehta

My association with the Bajaj family predates my personal relationship with Rahul-bhai. My grandfather, Dr Mohan Singh Mehta, knew Shri Jamnalal Bajaj, and from what I gathered from conversations with my grandfather, their relationship was based on deep mutual respect. One was a Marwari businessman and the other a Fabian socialist and public administrator in feudal Mewar. My family had for generations served the court of Mewar (Udaipur), and although my grandfather wanted to teach on his return from the London School of Economics with a PhD in economic history, he was compelled by tradition and familial pressure to join the Mewar administration.

Both were deeply committed to the national movement, to societal progress and to Mahatma Gandhi. I am not sure where their paths first crossed, but they were in touch through letters. The philanthropic contributions of the Bajaj family were often the subject of conversation between me and my grandfather when we talked about the role of business in society.

I first met Rahul-bhai socially through common friends in the business community. He was always the dominant figure at these gatherings, and I did little more than listen to his clear and forcefully articulated thoughts on the 'state of the nation'. I got to know him better at the meetings of the Confederation of Indian Industry (CII) national council, where his blunt, incisive, often amusing and provocative interventions enlivened an otherwise pedantic roll call of government achievements by senior officials. It was a particular pleasure to hear him call a spade a shovel.

I cannot claim, however, that these interactions created a bond of deep friendship between us, for they were intermittent and somewhat impersonal. What transformed our relationship were two unrelated but personal developments. I narrate them below not because they track the evolution of my relationship with Rahul-bhai but because they revealed to me the person behind his larger-than-life personality.

My wife Tasneem Zakaria Mehta is an art historian and formerly the vice chairman of the Indian National Trust for Art and Cultural Heritage (INTACH) and convener of the Greater Mumbai INTACH chapter.

Late in the 1990s, my wife persuaded the Municipal Corporation (MC) of Mumbai to allow INTACH to restore the Bhau Daji Lad museum (the erstwhile Victoria and Albert Museum), the oldest museum in Mumbai. At the time it was derelict. The plaster was peeling off the walls; the woodwork had rotted and the display cabinets were so encrusted with dust you could barely see the objects. Tasneem convinced the MC that she would raise the funds and provide the expertise to return the museum to its pristine glory. It took time and patience to convince the municipality, but eventually the MC agreed.

Tasneem had set herself a tough challenge to secure private funding. She approached several industrial houses. Many expressed interest, but internal corporate bureaucracy or whatever drove a wedge between intent and outcome. Rahul-bhai came to the museum at the request of Tasneem, and within minutes he approved the entirety of Tasneem's funding request. He asked pertinent questions, but his sanction was on the spot. He followed up this financial commitment by joining the board of trustees.

Henceforth, he stood solidly behind Tasneem as she navigated the complex cross-currents of politics, bureaucracy, management and public interest. It was a matter of great personal satisfaction to him that UNESCO recognized the restoration with the award of its Asia-Pacific Award of Excellence for Cultural Conservation, the only award of excellence given to an Indian institution that year, to the museum, which came to be ranked alongside Mumbai's Gothic architecture as an essential stop in the itinerary of visitors to the city.

I was at the time chairman of Shell India and therefore familiar with corporate procedures. What struck me was the speed of bhai's decision-making. It took him minutes to recognize that the proposal warranted support; that the promoters of the proposal were individuals of integrity and expertise; that they could deliver what they promised; that this would indeed make a huge impact on the city; that the money requested was minimal relative to the upside; and finally, that if corporate India did not step up to support such public-interest projects, they did not deserve the profits they made.

Rahul-bhai's association with the museum brought me closer to him. I met him outside conventional social and business circles, and on such occasions he would inevitably introduce me by reference to Tasneem. 'Vikram is chairman of Shell but his claim to recognition, if any, is his wife. He is married to . . .' – this was his favourite opening refrain.

These bonds of friendship strengthened further when I agreed to help the Brookings Institution set up the Brookings Institution India Centre (BIIC) as its first executive chairman between 2012 and 2020. Rahul-bhai was at that time a trustee of the Brookings Institution.

I had set out three conditions to Strobe Talbott, the president of Brookings Institution, prior to accepting his offer. One, BIIC must be an Indian think-tank focused on matters of policy important to India; two, in consequence, it must be led by Indian scholars, and three, it must be supported by a wide phalanx of Indian corporations so as to ensure it was perceived to be independent and not under the control of any one or more corporate entities.

These conditions were accepted, but they made the task of raising funds that much more difficult. There were a few companies that understood the need and importance of analytically rigorous, independent and empirically solid policy research and were prepared to support such work. But the majority had not really thought of think-tanks as potential recipients of their CSR funds.

Rahul-bhai provided stellar support to me in changing this perception. Not only was the Bajaj Group amongst the first to join Brookings India's Founders Circle (FC), but Rahul-bhai also went out of his way to persuade other corporate leaders to support my efforts. As a result, in time Brookings India was able to garner funds (the same amount from each) from twenty-five corporations, all of which are today recognized as members of Brookings India FC.

Later, in 2020, when Brookings India decided to change its name to Centre for Social and Economic Progress (CSEP),' Rahul-bhai gave me unstinted support in managing the transition. He joined the CSEP board, and it would be no exaggeration to say that it was because of his meticulous eye for detail and refusal to accept anything less than excellence that CSEP has more than doubled in size since its inception and is now recognized as one of the premier multidisciplinary think-tanks in India.

There are few business families with as strong a claim to corporate philanthropy as the Bajaj Group. It is not for nothing that Mahatma Gandhi referred to Shri Jamnalal Bajaj as the 'merchant prince'. Rahul-bhai nurtured similar values. He was a hard-nosed businessman, and had he not been so, '*Hamara Bajaj*' would not have become the top-selling scooter in the world. But profits were not his singular purpose. He operated on a broader canvas. His support to Tasneem's museum and his readiness to put his weight behind the creation of a world-class think-tank in India without looking for any 'quid' for his 'quo' were illustrative of his philosophy that whilst companies needed to make profits to afford principles, they did not deserve profits if they abridged principles. That was his value credo, and it had been the credo of his family for generations.

Rahul-bhai was a friend who helped when help was most needed. Tasneem and I owe him a huge debt of gratitude.

VIKRAM SINGH MEHTA, *former Chairman, Shell Group of Companies (India), and currently Chairman, Centre for Social and Economic Progress*

Tasneem Mehta

My first formal meeting with Rahul-bhai, as Rahul Bajaj was known to his family and friends, was when he came to the Dr Bhau Daji Lad Museum with his cousin Niraj Bajaj, sometime in late 2000. I had made a proposal to the Jamnalal Bajaj Foundation, of which he was president at the time, to fund the restoration of the museum, which was in a derelict condition. I had met Rahul-bhai briefly in New York several years earlier at a dinner, and his towering stature intimidated me at the time. I was anxious that he might reject the proposal or make difficult demands on the municipal corporation, who are the owners of the museum. I had been trying to raise funds for the project for almost five years, but conservation at the time was not a known subject, and getting a corporate house to fund a government project seemed an almost impossible task. I had been ditched at the altar, so to speak, by one of the largest business houses in the country, and most of the others were not convinced the project would succeed. This meeting with Rahul-bhai was therefore critical.

Niraj and his wife Minal had done a recce and due diligence of the project, and it was their foresight and faith that helped steer the way. I had just completed the site museum, master plan and restoration of the Elephanta caves with the Archaeological Survey of India (ASI). I was Indian National Trust for Art and Cultural Heritage (INTACH) convenor for Mumbai at the time.

To celebrate the successful completion of the project, which had been funded by the UNESCO, the ASI and INTACH Mumbai decided to host a gala event at the caves, which Niraj and Minal attended. The chief minister graced the occasion, and most of Mumbai's luminaries were present. Shubha Mudgal sang shlokas and Alarmel Valli danced in homage to Lord Shiva in front of the Trimurti. It was an unforgettable evening. Shortly after this, I approached Niraj with the proposal for the Dr Bhau Daji Lad (BDL) Museum.

I'm sure Rahul-bhai had been well briefed by Niraj, who had visited the museum previously and carefully studied the details of the project. Niraj had told me that Rahul-bhai would make the final decision. As I waited with trepidation for their cars to arrive at the museum that morning, I went through all the important points in my head. Rahul-bhai listened intently as I explained the importance of the museum, which was a forgotten relic in a highly dilapidated condition. I pointed out that the museum was a rich archive of the city's history, which should be beautifully showcased to the public. Rahul-bhai walked through the galleries and in half an hour decided and agreed to support the project. I was absolutely elated. This was in contrast to the experiences I had had with other corporate houses, where after many meetings and much confabulation nothing had happened.

Rahul-bhai's interest in the project was exemplary. He was a member of the board of trustees, and in the initial stages he attended all the meetings to ensure the parameters and functioning of the trust were on track. His presence galvanized everyone, and many issues were resolved quickly as a result of his attention to detail and determination to get things moving. When we won UNESCO's highest award of Excellence for Cultural Conservation in 2005, he was very happy and proud. We went together to meet the President Pratibha Patil at the Rashtrapati Bhavan to request her to open the restored museum to the public. That was a very special moment. When the museum finally opened to the public, Rahul-bhai hosted a special evening at the museum for important people in the city.

At the very first meeting of the board of trustees of the museum, I had flagged the idea of an expansion plan. Rahul-bhai understood the museum's tremendous educational potential and the importance of expanding the museum facilities. He offered to fund the plan, if the Bajaj name was associated with the museum, for an extended period of time. However, the proposal took a long time to materialize. Eventually, a more elaborate version of the expansion plan was prepared under the chairmanship of Municipal Commissioner Sitaram Kunte and a very successful international architectural competition was held in 2014. That plan too is in abeyance, but it is hoped it will come to fruition someday soon.

Rahul-bhai was one of the most remarkable people I have met. His eye for detail and his quick grasp of issues made him a formidable person to interact with. He was always prompt in his responses, which often included a touch of humour. He was deeply committed to the public good, and his interest and support contributed significantly to the success of the BDL Museum project. I feel fortunate that I had the opportunity to work with him, and I owe him a huge debt of gratitude for his belief in me and his unstinting support to me.

TASNEEM MEHTA, *Honorary Director and Managing Trustee, Dr Bhau Daji Lad Museum*

Ashok Misra

I wish to thank Tarun Das for asking me to contribute to this book on Rahul Bajaj, and it is my immense pleasure to do so. I was privileged to enjoy a special relationship with Bajaj, starting in 2003 when he took over as the chairman of the board of governors of the Indian Institute of Technology Bombay (IIT Bombay), where I was the director. I was on a short sabbatical at the University of Cambridge as a visiting professor when he took charge. My first conversation with him was over the phone from Cambridge. He was in Pune. In his typical inquisitive manner, and with his characteristic insatiable curiosity, he asked a lot of very detailed questions about IIT Bombay! A few weeks later, a Confederation of Indian Industry (CII) delegation had an event at the London Business School. By coincidence, I was independently invited and unexpectedly met him in person for the first time. But it was a very brief chat as he was busy with the CII event. It was only later, when we were both in India, that we had our first long personal conversation at the Taj hotel in Mumbai. That conversation was the start of a long relationship, one that I will always cherish with respect, fondness and admiration.

I saw Rahul Bajaj as a towering personality and a great visionary whose enormous contribution to the growth of Indian industry is well known. People like him come once in a generation. His knowledge spanning a number of subjects was really enormous, and he was always on top of every situation. He was a strong leader full of ideas and suggestions for the growth of any organization. He was a true nationalist who put the benefit and growth of India foremost in his mind. In my experience, I found him a forward-thinking leader who inspired a lot of people. He was always thinking about how our organization could help the country.

He was very eloquent and shared his thoughts freely. His frankness in sharing his opinions was his trademark. Yet he was willing to listen to the viewpoint of others with patience. I also found him to be very fair-minded in his dealings with people. In addition, I remember him as a fun-loving person with a great sense of humour. He appeared to be tough at times, but then I noticed a very warm and soft side to his personality. He had a very high level of business ethics, which earned him the respect of all around him. I regarded him as a person of high thinking and simple living. The thing I most admired in him was his respect for all human beings. He never compromised on his values and managed to achieve a mind-boggling number of truly inspirational things in his lifetime. People like him are a great asset, not only to our nation but also to the world.

Perhaps the best way I can honour Bajaj is to recall some of my interactions with him in the context of our respective roles at IIT Bombay – he as the chairman and I as the director. It is such specific details that ultimately help define and understand the way great souls like him operate and serve as a road map for younger generations seeking to learn from high achievers.

Our interactions began with the start of his three-year term as the chairman of the board of governors of IIT Bombay from 2003 to 2006. During our first few meetings he told me he did not know much about academic institutions, especially IIT Bombay, and he would like to learn. I soon realized that he knew a lot more than he let on since he had done his homework and was always very well informed! He would ask me and my colleagues very pertinent questions about the workings of IIT Bombay and its progress over the years. He would lay special emphasis on plans for the institute's future progress. He made enormous contributions to the institute, and it was during his tenure that IIT Bombay surged ahead to become the leading IIT among its peers in India. The decisions taken at the board meetings helped us put new systems in place to attract high-quality faculty and excellent students. Overall, there was a huge cultural change and a paradigm shift at IIT Bombay. It became a very vibrant place, one that marched confidently ahead to its tryst with excellence and its goal of becoming a leading global institution.

His first major visit to the institute was when he came for the convocation scheduled for 8 August 2003. The convocation was held in the afternoon and the board meeting the same day, in the morning. He came to the institute on the evening of 7 August and we discussed in detail the full agenda of the board meeting to be held the next morning. He had a lot of questions, most of which I managed to answer to the best of my ability. He offered some excellent suggestions to be taken up at the board meeting. In particular, he made several observations about the institute accounts, this being one of his strengths. We had our first board meeting under his chairmanship the next morning and he was introduced to the board members, including some senior faculty. Even though he was such a towering personality, he put all of us at ease with his friendly conversations and openness. He clearly brought a breath of fresh air to the board, and we all realized that the institute would progress greatly under his leadership as the chairman.

We had sent him the video recordings of the previous convocations since he wanted to get a good feel of the flow of events during this ceremony. The students of IIT Bombay wear traditional kurta–pyjama at the convocation, and he asked me if it would be okay for him also to do so. As we know, he loved to wear kurtas for most occasions, and I said of course yes.

Subsequently, I also decided not to wear a suit but a kurta for future convocations. At the 2003 convocation, Rajiv Lochan Gupta, CEO of Rohm and Haas, was the chief guest, and N.R. Narayana Murthy received the Honoris Causa degree. Bajaj chaired the convocation proceedings in an outstanding manner with his elegant touch and provided a different ambience to the function from what it used to be earlier.

He had to hand over the Honoris Causa degree to Narayana Murthy, and he did so with elegance and some humour. His first convocation address as the chairman was brilliant, and he gave several ideas for the growth of IIT Bombay. He congratulated the graduating students and gave them sound advice for their future endeavours. He set the tone for the institute towards enhancing industry–academia interactions.

At the 2004 convocation, Mukesh Ambani was the chief guest and Faqir Chand Kohli received the Honoris Causa degree. He knew both of them well and appreciated their respective contributions to Indian industry. He talked about the technology incubation centre that had started functioning on campus. At the 2005 convocation, Arjun Singh, the minister for human resource development at the time, was the chief guest, and Anil Kakodkar received the Honoris Causa degree. All of Bajaj's convocation addresses were very thought-provoking. He always encouraged the graduating students to be bold and contribute to the growth of the nation. He shared with them the common traits of the engineers that worked at Bajaj Auto. They were: passion, focus, excellence, commitment and determination. He said an organization that had employees with these traits would be the darling of its customers and a terror to its competitors, and that the graduates should try to imbibe these qualities.

He was a chairman from the business and industrial community after a long string of senior scientists had led IIT Bombay. He took over from Professor M.G.K. Menon, a towering figure in the world of academics and science. I was fortunate to have two leading personalities in their respective fields to guide the institute and me. The enormous experience Bajaj had in the corporate world made a great difference in the working of the IIT, since he brought in a new kind of thinking and energy to the board as well as to the institute. For the board meetings, he would go through the board agenda and discuss every item with me the day before, along with his comments. Subsequently, at the board meeting he would discuss every item in detail and offer solutions to those that needed the intervention of the board. In a short time he grasped the workings of IIT Bombay and offered a number of constructive suggestions and out-of-the-box ideas for making it a truly global institute. He always had the big picture about the future of IIT Bombay in mind, and at the same time he had a very good grasp of the details. His prime focus was always the growth of the institute. One of the things we admired most about him was that he always found the time for IIT Bombay meetings and events. All the meetings were held on the institute campus, and he would often come by his own helicopter.

The chairman of the board of governors (BoG) at IIT Bombay is also the chairman of the finance committee, and Bajaj focused on the financial aspects as he was very strong in this area. He would often point out things that we may have overlooked. This helped us to tighten our financial systems and bring changes in our accounting system, which was a great step forward. Another initiative that we took was to engage the services of an internal audit firm before the accounts were sent for audit to the comptroller and accountant general. In the years to follow, the objections raised by the Comptroller and Auditor General of India (CAG) came down considerably.

Another significant contribution by him was to bring about a major change in the governance structure. We took the help of McKinsey to go through our governance processes and to suggest changes. This task was led by IIT alumni who were working at McKinsey. Bajaj played a major role in building a new structure for smoother and more efficient running of the institute. His knowledge of good practices from industry helped bring about the needed changes.

After the board meetings we would visit a couple of selected departments, and he took interest in learning about academic activities from the faculty and always gave them encouragement and imbued them with enthusiasm. Often, he would point out that the infrastructure in the departments was getting old and needed renovation. His visits helped us to get the required approvals from the board and other committees to improve the infrastructure in the departments and centres.

At that time, IIT Bombay was the only institute to have an advisory council, chaired by the chairman of the BoG, which would help bring up new ideas and initiatives for the institute. We had leading people from the corporate world, leading academicians and distinguished IIT alumni as members of the IIT Bombay Advisory Council (IITBAC).

The members included Mukesh Ambani, Naushad Forbes, S. Ramadorai, Adi Godrej, Prof. M.G.K. Menon, Prof. M.M. Sharma, Prof. S.P. Sukhatme, Alyque Padamsee and Nandan Nilekani. The IITBAC would deliberate on the current status in selected areas and focus on the new initiatives put forward by the institute to take it to greater heights in its quest to become a global institute. The IITBAC did not have to deal with the working of the institute, as that was taken care of by the board; this was basically a brainstorming forum. The ideas suggested by the IITBAC would then be converted into projects and finally implemented after the approval of the board. Further, the IITBAC enhanced the interactions between the members and IIT leaders – the deputy director and the deans.

Bajaj's contributions at the IITBAC were enormous. We would often call him for advice in following up on the recommendations made by this body while building the framework. With his support we could take new and bold initiatives at the institute.

As an example, the starting of the Society for Innovation and Entrepreneurship (SINE) and the laying down of its details were guided by him. In fact, at one advisory council meeting, Rahul Bajaj and Mukesh Ambani laid out the entire plan for developing SINE, and that became the blueprint for us to follow. The foundation laid at that time made SINE the best technology incubator in any academic institution in India, and it remains so to this day.

Rahul Bajaj helped IIT Bombay take so many new initiatives through the board and the advisory council that it is difficult to list them all. Some of the major decisions and actions taken during his tenure were:

1. Given the changing times, the governance system at IIT Bombay had to be reviewed and updated. His enormous experience in the industrial sector and his valuable inputs helped us put in place systems for an improved governing framework. He gave us excellent suggestions for improvement of our governance and helped me personally to deal with it. Alongside, he helped us refine and upgrade the financial systems.
2. He always emphasized the need for enhancement of interactions between industry and the institute. During his tenure we saw an increase of interactions in this area. He helped to connect us with several companies. He would, however, point out that the IITB was slow in responding, and we tried our best to address this shortcoming.
3. A major increase in the number of PhD students took place

during his tenure. This was done to enhance the research focus of the institute, and it paid dividends in the years to follow. At the 2008 convocation, the number of PhDs reached 200 for the first time at IIT Bombay. The PhD students take about four years to graduate.

4. Another of his major contributions was in helping us put together a road map for establishing an excellent technology incubation centre and enhancing our entrepreneurship activities. We established SINE, with a framework that was robust. He helped us fine-tune the financial aspects of SINE, which eventually became a role model for other institutions to emulate.
5. There was an enhancement in interactions between our institute and other leading educational institutions round the globe for mutual benefit during his tenure. Several memorandums of understanding (MoUs) for collaboration were signed with his approval. A major collaboration was with Monash University, Australia, to establish the IIT Bombay–Monash Research Academy for joint PhD programmes. This helped us get higher-quality students for pursuing doctoral work and to obtain joint degrees from both institutions. This model was entered into for the first time at an Indian educational institution, and it has become very successful. It has become a model for other IITs to emulate. The other major MoUs were with Washington University, University of Cambridge and National University of Singapore, among others.
6. Bajaj helped the IIT system bring about significant changes through the IIT council. He made some bold remarks at the IIT council and helped to bring about constructive changes in the practices that were in place. One such decision was the hiring of faculty of Indian origin – with PIO cards but with foreign passports – on a permanent basis. Earlier, we could

offer positions to such people on contract only, hence we were missing out on some very capable people. Such decisions helped all the IITs.

7. The master plan for the institute was made during Bajaj's tenure, and this helped enormously in the matter of future construction activities on the campus. This was much needed for expansion of the institute as student enrolments grew.
8. We managed support for the construction of several buildings on campus, with novel approaches to quality under his leadership. With his help and support, we could start to construct buildings with facilities of high quality. He would examine each case very critically and gave sound advice. The major constructions included the iconic convention centre, named after Victor Menezes, a distinguished alumnus of the institute who contributed generously for this, the lecture hall complex, faculty housing and several buildings for departments and centres.
9. Upgrades of the infrastructure of departments and centres happened when Bajaj was helming the board. The institute was about forty-six years old and the structural infrastructure had started to deteriorate owing to the weather conditions in Mumbai and were looking shabby. His support helped us to renovate most departments and centres.
10. One of the shortcomings in the system was lack of post-retirement medical benefits for faculty and staff. The institute put up a proposal for this, and Bajaj examined it himself very closely, suggested several steps that we needed to take, and asked us to bring it to the board later. His invaluable inputs helped us put together a scheme that would benefit the employees and at the same time was financially viable. It was such a relief for the faculty and staff as they used to struggle for proper medical care after their retirement.

11. IIT Bombay alumni are an enthusiastic group with a passion to give back to their alma mater. On several occasions they wanted to meet and interact with the chairman of the BoG. Bajaj always made time in his busy calendar to meet them. One such meeting was held in the New York area. We had a wonderful dinner meeting at the home of Parag Saxena, a distinguished alumnus. This was followed by a formal meeting in New York City. At both these events, Bajaj clearly outlined the vision of IIT Bombay, its quest for excellence and how the alumni could contribute.
12. He was always available to hear about the welfare of the faculty and staff. Very often, the non-academic staff association representatives would want to meet him, and with his concurrence I would arrange a meeting. He always gave them a good hearing and then took his own decisions on their grievances and demands.

The above incomplete list of Bajaj's contributions offers a glimpse of his enormous involvement with IIT Bombay, which will be remembered for a long time. As the director during his tenure, I learnt a lot from him and he guided me greatly with his visionary and progressive approach, thus helping me perform my role better. One of the features I admired most in him was that he was available at any time if needed for consultations. I remember that I needed to speak to him on a very urgent matter and he was attending the World Economic Forum at Davos. I sent word to him through his office and he called back as soon as he could, thus helping us resolve the issue.

In 2005, I had got a second term of five years at IIT Bombay, and he was the first one to call me to congratulate me as soon as he found out about it. I was of course delighted and promised him that I would try to do my best in my second term. I would get invitations to be on the boards of companies and educational institutions. I consulted every case with him in detail and he always gave me very sound advice, which helped me make my decisions. The welfare of the institute was his prime focus, and he emphasized that looking after the institute had to be my priority. Later on, I received an excellent offer from an American company to be the chairman of their Indian operations in 2008. The first person I called for advice was Rahul Bajaj, and he gave me several important points to think about before changing jobs. Clearly, his insights were enormously useful.

He will always be remembered at IIT Bombay as an outstanding chairman who brought new energy to the board of governors. His aspirations and push to take the institute to the next level was always inspirational for all of us. His passion to see that we attained excellence in all our activities and his support for improving our management have been most helpful. We were indeed very privileged to have Rahul Bajaj guide IIT Bombay to the next levels in its education and research programmes.

I always admired his enormous energy and his out-of-the-box thinking. Working with him was challenging, inspirational and fun. From him I learnt how to deal with difficult situations and find solutions. He would appreciate the good practices of the institute and make critical remarks on the not-so-good ones. His flamboyance and clarity of thought were the trademarks of his personality, which we all admired. Together we took IIT Bombay to greater heights, and by the end of his tenure it became the leading IIT in India.

After the end of his tenure, Bajaj offered to support the technology innovation centre at IIT Bombay by making a generous donation. We worked out the logistics and invited him for the inauguration of the centre. We wanted to name it after him, and with a bit of persuasion he agreed. It is thus called the Rahul Bajaj Technology

Innovation Centre, in appreciation of his contributions to it. We could not arrange a formal farewell for him at the end of his tenure at IIT Bombay, and hence organized a seventieth birthday celebration for him to coincide with the inaugural event. It was an excellent occasion for the faculty members who had worked with him closely to pay their respects and convey their good wishes to him.

The readied Rahul Bajaj Technology and Innovation Centre building was inaugurated on his birthday in 2022. It is an eight-storeyed building with a single-level basement. It is a multi-department academic building with an overall area of about 19,900 square metres. The building is designed to have semi-open spaces welcoming the outdoors and integrating it with the interior spaces, making the building lively and conducive to creative output. The building provides ample space to accommodate a large welcoming lobby, two large exhibition halls, a few academic and conference spaces, classrooms and office spaces. It houses the Society for Innovation and Entrepreneurship (SINE), the Industrial Research and Consultancy Centre (IRCC) and IDC School of Design. This centre will always remind IIT Bombay of Rahul Bajaj's contributions to it.

In addition, he sponsored several chair professorships at IIT Bombay, and they were:

1. Rahul Bajaj Chair Professor in the area of Mechanical Engineering
2. Kamalnayan Bajaj Chair Professor in the area of Electrical Engineering
3. Bajaj Group Chair Professor in the area of Computer Science and Engineering
4. Ramkrishna Bajaj Chair Professor in the area of Design

The faculty members appointed on these chairs over the years have benefited and have contributed to teaching and research in their respective disciplines.

On a more personal level, I have many fond memories from the quality time I spent with him, both at the institute and at our home over dinners and get-togethers. His pleasant manner put everyone at ease and he always shared interesting anecdotes. At times our meetings included the faculty of IIT Bombay, and Bajaj, with his enormous knowledge of quite a few subjects, would enthusiastically share stories with us.

One of my memories of him is from our trip to IIT Roorkee in his helicopter from Delhi to Roorkee. He was to receive an honorary doctorate degree from IIT Roorkee and he wanted me to accompany him. We had a wonderful trip and a marvellous visit to IIT Roorkee. His insights about the corporate world were fascinating and I learnt a lot from our conversations. His perspective on a number of matters was excellent.

My wife Rashmi runs an NGO named Vidya Integrated Development for Youth and Adults (VIDYA), and Bajaj always made it a point to inquire about it. He made a generous donation to VIDYA. He had introduced us to his cousins Shekhar Bajaj, Madhur Bajaj and Niraj Bajaj and their families. Niraj often accompanied Rahul-ji to the functions at IIT Bombay, and I got to know him quite well. Rashmi and I were fortunate to be invited to Rahul-ji's annual get-togethers at his home in Pune in January every year. He introduced Rashmi and me as his good friends to the leading industrialists in Pune. This was really very generous of him, and we enjoyed these excellent events thoroughly. These events gave us the opportunity to meet Rupa-ji, a very affectionate and loving person. It was great to see the togetherness between Rahul-ji and Rupa-ji. We also got an opportunity to meet other members of Rahul Bajaj's family.

As we all know, he was actively involved in the activities of the Jamnalal Bajaj Foundation, which gives annual awards to outstanding individuals who follow Gandhian values and have contributed towards the welfare of humanity. Clearly, he had a highly philanthropic side to his personality and had the welfare of people in mind. He always invited Rashmi and me to the annual awards ceremony. At these events he would introduce us to the dignitaries who attended these events.

I continued my interactions with him after his three-year tenure with IIT Bombay ended in 2003. I contacted him every time I visited Pune, and if he was in town he would find the time to meet me, and often we had lunch together. He always asked me about my work and the welfare of my family. He also inquired about the welfare of my sons, Harsha and Kanishka. He attended the weddings of both our sons. I have valued my friendship with him – in fact he was like an elder brother to me. Under his mentorship and guidance, I grew in stature at my job at IIT Bombay, and in fact in all my future endeavours.

During one of my visits to him, he asked me about the activities I was involved in. I told him about the IIT Alumni Centre in Bengaluru (IITACB) that we had set up, with me as its founder president. He asked about the objectives of the centre and the proposed activities. The main aim of the IITACB is to bridge the gap between the IITs and industry. IITACB was to have its own building, the first IIT alumni group to do so. He also asked me how we were funding it. After hearing the details, he promptly offered a generous donation of ₹1 crore towards it. I was delighted, as we were raising funds and his generous donation was very timely.

In conclusion, Rahul Bajaj contributed greatly to the academic world as chairman of the BoG of IIT Bombay and through the IIT council. His contributions to IIT Bombay will always be fondly remembered. As I have mentioned earlier, his fantastic inputs and encouragement pushed IIT Bombay towards becoming a truly global institution. The outside world may not know how enormous his contributions to it were.

My salutations to a great personality, my mentor and good friend.

PROF. ASHOK MISRA, *Distinguished Professor, Indian Institute of Science, Bengaluru, and former Director, IIT Bombay*

Rakesh Mohan

I first met Rahul Bajaj in January 1990 at the World Economic Forum (WEF) in Davos. I was then a 'young' economic adviser in the ministry of industry and the juniormost member of the official Government of India delegation. This delegation was headed by a Cabinet minister who had substituted for the then industry minister, Ajit Singh, at the last minute. Consequently, the minister had a very minor role at the meetings since it was Ajit Singh who had been briefed in detail for his participation in the meetings.

So I was relatively free during the meetings to become familiar with all the members of the Indian private-sector delegation at the forum. Rahul was clearly the de facto leader of the Indian industrial titans attending the forum. He had obviously been a regular visitor to Davos since he appeared to know many of the delegates from many countries. His presence there was larger than life, as it always was. Despite my being a nonentity at the time, he was very warm and generous in his interactions with me at the meetings. As I went on to spend the following twenty years or so in policymaking positions in the government, where I had to interact with businessmen, I felt I already knew him well and could have interesting and formal interactions with him because of these first meetings with him at Davos.

Among the many Indian business leaders whom I got to know in subsequent years, he was the most outspoken and straightforward in his views, in his public and private statements alike. One of his qualities that I admired the most, both in his interactions with me and with others, was that you could have vehement disagreements and vociferous arguments with him, but it did not have any impact on his relationship with you and the warmth he exuded. He was always forthright, and even stubborn, about what he thought and felt.

He was the leader of the so-called Bombay Club, which protested the 1991 major economic reforms. As one of the originators of the reforms that opened the Indian economy to both domestic and foreign competition, this was obviously a matter of great irritation to me. Given my respect for him as a business leader, I felt somewhat saddened that he was the leader of this emerging view at that time. I was somewhat surprised at his views too, given his exposure to foreign business and business leaders, as exhibited by his regular participation in the WEF at Davos. Despite this significant difference between us during those early years of reform, I was gratified to see that it did not affect his relationship with me or his warmth towards me. We continued to share a mutual respect.

Unlike some of his colleagues, however, he realized quite soon that the country, and his own firm, would benefit greatly from the reforms. He then took his company to greater heights, taking advantage of all the new opportunities presenting themselves with the opening of the country's domestic and international markets. He was among the foremost Indian business leaders who promoted India internationally, particularly through his participation in and leadership of the WEF in Davos, and his promotion of the annual India Economic Summits.

Through his sagacious leadership during the licence raj, he built Bajaj Auto brick by brick into the two-wheeler leader that it became. He, of course, benefited greatly, like other industrialists, from the command-and-control regime, where he could dominate a limited market through the production of the limited number of scooters that he was allowed, regrettably without any innovation, throughout the period. But Vespa became the most loved Indian brand: a symbol of the Indian middle class arriving at the market.

As I understand, Rahul Bajaj was among the movers and shakers of the Confederation of Indian Industry (CII), as it evolved from its origins as the Association of Indian Engineering Industry (AIEI) and transformed into the Confederation of Engineering Industry (CEI) before finally emerging as the leading Indian business organization with a predominant international outlook. Despite his own initial reservations on the speed of liberalization in the 1990s, which I have mentioned, he helped the CII to play a very significant role in supporting the government's efforts in carrying the country through its major economic transformation over almost twenty-five years. He was essentially an institution builder devoted to furthering the broad interests of the country at home and abroad.

What can be characterized as some of his shortcomings? I feel that he was slow in seeing the transformation in consumer preferences, which were moving away from scooters to motorcycles: but he listened to the next generation and, once he was convinced, moved full speed ahead, making Bajaj Auto a powerhouse in that segment too, in the face of stiff competition.

Similarly, he exhibited insufficient interest in promoting technology and research in his companies: perhaps understandable, given the very protected market that his company grew in, with ten-year-long queues for the coveted Vespa. Once again, he seems to have listened to the next generation, and Bajaj Auto is reportedly displaying much greater interest in this aspect of business development too. I do wish that he had led Bajaj Auto to venture into developing an indigenous four-wheeler vehicle too during his lifetime.

Like other busy business and political leaders, he apparently neglected his growing family in their early years, according to his own telling; but he made up for it in later years. In fact, during my association with him I was always impressed by the devotion and attention that he showed to his extended family, and he was indeed a true patriarch.

Among Indian business leaders, Rahul had an unusual upbringing, which probably shaped his outlook on life, business and family alike. After Gandhi's return from South Africa, Rahul's grandfather, Jamnalal Bajaj, was among his earliest colleagues and friends; his father, Kamalnayan Bajaj, followed suit and lived in the Wardha ashram much of his life; and his mother, Savitri, was active in the freedom struggle, even suffering jail terms. Consequently, Rahul grew up in a traditional Marwari business family but was imbued with the Gandhian ethics of truth, austerity, honesty, kindness and respect for others, along with an overall sense of duty, which he endeavoured to transmit to his children.

As I got to know him over the years, I began to understand Rahul's evolution as a person: ethical business leader, son, father and patriarch. He always spoke truth to power, regardless of the regime in power, and exhibited his independence despite intolerable business and personal pressures at different times. When he agreed to be a member of Parliament, he insisted on standing as an independent candidate rather than joining any political party.

He was also a generous philanthropist, but in contrast to his outgoing and otherwise boisterous profile, his philanthropic activities were done relatively quietly, with little publicity. He was among the pioneering founders who set up the then Brookings India in 2013, making the largest donation with no strings attached. When Brookings decided to withdraw their association with Brookings India in 2020 and the institution became the Centre for Social and Economic Progress (CSEP, with which I am currently associated), he gave full-throated support for the transition and to the Indian team. He was also the first donor as we launched a new fundraising effort after the transition. It was at the CSEP board meetings, during the last couple of years of his life, that I observed his incredible personal interest in the institution, along with his amazing attention to detail. That illustrated to me the way he must have run all his companies and why they have done so well.

In her excellent biography of him, Gita Piramal has chronicled Rahul's evolution as a patriarch and his increasing devotion to his extended family. This is amply illustrated by the touching, heartfelt tributes to him by his children and grandchildren at the end of the biography. It was this devotion that helped in engineering a smooth succession plan for the next phase of the expanding Bajaj business empire.

This has not been without its problems, but Rahul Bajaj succeeded in making adequate space and potential for growth for different members of his extended family. To be given leadership positions in the expanding Bajaj group, each of them had to demonstrate their business acumen: nothing was given on a platter. As he slowly eased himself out of active management, he listened more and more to the next generation as they persuaded him to diversify the Bajaj group into the financial sector, in both insurance and non-bank financing, with each arm emerging as a private-sector leader in its respective segment.

One can hope that, given the ethical upbringing of the whole

Bajaj family, also imbued with the practice of hard work, the next generation will continue to be inspired by the example set by their late patriarch.

He was one of a kind and is greatly missed by all who had the good fortune to have known him.

RAKESH MOHAN, *President Emeritus, Centre for Social and Economic Progress, and former Deputy Governor, Reserve Bank of India*

Bhaswati Mukherjee

An icon is no more. Marking the end of an era, India mourns the passing away of Rahul Bajaj, the charismatic and pioneering leader of India's strong and competitive automobile industry.

While speaking of Caesar in Shakespeare's *Julius Caesar*, act I, scene II, Cassius spoke thus to Brutus:

Why, man, he doth bestride the narrow world
Like a Colossus, and we petty men
Walk under his huge legs and peep about
To find ourselves dishonourable graves.

So it was with my friend Rahul Bajaj, who strode the world of corporate finance like a colossus. He was not just chairman emeritus of Bajaj Auto. He was a legend, a corporate leader, a strong nationalist and a visionary who understood that the mobility of India's vast and untapped middle class could unleash the forces that would propel India's economy to its present strength. Today, as president of the G20, India is set to be the second-fastest-growing economy in the G20 in financial year 2022–23.

The realization of Rahul Bajaj's dream was a social revolution with the ubiquitous Bajaj scooter, to be followed by the popular Pulsar motorcycle. '*Hamara Bajaj*' was a strong affirmation of an India in transformation. It was an instrument of empowerment, not only of the middle class but also the youth, including girls, who had never dreamt of owning their own transport. Today, Bajaj Auto, in the capable hands of Rahul Bajaj's elder son Rajiv, has a market cap in excess of around $12 billion. As of June 2023, Bajaj Finance had a market cap of $52.49 billion. This makes Bajaj Finance the world's 309th most valuable company.

I met Rahul-bhai, as I called him, when I was joint secretary (West Europe) in July 1999. We built up an excellent camaraderie, which continued after my departure for Paris in September 2004 and subsequently to the Netherlands. He always called me his 'most favourite joint secretary', even when I explained that I had been promoted! In return, I used to call him, innocently, 'my most favourite crorepati', until he explained to me that billionaires, as distinguished from millionaires, have a different Hindi word to describe them!

At that time, from 1999 till 2004, I was the secretary of the Indo-German Consultative Group (IGCC), whose Indian side was dominated by him. We were lucky to have such a strong Indian component led by Rahul Bhai. His energy and enthusiasm held the group together. The Confederation of Indian Industry and the Federation of Indian Chambers of Commerce and Industry were represented respectively by their DGs, Tarun Das and Dr Amit Mitra, both men of outstanding competence, integrity and commitment to building a prosperous nation. The members on our side had been selected by our prime minister, and on the German side by the German chancellor.

The group met annually in Germany and India. Its intention was to push investment and business opportunities on both sides. Bilateral trade and investments flows increased dramatically as a result. It was Rahul-bhai who persuaded the Germans to consider a 'German green card' for regular Indian business travellers. The Indian side reciprocated, and the system gradually spread to all of India's major business partners. It was a great innovation and revolutionized the Indo-German partnership.

Rahul had wonderful contacts with western corporate leaders, who greatly respected him. As an early member of the World Economic Forum (WEF), he used his annual presence at Davos to make a convincing 'tour de horizon' of the great strengths and resilience of the Indian economy. As a convincing and compelling speaker and a true patriot, making the case for India came naturally to him.

The Confederation of Indian Industry (CII) was beholden to him for his support since 1976. He was the only business leader who was twice elected as CII president, in 1979-80 and in 1999–2000. He was strongly supportive of the business summits organized by the CII around the prime minister's visits to key countries, including the first India-EU Summit in Lisbon in June 2000.

Once I reached the Netherlands as ambassador in July 2010, I persuaded Rahul-bhai, with the support of the DG of the CII, Chandrajit Banerjee, to head a CII delegation to an important Indo-Dutch business conference in Amsterdam. He readily agreed to be hosted at the ambassador's residence, surprising his devoted wife Rupa, who warned me on the telephone that he was a demanding guest! On the contrary, he was a delightful visitor, easy to entertain and with many helpful suggestions.

The event was a huge success. He charmed the Dutch and the Indian diaspora, including the huge Indian business community in the Netherlands. He patiently and painstakingly responded to all questions, including questions on social issues, with great élan. When I felicitated him, he said with a chuckle that he did have diplomatic skills when he wished to use them!

Since he was a close friend of the late mayor of Amsterdam, the equally charismatic Eberhard van der Laan, he invited the mayor to Mumbai to come with a business delegation. The mayor obliged, and Rahul-bhai was able to get some excellent business opportunities for India during that visit. Later, when the mayor was fighting lung cancer, he called me to ask if he could speak to his friend Rahul in Mumbai. I immediately called Rahul-bhai, who telephoned the mayor many times to counsel, advise and encourage him to fight to the last.

These traits should not surprise anyone. Rahul-bhai had an extraordinarily large heart and was a true friend when in need. He was a family man and always told me that it was important to give space within families for the aspirations of others, to keep the family together. He took me once to lunch at his factory, where everyone sat together and ate simple but nourishing vegetarian fare. There was no separate table for the boss! That was typical of his Gandhian heart.

He promoted these Gandhian values with zeal. At the Jamnalal Bajaj Foundation, with which I have been associated for some years, Rahul-bhai was passionately involved in the search for the four annual awardees. The most high profile was the one for promoting Gandhian values outside India by individuals other than Indian citizens. On the birth centenary of Jamnalal Bajaj in 1990, the Foundation presented a special award to Nelson Mandela, including a specially sculptured trophy honouring his fight for freedom and the liberation of his homeland.

I last met my friend Rahul-bhai at the forty-second Jamnalal awards ceremony in 2019 in Mumbai. We were in touch throughout the pandemic. When he was unwell, I used to call his devoted colleague, Mohan, for news. It seems difficult to imagine that when I visit Mumbai or Pune I will not be able to call and see him ever again.

Yet, for all of us, his extended Bajaj family, who knew and admired him, who believed, like him, in the greatness of India, who appreciated his qualities of compassion and love, he is still with us.

As Gurudev Rabindranath Tagore said:

Remember me, still remember me,
If I go far away,
Still remember me.

Rahul-bhai, we will always remember you. You will always be there for us. May your soul rest in eternal peace.

BHASWATI MUKHERJEE, *President, India Habitat Centre, and former Ambassador of India*

N.R. Narayana Murthy

It was sometime in November 1974. I was in Pune working at the Systems Research Institute (SRI). One evening, Sudha Kulkarni, my then friend and now wife, thought it was a good idea to go and listen to a Pune celebrity. She described him as one who brought confidence, hope, joy and pride to every Indian. Her logic was simple. Being the owner of a Bajaj Chetak scooter brought much pride and joy to youngsters of the 1970s in India. There was a long waiting list of several years for owning the much-appreciated vehicle. Production was limited, thanks to the restrictive government policies!

We went and listened to a smart, youngish man in his late thirties or early forties. He was clad in a simple bush shirt. There were about 3,000 or 4,000 people in the audience in a big maidan. He acknowledged with grace and charm the clamour of youngsters for allotment of a Bajaj Chetak. He bemoaned his inability to produce more scooters for people because of the restrictions imposed by the government. He followed it up with a brilliant lecture, in layman's terms, on what economic policies our country should follow. We were exhilarated, enthused and inspired by that lecture.

My father-in-law was allotted a Bajaj Chetak in 1979 after five years of waiting! He was kind enough to loan it to me for a few years. That scooter became the first official vehicle of Infosys in Bangalore. Two founders – my colleague N.S. Raghavan, as the driver, and me, as the pillion rider – used it to go to Motor Industries Company Ltd. (MICO) to negotiate a five-year, multimillion rupee contract. After a few weeks we were advised by a MICO officer that coming to an MNC on a scooter to negotiate a multi-year, multimillion rupee contract was not going to raise the confidence of the purchase department in our financial soundness. Very reluctantly and with much sadness, we had to give up this prized possession to rent a battered second-hand car.

The next time I met Rahul was at a function in Mumbai in 1994. I was a puny nobody, jostling with other entrepreneurs to speak to the business celebrities there. Rahul was obviously one such celebrity. He was the centre of attraction at the function. I was in awe of him. He was my target. Finally, it was my turn to ask Rahul for advice. That booming and confident voice, that nonchalance towards bureaucrats and politicians, and that irreverence towards the silly and enigmatic rules of the government, had not changed a bit since I heard him in 1974.

I asked him which management guru's books he would recommend to me, a novice in management and entrepreneurship. He looked at me as if I was an idiot and said, '*Young man, it does not look like you have much money. So, please do not waste your money on management books. Instead, realize that competition in the marketplace is the best management guru. You can learn everything you want in management from keenly observing and studying competition and learning from it.*'

It was the most useful advice I got in shaping the future of Infosys. We had gone public in 1993. We had adopted the developed world as our market. Exports contributed about 98 per cent of our revenue then, as they do even today. I came back to my office, took Rahul's advice as my gospel, sat down with the brains trust of the company and explained what Rahul had advised me to do. They largely agreed that the leading competitor in our field was indeed the best management guru. So we requested all the function heads – sales, finance, HR, software development, quality and productivity, technology and physical infrastructure, and education and research – to benchmark themselves with the best global player in the market in their field, create a plan to emulate that competitor in their field, and use innovation to become better than them. It was this principle that helped Infosys become the leader in most functions in our industry during the 1990s.

Davos was clearly Rahul's theatre. He enjoyed being there. He was quite close to Klaus Schwab, founder of the World Economic Forum (WEF). Every CEO knew Rahul. Every WEF employee respected him. It was nice to spend some quality time with him in the evenings when things slowed down a little bit at Davos. For Rahul, attending the WEF at Davos in January was a sacred ritual not to be missed. I am certain his mind must have been focused on whatever new ideas he could derive from the myriad industry-leading companies and highly accomplished leaders assembled there, use them and improve upon them.

How would I characterize Rahul? He was honest, courageous, patriotic, warm and kind. He would joke a lot with me. He was open to discussing and debating any issue. He was not afraid of telling someone the unpleasant truth, no matter how bitter it was. He was open-minded in the matter of accepting others' ideas if they were clearly better than his. He was fun to be with. He was fearless about articulating his views on politics and economics in India. I am happy that his sons – Rajiv and Sanjiv – have proved to be very successful business leaders in their chosen fields and have stood for good values. I miss Rahul. May his soul rest in peace forever.

N.R. NARAYANA MURTHY, *Co-Founder and Chairman Emeritus, Infosys Ltd*

Harshavardhan Neotia

My father Vinod Neotia and Rahul Bajaj were cousins. My father, his elder brother Suresh Neotia and Rahul Bajaj were very close. During their childhood, the families would often go on holidays together during their school vacations. Since they were all about the same age, they developed a warm relationship among themselves. However, as they grew up and took up the responsibility of their businesses, their meetings became less frequent. Moreover, the Bajaj family settled in Pune while we were in Calcutta. However, their shared childhood memories held the bond they carried throughout their lives.

As a child, I knew Rahul Bajaj theoretically as an uncle, but we never spent time together since we were separated geographically. I knew him more from folklore rather than as a person. He was, after all, my father's most successful and famous cousin and friend, whose accomplishments were discussed at the dinner table. I would meet Rahul uncle at family functions and weddings, where I would greet him and do pranam, but that was about the extent of our interaction.

In the early 1990s, I applied to Harvard Business School for an executive management programme. I needed a recommendation letter as part of that application. My uncle Suresh Neotia suggested I take it from Rahul Bajaj, since he was an alumnus. He called up

Rahul Bajaj, who happened to be in Delhi. Coincidently, we too were travelling to Delhi at the same time. Rahul uncle wanted to meet me before writing the letter and called me to his suite at the Taj hotel where he was staying.

He gave me about an hour, and we chatted. He was handsome, articulate and charming. I was about thirty years old at the time and had just entered business; he was already a legend. And here I was, having a one-to-one conversation with him. I was more than a little awed and intimidated. However, he quickly made me comfortable. He asked me about my work and what I wanted to do. I still remember every word of that conversation. It was an inspiring talk where he shared his thoughts with me.

Rahul uncle did not believe in brevity. Even when he spoke he was detailed and lengthy. While I had come expecting a paragraph or two recommending my admission, he called his secretary to dictate a thorough and exhaustive recommendation letter running into two pages. After such a recommendation, what could go wrong! Obviously, I secured the admission.

In the late 1990s, I began to know him more as Mr Rahul Bajaj, as opposed to Rahul uncle. I was actively involved with the Confederation of Indian Industry (CII) when Rahul Bajaj was in his second stint as president of the CII. This was in 1999. Since I was involved with the CII (eastern region) and he was the national president, there were more occasions to meet him, I being a co-member of the CII. That's when I saw him dealing with heads of state and ministers with so much confidence. He always spoke his mind. While we ordinary mortals were always in deference to them, Mr Rahul Bajaj sat there speaking his mind, looking them straight in the eye. He became a bigger hero to me than he already was.

Mr Rahul Bajaj was known for his forthrightness and honesty. He would always call a spade a spade, irrespective of the discomfort it caused to those around him. Surprisingly, people did not take offence at what he was saying as much as I perhaps imagined they would. In some way, they grudgingly respected him even if they disagreed with him.

I think there was also an underlying acceptance of 'Rahul being Rahul'; of his straightforwardness being par for the course.

He would say things that others wanted to but did not have the courage to. Also, he may have been straightforward but he was never malicious or abrasive. Mr Rahul Bajaj harboured no ill will, nor did he bear any grudge against anyone. I think he saw straight talk as dispensing a bitter pill to cure an infirmity.

He was equally candid about his own shortcomings. I admired his immense humility and refreshing honesty in looking at himself and admitting to his mistakes very, very openly. He was the first to admit that while he was concentrating on making efficient scooters, the Indian consumer had moved to motorcycles. He admitted that they had blinked and missed the boat and let Hero Honda surge ahead. Of course, Bajaj has since fought back and recovered market share.

He was also a man of simple tastes. He came to Delhi often and he had a fixed suite at the Taj Palace, where he was provided specially cooked food which was almost like home-cooked food.

That is my personal story about him.

Much has been written about him as an industry leader. On that front I can contribute little that is not already known. We all remember that when a daughter was born in many a middle-class family, they would book a Bajaj scooter in her name. The waiting period for a Bajaj scooter was fifteen to twenty years. The scooter was reserved for the girl's dowry when she got married. In a way, it was awful for India to be in a situation where you had to wait fifteen to twenty years to buy a scooter. On the other hand, think about the trust the Bajaj name had that a person was unhesitatingly ready to pay up for something that would be delivered after twenty years!

Perhaps an often-ignored fact about Mr Rahul Bajaj was his nationalism. He was deeply and strongly patriotic. His family had very close ties with Gandhi-ji. He was born and brought up in that milieu of belief in self-rule, nationalism and nation-building. The seeds of patriotism and nationalism were embedded in Rahul-ji from his birth. He believed in the potential of Indian entrepreneurs and the spirit of our people. He was equally happy to engage with the western world and was a hot favourite at Davos. He was an eloquent speaker, communicating the Indian point of view at international forums. He was indeed *Hamara Bajaj*, both in spirit and emotion. He himself was the most celebrated brand ambassador of the slogan his company created.

In the last decade of Rahul uncle's life, I became much closer to him because he had retired and was not so busy. He was not as active in the CII as he was earlier, though he was still a father figure there. Every month I would call him to ask him how he was doing. And we matched diaries to figure out if I would be in Delhi when he was there. We would meet up for a meal almost every other month. We connected at a more emotional level.

Then the COVID pandemic hit us all. When we could finally travel, I wanted to go and see him in Pune. However, he was not keeping well. I kept postponing my visit, waiting for him to get better. He didn't get better. That's one regret I will always have to live with.

HARSHAVARDHAN NEOTIA, *Chairman, Ambuja Neotia Group*

Nitin Nohria

From the bustling lanes of Pune to the boardrooms of multinational corporations, Rahul Bajaj's name echoes with respect and admiration. As one of India's most legendary business leaders, he exemplified persistent excellence, unwavering commitment and a vision that shaped India's industrial landscape.

Growing up in India, I marvelled, like many, at the success stories of industry titans like Rahul Bajaj. It was the era when buying a Bajaj scooter symbolized more than just buying a vehicle; it epitomized aspiration, determination and a new-found sense of mobility. Owning a Bajaj scooter wasn't just an economic choice but also a statement of personal control. Like countless others, many members of my family found solace in the reliability of a Bajaj scooter, especially when juxtaposed against the unpredictability of Indian public transport. And I always marvelled at how many people could sit on a Bajaj scooter!

My father, an active participant in many industry associations, often shared stories of Bajaj's tenacity, especially in the famed Bombay Club. Through him, I understood how fiercely Rahul Bajaj advocated for the interests of Indian businesses. He was a guardian of India's industrial aspirations, keen to ensure that domestic players had a level playing field before the country's doors opened to global competition. Like a true leader, when globalization came, Bajaj

Auto didn't retreat but led the march, showcasing Rahul Bajaj's formidable competitive attitude and fighting spirit.

My affiliation with Harvard Business School gave me a more personal insight into the man behind the legacy. Having him on our dean's advisory board was an honour and a learning experience. I could sense the pride he took in my appointment, acting as a pillar of support to me. Yet, true to his nature, he never held back from delivering candid feedback. His honesty taught me that true mentorship is rooted in fairness and a commitment to uphold the highest standards.

But what stands out most prominently about Rahul Bajaj is his trailblazing journey of leading the Bajaj Group and his ability to ensure its continuity. The transition of leadership from one generation to the next can often be tumultuous. Many great leaders stumble, relinquishing control too late or becoming overbearing shadows. Rahul Bajaj, however, masterfully navigated these waters. Entrusting the Bajaj Group to his sons Rajiv and Sanjiv, he displayed trust in the next generation and confidence in his foundational work.

It was a proud moment for all of us who looked up to him when a renowned Indian business magazine dedicated its cover to lauding the accomplishments of the next Bajaj generation. The cover rightly credited Rahul for the solid foundation he had built, symbolizing his timeless legacy. It was clear: Rahul Bajaj's brilliance wasn't just about building an empire but also about ensuring its perpetuity.

A book I wrote, *In Their Time*, chronicles the stories of America's greatest business leaders of the twentieth century. If I had ever considered writing a similar book on Indian business leaders, Rahul Bajaj would undeniably have been one of the central characters in that compilation.

In paying tribute to this giant of Indian industry, words might fall short, but his legacy stands tall, speaking for itself; he is an inspiration for generations of entrepreneurs and leaders. His journey, marked by adaptability, tenacity and vision, will continue to inspire countless hearts, including mine, for years to come.

NITIN NOHRIA, *George F. Baker Jr. Professor and former Dean, Harvard Business School*

Ranjit Pandit

This is for my good friend Rahul Bajaj: bon vivant, iconoclast, entrepreneur extraordinaire, philanthropist.

Rahul established world-class manufacturing in India at a time when few gave the country a chance. He built global scale in two-wheelers and took on the world. He showed that you could build a business in India based on cash and cash flow and not debt. He demonstrated that you could diversify, not stick to your knitting and yet create huge value, as he moved into financial services. In each of these endeavours, he upended conventional wisdom.

Rahul lived life king-size, but it was simple pleasures that gave him the most joy. For instance, he loved his 'gharguti' Pune food. He loved his kurta–pyjamas.

He always placed his workers' interests at the top of his agenda. He played sports with the workers and management regularly in order to get to know them. One of the things that affected him deeply was the strike at Bajaj Auto.

Rahul donated generously. Unlike most others who donated, he was not looking for recognition. He was driven by the cause – for example, healthcare.

Rahul was imperious and did not suffer fools lightly. Once at a Bajaj Auto annual general meeting, a shareholder suggested that the huge cash balance sitting on the company's books be returned to the shareholders. Rahul dismissed him with a wave of his hand

and told him that if he did not like what the company was doing he should sell his stock.

Rahul had his share of critics. But love him or hate him, you could not ignore him.

Rahul will be missed. He has made India proud. He has made our founding fathers proud. He showed that India could convert licence raj into global raj. That India could become self-sufficient and take on the world by building world-class, world-scale enterprises right here in the country.

RANJIT PANDIT, *former Director, McKinsey & Company and former Managing Partner of General Atlantic for India*

Deepak Parekh

Hamara Bajaj stood tall, defiant; a goliath of a man who pioneered innovation to move India on wheels. To some of us, he was traditional and yet a contrarian, challenging established beliefs on how business should be conducted in a given economic scenario. Unafraid and potent were his views; when Rahul Bajaj spoke, people took heed.

Rahul was the vociferous spokesman of the Bombay Club in the 1990s. It was an era when foreign manufacturing companies were trying to make hostile takeovers of well-run family-owned, listed Indian companies. He was a staunch believer in the potential of the Indian manufacturing sector. Although a philanthropist widely involved in many trade and industrial associations, he had a finger on the pulse of his own enterprise and he was minutely aware of the everyday deliberations of the Bajaj clutch of companies.

We were an intimate group comprising Anami Roy, Ranjit Pandit, Jaideep Bose and Dilip De, who met whenever Rahul was in Mumbai for an open conversation about the story of the day and everything that came to mind. There was never any agenda; we were simply a bunch of backslapping friends Rahul enjoyed meeting. Towards the twilight of his life, when the mind was able but body not quite so, Rahul hosted us at his Pune home. He was the quintessentially gracious host.

His legacy carries on in the hands of his extremely competent sons, Rajiv and Sanjiv. He imbued in them a sense of integrity and pride in their products and their people. He lives on in the consciousness of every Bajaj employee, the people whose lives he touched, his immense connections, his cherished family.

You live on in the heart of India, my friend, missed and never forgotten . . .

DEEPAK PAREKH, *former Chairman, Housing Development Finance Corporation (HDFC) Ltd*

Sharad Pawar

The Bajaj group, one of the oldest and largest business conglomerates in India, was founded by Jamnalal Bajaj in 1926. Influenced by the principles and way of life of Mahatma Gandhi, he participated in the freedom struggle and suffered incarceration. He also dedicated his life to the upliftment of people by creating jobs and making people self-reliant. Since then, each of the members of the Bajaj family has followed in the footsteps of Jamnalal-ji, and as a result we all see the Bajaj Group as one of the most respected business houses in India.

After the long walk to freedom, it was an uphill task for Indians to enjoy their freedom as they were weighed down by poverty and unemployment, which was aggravated by poor infrastructure. The people of independent India had to have better and affordable means to commute. The Britishers brought the bicycle to India; slowly, it passed from elite and affluent hands to the lower-middle and middle class. As it seeped further down the income ladder, to the poor and marginal class, the automobile two-wheelers started replacing or adding to the bicycles in middle- and lower-middle income groups.

The Bajaj family got an inkling of the situation and ventured into the automobile business. Bajaj, the family of freedom fighters, assumed the new role of nation builders by taking up the cause of the common man, easing his life, enabling him to move and to enjoy the fundamental right (to move freely throughout the country) enshrined in the Constitution.

Ramkrishna Bajaj, the younger son of Jamnalal Bajaj, was the first Bajaj scion with whom I had become acquainted. Like me, he too was associated with the students' and youth organizations. He would call himself a 'coolie of Mahatma Gandhi', but he was a leading industrialist who served the country as a true disciple of Gandhi-ji. In the mid-1960s, I met a vibrant and vivacious youth, Rahul Bajaj, who had just finished his MBA from Harvard Business School. He would later become the icon of the automobile industry in India.

My journey in public life coincides with Rahul's growth in the business sector. In 1967, my public life began with my election as a member of the Legislative Assembly of Maharashtra. Within a year of this, Rahul became the CEO of Bajaj Auto. In 1972, I became a state minister with important portfolios, and in the same year Rahul was appointed as the managing director of Bajaj Auto.

The Bajaj Group had earlier, from the 1950s to the 1960s, experienced a smooth ride because of the restricted policy regime, but under the dynamic leadership of Rahul Bajaj, Bajaj scooter changed gears and made rapid strides. '*Hamara Bajaj*' reached the fastest speed, like a 'Chetak horse', and went to almost every corner of India. Rahul's straightforwardness and foresight brought him close to me, and our friendship grew with the rise in our respective careers: mine in politics and his in industry.

He would openly and loudly say, '*Sharad Pawar mera khas dost hai!*' The Bajaj family had never been aloof from public life. Since the days of Jamnalal Bajaj, this family remained inseparable from Gandhian ideology and rendered service to the nation. Naturally, I would always want Rahul Bajaj to represent the people in the Rajya Sabha.

In 2006, when I was in London, I saw a window of opportunity. I asked him if he was interested in entering the Rajya Sabha. Luckily, he was at leisure at his residence on the Bajaj campus of Akurdi. He immediately agreed, but on one condition – he would not withdraw under any circumstances, and he would remain independent. His vast experience in the industrial and social sector would be of immense importance to law and policymakers. His political views and opinions weren't attached to any political party. Knowing this, the 'like and unlike-minded' parties came together to elect him to the Rajya Sabha.

Soon, the doyen of Indian industry made his mark in the house. In spite of his busy professional schedule, he maintained an 88 per cent attendance in the upper house. He actively participated in debates of all types. He covered global issues like climate change, economic slowdowns, Indo–Pak and Indo–Afghan relations; national issues like the annual budget, disinvestment of PSUs, the situation arising out of closure of IT industries, the deteriorating financial condition of Air India; and also touched on issues affecting the common man, like the diversion of kerosene and food grains from the public distribution system, fuel price hikes, health and education policies.

His political views were progressive and balanced, and he would never hesitate to speak his heart out. In 1975, he invited IT raids by criticizing the imposition of Emergency, and in 2019 he voiced the wishes of the people and the business community for an environment free from fear. He took a swipe against the government when Nathuram Godse, the man who murdered the Mahatma, was termed a patriot by a politician. Sometimes his political views seemed very idealistic. Once, he had appealed to both the BJP and the Congress to work together on economic policies, keeping their core differences apart.

As a businessman, Rahul Bajaj was a protectionist but one pragmatic in approach. He would call himself 'a pragmatic optimist'. He believed in 'inclusive growth for India' and would assertively demand a level playing field for Indian companies. As far as the Bajaj Group went, he was open to foreign technology and investment but would not offer his shareholding to foreign entities. He was a firm believer in the Hindustani man and in his ability to do something for the nation. He might be the only big industrialist who lived at the factory site to maintain a constant connect with his employees.

Rahul Bajaj developed a conglomerate that cared for the common man. He made a conscious decision not to enter into car manufacturing, because for him two-wheelers were the need of the hour and the symbol of the middle-class and marginal sections of society.

The name 'Bajaj' is synonymous with philanthropy. Jamnalal Bajaj-ji sowed the seeds of humanitarian work in the family, and the legacy is continued by each member of the family.

Rahul spent much of his childhood in and around Wardha and cherished his relations with Wardha throughout his life. Keeping the Gandhian flame alive, he supported social initiatives, especially when it came to bringing holistic development to rural areas. I can't forget his continuous and unstinted support to my social work, especially in education, rural development and health. In recognition of his generous help, we the trustees of Vidya Pratishthan, Baramati, decided to name our engineering college after his father, Kamalnayan Bajaj.

On 17 October 2015, Arun Jaitley had inaugurated the Kamalnayan Bajaj Institute of Engineering and Technology, Vidyanagari, in Baramati. At that function, Rahul Bajaj opened his heart and went on to say, 'Sharad Pawar is the best prime minister India never had!' That lofty praise embarrassed me, and I couldn't respond to it! Those words might have created ripples in political circles as Arun Jaitley was sharing the same dais with us. Jaitley went even further, stressing the need to replicate the 'Baramati model of development' at at least a hundred places in India. Rahul was such an open and lion-hearted man!

During my Pune stays, I would invariably go to his Akurdi residence for dinner. Rahul, a boxer during his school days, would openly throw straightforward punches at any system or establishment that was against the national interest. Our rendezvous used to be full of humour, happiness, laughter and sometimes a bit of anguish. In 2013, the loss of his wife saddened him deeply, so I and Vithal Maniar started meeting him frequently, either at my or his home. Two years back, he stepped down as chairman of the Bajaj Group, passing the baton to his brilliant sons. The void that such events result in takes a toll on one's health, especially of an industrious person like Rahul Bajaj, who always found himself surrounded by people.

A year before, I heard about the death of this true patriarch, a veteran businessman and my close friend. It was a disturbing and painful moment to see him resting in silence when I visited his mansion at Akurdi. It took me some time to cope with the loss. Since then, during my travels, whenever I see a two-wheeler pass me by, it reminds me of my zealous friend Rahul Bajaj. The generations to come too will remember him as a generous industrialist imbued with the national spirit, who transformed the lives of millions with his two-wheeler technology. I pay tribute to his work and to his eternal soul!

SHARAD PAWAR, *former Cabinet Minister, India, and former Chief Minister of Maharashtra*

Sam Pitroda

I first met Rahul Bajaj in 1985 at an event organized by Tarun Das, director general of the Confederation of Indian Industry (CII), in Delhi. Rahul was a leading industrialist, known as the champion of two-wheeler scooter manufacturing in India. He was determined to change the availability of and access to scooters in India. I was then working for the Prime Minister of India, Rajiv Gandhi, on telecom and technology-related initiatives. I remembered the days when it used to take months to get a scooter in India and priority was given to people paying in dollars and pounds. Rahul provided the impetus to ultimately change that. Today, India is one of the global leaders in two-wheeler manufacturing.

Rahul Bajaj was tall, handsome, witty, outspoken, frank, energetic and full of enthusiasm about India's future. We immediately connected and clicked. He was four years older than me. Over a period of time, we became personal friends and enjoyed many interesting conversations, as well as lavish dinners and a few fancy parties.

Rahul came from the distinguished Bajaj family. His grandfather was a close associate of Mahatma Gandhi and actively participated in the Indian National Congress and played an important role in the Independence movement. Rahul had inherited his character and values rooted in democracy, freedom, justice, diversity, simplicity, openness, accountability, truth and trust from his grandparents,

parents and uncles. He also had the right education – from St. Stephen's College and Harvard University – that augmented his values and imparted him the wisdom needed to lead business and public opinion in India.

From my interactions with him, it was always clear that he was fully committed to a thriving democracy, independent institutions, a free-market economy, a scientific mindset, and free and fair conversations on important issues of national interest. He had very strong views on several social, political and economic issues, and he was quick and bold to express them. With me, he talked less about business and more about national development. At times, some people thought he was too outspoken for an Indian industrialist. To me, that defined Rahul Bajaj and separated him from others who valued personal interest more than public interest.

Once, at a small private party in his suite at the Taj Palace hotel, we spent two hours talking about privatization and liberalization in India. He was committed to increasing private-sector participation in India to help expedite growth and build infrastructure. At the same time, he rightfully believed that Indian industry needed time, investment and support to strengthen its base before fully opening to global competition. He believed in young Indian talent and in the role of new technologies in developing Indian industries to be globally competitive. He understood, appreciated and supported the role of communication and computer technology developments for India, especially during the Rajiv Gandhi government. We had many long conversations on technology missions related to literacy, drinking water, immunization, oil seeds, dairy development and telecom to help take technology to the people of India.

Rahul Bajaj was always interested in new technology ideas for modernization of Indian industry. Once, in 1990, over drinks, we collectively thought of building robots for various applications in agriculture. Based on our conversations I even did a brief report for him on the product development. However, in the end we both realized and agreed that it was too early for India to work on robots and drones. Later, in 1993, I did a brief business plan for him to offer scooters on short-term rentals to customers in India, like regular auto rentals in the western countries. However, at that time India lacked GPS and the internet to track and monitor this scheme to make it a reality.

Rahul Bajaj made significant contributions to India beyond his role in the automotive industry. Here are some key areas that Rahul and I discussed, which made lasting impressions on me.

1. Corporate governance: Rahul Bajaj emphasized the importance of strong corporate governance practices. As the chairman of Bajaj Auto, he implemented transparent and ethical business practices, setting high standards for corporate governance.
2. Education and skill development: Rahul Bajaj was actively involved in promoting education and skill development in India. He contributed to initiatives aimed at improving the quality of education, supporting vocational training and bridging the skills gap in the country.
3. Industrial reforms: Rahul Bajaj was an advocate for the growth and development of the Indian manufacturing sector. He actively worked towards promoting policies that supported industrial progress, attracted investments and fostered innovation.
4. Economic reforms: Rahul Bajaj was a vocal proponent of economic reforms in India. He advocated for liberalization, deregulation and privatization to drive economic growth and increase competitiveness. He was actively engaged with policymakers and government bodies to provide insights and recommendations on various issues affecting the Indian economy and industry. His participation in policy discussions helped shape government policies and initiatives at various levels.

5. Philanthropy and social initiatives: Rahul Bajaj was involved in various philanthropic activities and social initiatives. He supported causes related to healthcare, education, rural development and empowerment of women. Through the Bajaj Foundation, he developed and supported projects to uplift marginalized communities and improve their quality of life.

His leadership, entrepreneurial spirit and commitment to nation-building made him a respected figure in both the business community and the wider society. At a personal level, he was a loyal, reliable, dependable and helpful friend who was always full of life and fun to be with.

SAM PITRODA is an engineer, innovator and entrepreneur. He served as Adviser to three former prime ministers of India.

Anuj Poddar

Some people lead lives that have an outsized impact on others. Rahul Bajaj was one of them. And not just as a doyen of Indian industry. His contributions span many spheres. He was an inspiring person in many ways. But amongst all the traits one can pay tribute to him for, the ones most commonly picked out will be his candour and his fearlessness in speaking truth to power – traits that made him the voice of industry over several decades.

Beyond that lay the many values (integrity, humility, graciousness, shunning of ostentation) of the Bajaj family that he inherited, lived with, and strengthened and passed on to the next generation. These values are something that the Bajaj family and the Bajaj Group continue to live by and practise.

His characteristic frankness and bluntness transcended all situations – public, professional and personal. For those who didn't understand him, it could put them off. I have experienced it too. I had once asked for something really simple (this was in the space of our personal connect, much before my professional involvement with the Bajaj Group), to which he replied with a straight 'no'. I was initially a bit put off. But over time one learnt to understand and appreciate his matter-of-fact approach, which many of us could do well to emulate.

While his many achievements are all stuff for the history books, what he will really be remembered for by those who knew him was his personal warmth, his care and attention to little details and to every person, his remembering of things that you would not expect him to – all belying his larger, busy public persona.

I will share just one anecdote that illustrates this: I had once forgotten my mobile charger in his car in Pune. And I realized that only the next day, once I was back in Mumbai. Initially, I thought I would just let it be, but then I happened to mention it to him. He not only ensured that it was found, but also kept personally following up its dispatch to me till I received it in Mumbai two days later. Everyone who knew him will have several anecdotes to vouch for his qualities. And that was what made him even more special.

We will all remain inspired by him and his values.

ANUJ PODDAR, *Managing Director & CEO, Bajaj Electricals Ltd*

Suresh Prabhu

I grew up listening to the jingle '*Hamara Bajaj*'. And the back page of the newly born magazine *India Today* was reserved for the iconic Bajaj scooter advertisement. It wouldn't be an exaggeration to say that many read the back page first to ensure that 'their Bajaj' was still on the roads.

I have never driven any vehicle till date, nor do I even have a driving licence, so owning or driving a Bajaj scooter was never in my scheme of things. Despite this, the name 'Bajaj' made a permanent impression on my young mind. As a student I used to attend events organized by the Kamalnayan Bajaj Foundation. I was always driven by the virtues and values of Kamalnayan-ji, the great philanthropist, nationalist and industry leader.

I developed further respect for the 'Bajaj' brand as the name seemed associated with our national heritage and at the same time signified the new strides we were making as a free nation.

I was interested in several extra-curricular activities, which probably occupied more of my time than my formal studies in the classroom.

Sports, apart from reading books, took much of my time. I would invariably take the Mumbai suburban train to reach 'town' (as south Mumbai was called), to watch table tennis matches at the Mumbai University Club.

The star attraction of the TT matches was Niraj Bajaj. He was my hero. I never interacted with him then, but I was his fan. The way he played, his demeanour . . . everything about him was extremely praiseworthy. His artistry and masterful skills in table tennis were a treat to watch.

I fought against the undemocratic Emergency rule in 1975–77 while completing my chartered accountancy course. During this challenging period, I often heard a name mentioned with respect and awe by many others who were working towards restoration of democracy in India.

Many of these 'freedom fighters' would talk about a towering personality, an exceptionally brave person, a leading industrialist who was steadfast in his values and opinions – Rahul Bajaj.

I became the chairman of the largest Indian cooperative bank, Saraswat Bank, while pursuing my practice as a chartered accountant. The bank had a significant presence in Mumbai, Pune and Aurangabad. I experienced the big impact Bajaj Auto and other Bajaj Group companies had made on industrial landscape of Maharashtra.

It was at Waluj in Aurangabad and at Pimpri-Chinchwad in Pune that the Bajaj Group had not only developed their big manufacturing facilities but also sustained a large ecosystem of small and medium enterprises (SMEs) that created employment. Such was its magnetic pull that the iconic brand created a spirit of entrepreneurship in many and inspired several others to develop their own businesses.

The Bajaj two-wheeler became a household necessity, with thousands – industrial workers, white-collar employees, students – becoming proud owners of what everyone lovingly called '*Hamara Bajaj*'!

Our bank had financed such buyers, and also several ancillary SME units in the Bajaj orbit.

In 1991, when Prime Minister Narasimha Rao and Dr

Manmohan Singh introduced new economic thinking in India, one voice that expressed its opinions loudly was that of Rahul Bajaj.

In 1996, I was elected to Lok Sabha and was immediately sworn in as the industry minister in the Atal Bihari Vajpayee government. The very first person to visit me in my office at Udyog Bhawan was the legendary Tarun Das. He invited me to an event planned by the CII to felicitate me. Of course, the event never happened, because even before invites could be sent out our government collapsed, just thirteen days after it had been established. But my association with the CII never ended. Rahul was a pillar of the CII.

I was a great fan of the giant leader Atal Bihari Vajpayee, but had never met him in person till I was sworn into his cabinet. He showered paternal affection on me, and I got innumerable opportunities to meet him and learn many a life lesson from him.

As I was closely associated with Atal-ji, L.K. Advani-ji, George Fernandes and many such stalwarts, I would often be part of important discussions initiated by them on various issues. One name that would invariably crop up in any such discussion on important issues related to industry would be that of Rahul Bajaj.

From the time I was a young, impressionable student, a diehard opponent of the Emergency, and later becoming a banker and then a politician, I have always witnessed different facets of this fascinating personality, Rahul Bajaj.

Rahul-ji had his own independent thought process. He had strong opinions on various issues, which he expressed fearlessly. He spoke without mincing words even in presence of the powers that be, and sometimes he paid a huge price for his truthfulness. He stood steadfastly for his own well-cultivated value system, even if it meant he had to be politically incorrect.

For him, his country always came first. While his own business was certainly important, it was not as much a priority as his love for the country.

My political journey continued for another twenty-six years. I handled ten Cabinet positions under two towering PMs, Atal-ji and Modi-ji. I also served four consecutive Lok Sabha terms and two Rajya Sabha terms. I was also on the Opposition benches for some time. Each of those responsibilities offered me opportunities to meet the icon Rahul Bajaj. It was great interacting with Rahul Bajaj the public figure, the industrialist, understanding his point of view and getting valuable insights from him regarding business.

However, it was even more interesting and fulfilling to meet the real Rahul Bajaj – it was a completely different experience to meet the business icon as a human being! This man had feet of steel. He was a far greater person than I had imagined him to be. His every action was unambiguous, clear and focused. He never wore different identities for different occasions, like dress codes meant for different events. He was the same person, with a clear mind, well-articulated thoughts and the courage to express his mind irrespective of who was in front of him.

He never had an 'off-the-record' conversation, as is the prevalent culture.

He cared for the people of India and for his country, and took to task anything and anyone that he thought was not serving that interest or caring for the consequences.

On many occasions he publicly hailed my actions as a public figure. I had resigned as the power minister just after I had introduced the Electricity Act in parliament in 2001. There was a huge outpouring of public support for me and opposition to my resignation. Atal-ji didn't accept it for a long time. Rahul Bajaj was one of the first few persons to visit me after that incident. I can't describe today what transpired between us, but his words are etched in my mind. There are many such personal experiences I have had with him.

Rahul-ji attended the World Economic Forum (WEF) for the most number of times. I saw the awe and respect with which world leaders regarded him. He was a global icon, unmatched, taller than most and better than many.

India's role at the WEF would never have been what it is today without Rahul-ji playing a crucial role there at critical times.

There can't be business as usual without Rahul-ji at its helm – his shadow highlights the country's business-scape!

Rahul-ji, you live in many parts and many hearts. You can never go away from our memories. You are immortal. Live long, wherever you are.

SURESH PRABHU, *former Union Minister, India, and Chancellor, Rishihood University*

Azim Premji

Rahul is one of the business leaders that I admire the most. This has little to do with his business acumen and organizational leadership capacities, all of which he had in plenty. Three things made him truly special.

First, his capacity to be straightforward and direct. Most of us are familiar with this nature of his. However, it's only when we try to practise this ourselves that it becomes clear how difficult it is. The courage, the conviction and the equanimity required to be as straightforward as Rahul was can only be an inspiration to all of us.

Second, he was truly down to earth. This is not about what cars he owned or how his houses were appointed. It is about his natural ability to see things from the perspective of somebody who is the average Indian living an average life. It's remarkable that he could relate to the experiences of the average person. I feel that this had a significant role to play in the solid success of Bajaj, the company.

Third, while he was a business leader, he was first a good citizen of this world. In all his actions it was clear that while business was very important, clearly, society and the country, and what was fair and just, always came ahead.

If I have a regret, it is that our interactions were not as frequent as I would have wanted. Without doubt I can say that not only his grandfather, whom all of us admire, would have been proud of him,

I think his grandfather's guru, the Mahatma, would have also been equally proud of him.

AZIM PREMJI, *Founder and former Chairman, Wipro Limited*

Prathap C. Reddy

One of my dearest friends for many decades, Rahul Bajaj was a compassionate and dynamic leader, a great industrialist and an exemplary nation builder. Since the 1970s, Indians have called him 'scooter king'!

I witnessed him don several hats – as a fiery champion of corporate India, a global representative of the country, a philanthropist, a loving family man. Furthermore, we also had a lot in common. Both of us firmly believed that India had the innate capability to innovate and achieve scale, as needed to serve its people. This was because we were aware that India had the talent, resources and the resolute intent that would guide the country in achieving all that its citizens wanted of it. Rahul was an institution builder and was passionately involved in the industrialization of India.

I will always cherish the memories of our being together on the board of Indian Airlines in the 1980s, when he was the chairman and I a member. It was during this point in time that India, for the first time, acquired twenty-one Boeing aircraft. This was a leap forward in the aviation sector, and there was a lot of discussion about developing business and economy class in the new planes. Back then, passengers in a few rows of the economy class and one row in business class were allowed to smoke inside the aircraft. On account of this, the non-smokers unfortunately suffered from passive inhalation of cigarette smoke. Rahul and I together brought in a resolution to ban smoking inside the aircraft. India was the first in the world to introduce such a revolutionary initiative in the field of aviation.

Now all airlines follow this best practice that keeps non-smokers safe and well. It was interesting that Rahul implemented this revolutionary initiative even though he was a smoker at that time.

On a similar note, when Rahul was chairman of the CII, he would often invite me, as a member, to participate in discussions on healthcare. He recognized the importance of health in nation building, backing our recommendations and giving them a lot of visibility. This encouraged the healthcare sector in India to scale newer heights in clinical excellence. Today, India's healthcare system has become a beacon of hope for patients from across the world.

In addition, I also had the privilege of being a member of the India–US CEO Forum along with Rahul. Only ten industry leaders from India, including Rahul and me, and ten from the USA made up this think-tank to promote bilateral trade and investment between the two countries. It was for a period of five years, which were truly memorable for me as we encouraged collaborations, which have been making a difference in the lives of citizens in the world's largest and oldest democracies.

A large-hearted philanthropist, Rahul Bajaj was equally committed to dedicating his family's wealth and time for the greater good.

Above all, Rahul had a great sense of humour, and I deeply cherished his warm friendship. He had attended many of our family functions, and my daughters too were very fond of him.

In his passing away, India has lost 'a giant of a man', a nationalist who was incredibly courageous, and an outstanding visionary!

DR PRATHAP C. REDDY, *Founder Chairman, Apollo Hospitals*

Frank-Jürgen Richter

The world knows Rahul Bajaj as a great business leader who was never afraid to speak his mind, a contrarian with conviction in his beliefs, a philanthropist and a Padma Bhushan awardee; but I remember Rahul as a compassionate man and a dear friend.

Rahul was a successful industrialist who almost single-handedly pioneered the two- and three-wheeler vehicle industry in India. In doing so, he has arguably had a more profound impact on the Indian middle class than any other businessman to date.

I first met Rahul in 2001 in Mumbai. I remember feeling a bit overawed at the thought of meeting him, but he had this wonderful way of putting one at ease. Humble and sociable, he was particularly easy to engage with, especially as he had a knack of making one feel comfortable through his warmth.

Rahul once invited me to dinner, and as he was devouring a plate of spaghetti arrabiata, his favourite dish, we got talking about my idea for a potential Horasis India meeting that would bring together business leaders from India and around the world to discuss issues of economic and business importance. Rahul provided me with some of the best advice I could get at that time and became the most ardent supporter of my endeavour. He helped in a myriad ways, including connecting me with several of his friends and acquaintances. He was a constant source of inspiration.

Once the Horasis India meeting was up and running, Rahul expressed his support by attending almost all the editions of the gathering over the years. I owe much to him for the success of the Horasis India meetings, of which we have hosted more than fifteen editions so far. Each night prior to the start of the event, he would bring together some key attendees and friends over dinner to discuss the agenda for the event, the key talking points and the themes. Almost invariably, Rahul led the discussions and laid the ground for the following day's summit. He talked, and we listened. He had this way of captivating the group with his insight, clarity of thought and candidness. And captivated we were.

A sharp mind

Rahul made Bajaj a household name in India, and even as Bajaj Auto's market share in India continued to increase rapidly, Rahul refused to compromise on the quality of the company's products. He never took the success of the company for granted and never forgot his commitment to the consumer. It is no surprise that he enjoyed such a high standing in India and got so much respect from all sections of society as he did.

He was a hugely successful businessman, and often critical of government, but always fiercely Indian. In all my interactions with him, Rahul was inevitably thinking not about how his company could do better but how Indian industry could do better and become globally competitive. He was an intellectual who thought deeply about how to further the cause of India's industrial sector. His mind was always running, whether during interactions with friends and peers or when chairing the Confederation of Indian Industry, which he did twice, twenty years apart.

He knew his words carried weight, and he was measured by them. But when he spoke he did so freely, irrespective of whether what he was saying would irk the dispensation of the time or not. Government leaders and administrators listened to him.

Rahul Bajaj was a visionary, and Indian industry looked up to him for his views, advice and guidance on all things related to business and the economy. I am fortunate to have known him personally, and I learnt a tremendous amount from him over the years I knew him.

More than a businessman

The business world was only part of what defined Rahul. He was passionately interested in the arts and in philosophy, and had a keen awareness of geopolitical trends and ebbs and flows.

Many say Rahul was not a flamboyant man, but I say he was – he was flamboyant in his thoughts. A man who led a simple, unpretentious life, he was a towering intellect. Through all of his business success, I did not see this aspect change.

He mixed with global business and political leaders, and was an ambassador for Indian enterprise at various international forums and conventions. Despite being a successful business tycoon, he was always a people person. This was most evident when, on his passing, the Indian state of Maharashtra accorded him a state funeral – something not seen before for an industrialist.

Rahul transcended different worlds comfortably – he was as at ease dining with royalty in Europe as he was speaking to a young college graduate in a small Indian town. He was as comfortable vociferously defending India overseas as he was outspoken in reviewing government policy at home. He could talk about protectionism and globalization one moment, and about European art history the next. Therein lay his greatness, and a sense of equanimity and awareness pervaded all his actions.

Rahul was unperturbed about what the world thought of him; what mattered to him was doing the right thing in the world. And that he did, right till the very end. We will miss you, my friend.

FRANK-JÜRGEN RICHTER, *Chairman, Horasis – a global visions community dedicated to inspiring the future*

Manashi Roy

Of grand heart and kind soul
He was a fine man, our great pride
Though we mourn him down here on Earth
In Heaven above, God wants him by His side

The devastating news of Rahul Bajaj's passing away on 12 February 2022 unleashed a wave of shock, sadness and sorrow through my mind and soul. He was my idol, my mentor, my guru. The very thought that I would not see him any more was unthinkable.

My association with Rahul Bajaj dates back forty-six years, to 1977, when I joined the Confederation of Indian Industry (CII). His mere presence charmed us all. He was tall, handsome, sharp, articulate; a charismatic figure with a towering personality and a mesmerizing larger-than-life presence.

Rahul Bajaj was straightforward and outspoken and did not mince words in calling a spade a spade. He could do so and nobody dared touch him because he was honest, transparent and a man of integrity, both at the personal and professional level.

His deep knowledge, clarity and precision of thought were impressive. He was a keen reader and always came thoroughly prepared for meetings, discussions and conferences. We had to be doubly prepared to answer his queries, very often unconventional ones. It was a great learning experience for all who ever interacted with him. He was a keen listener and thinker, respected the views of others and always added value to the deliberations.

He was focused and action oriented. He was very cost-conscious and vigilant of expenses. It is reported that as chairman of the Bombay Club, Rahul Bajaj vehemently opposed economic liberalization. That is not my understanding of Rahul Bajaj. My perception is that he was for fair competition, a level playing field, fierce domestic competition, and rooted for input duties to be lower than output duties. He was open to suggestions. Once you convinced him, he would support you fully and there would be no backtracking.

The CII was fully for economic reforms and was deeply engaged in interactions and discussions with the ministry of finance and the tax reforms committee set up under Dr Raja Chelliah for industry, trade and commerce. We were lobbying for fewer rates, lower taxes, better compliance and a broadened tax base. We advocated drastic elimination of the plethora of exemptions, numbering more than 2,000, which we believed complicated tax administration. We recommended correction of the inverted duty structure.

To convince the government was not, however, an easy task. We had organized multiple sectoral interactions and discussions and were able to narrow down and marginalize our differences and evolve a broad consensus. I remember that once we took a high-level delegation of the capital goods industry to meet Dr Arjun Sengupta, member of the planning commission. We asked Rahul Bajaj to join us, to which he readily agreed. Dr Sengupta was surprised to see Bajaj, who strongly supported the need for a strong, competitive domestic capital goods industry.

Rahul Bajaj was a hands-on man, a great thinker, a visionary and a strategist. He strongly believed in: (a) cost management, (b) time management, (c) quality management and (d) team management. His razor-sharp focus was on excellence. 'Whatever you do, you must excel.'

On the lighter side, he was an interesting conversationalist and could speak on any subject with ease. He was fun-loving, witty, full of humour and had an infectious enthusiasm for many things. He was a foodie, and also loved dancing and joking. He had an eye for detail. Style, elegance and sophistication were his forte.

His wife Rupa was a perfect match for him – pretty, charming, dignified, cool, composed, intelligent and balanced. She valued relationships, unity and togetherness. Behind every successful man is a woman – Rupa personified that maxim.

Rahul Bajaj was extremely large-hearted, generous, kind and caring. On several occasions, I shared personal issues in confidence with him. He gave very good advice and guidance and maintained confidentiality. Another amazing quality of his was that no matter where he was in the world, if you messaged him he would reply within ten minutes.

Rahul Bajaj was very popular with the media, and he was equally at ease with electronic, visual and print media. The media would swarm around him like bees to honey. They would crave his sound bites, interviews and photographs.

Rahul Bajaj was one of the most accomplished businessman ever born in India, or anywhere for that matter. He will be long remembered for his ideals and his many qualities of head and heart.

I salute him.

MANASHI ROY, *former Deputy Director General and Head - Economic Policy, Confederation of Indian Industry*

Kailash Satyarthi

Rahul Bajaj-ji was widely recognized as a visionary, a fearless leader, a stalwart of Indian industry and a pioneering nation builder of modern India. He embodied ethical business culture and always spoke truth to power. For me, he was all those things and much more – a close friend with whom I had shared a bond of love and mutual respect that extended to our families.

Everyone in my family looked up to him as an elder of the family. There were times when my children would complain to him that I was not looking after my health, and he would promptly call up to pull me up. This was how the special bond we had with each other and our families worked.

Beyond his professional accomplishments, Rahul-bhai was known for his humility, wisdom and integrity. In 2014, when I travelled to Oslo to accept the Nobel Peace prize, I was joined by my family and a few close friends. Among them was Rahul-bhai, who beamed with pride at the achievement for our country. At the hotel where we were staying, I heard the beats of the dhol. When I looked down from my balcony, I saw Rahul-bhai dancing along with other Indians, fully immersed in the joyful celebration. He had a strong love for food and enjoyed having a good time, often forgetting about any underlying health issues he had.

Rahul-bhai served as the chair when we established the Kailash Satyarthi Children's Foundation, while I served as a trustee for the Jamnalal Bajaj Foundation. When we organized the Bharat Yatra, one of the largest marches of its kind in the world aimed at combating child sexual abuse and exploitation of children, he walked with us for an entire day in Jaipur. He also visited us at Bal Ashram, where he became childlike amongst the children there.

Apart from being a personal loss for us, his passing away is an irreplaceable loss for the entire nation. He was a compassionate businessman and leader, championing *swadeshi udyog* (domestic industry) and Gandhian values. Rahul-bhai was a supporter of good causes, not only nationally but internationally too. We regularly attended the World Economic Forum (WEF), which was founded by his close friend Klaus Schwab. Schwab told me once that the WEF had started as a small initiative, but it was 'my Indian brother who helped me turn WEF into a global platform with his vision, conviction and energy'. I felt a lot of pride. Rahul-bhai has supported hundreds of charitable organizations, particularly Gandhian organizations working for rural development, women's empowerment, child rights and the environment.

Though Rahul-bhai is no more, his legacy of truthfulness, honesty and integrity will always be remembered. He will always be known as a far-sighted business leader who left an indelible mark on the Indian business landscape.

KAILASH SATYARTHI, *Nobel Peace laureate*

Dhruv M. Sawhney

My association with Rahul Bajaj goes back to the 1980s. He, along with Jhawar and Tarun Das, inducted me into the Confederation of Indian Industry (CII). At that time it was the Association of Indian Engineering Industry (AIEI) and had not yet become CII.

I was young and not really someone Rahul Bajaj knew well. Yet he went to great lengths to convince me that my DNA was an absolute match for the AIEI and that I would be a complete misfit in any other association.

Perspectives change when you get to know a person better. Over the years I got to know Rahul very well. Contrary to popular belief, he was a man who was open to change, especially structural change, and I can back this with a very solid example.

I will have to go back in time to when the AIEI had evolved into the Confederation of Engineering Industry (CEI) and I was its president. Rahul Bajaj, Tarun Das and I had frequent discussions on the need to broaden the horizons of the association so it would extend beyond the engineering industry. We felt that unless the CEI expanded to include other sectors, it could never become an international organization. The idea faced considerable pushback from members and office-bearers alike. People felt that the change would dilute our focus.

I requested Rahul to help push the proposition through. It speaks of the stature of the man and the respect he commanded that members finally agreed to the Confederation of Engineering Industry (CEI) becoming the CII. They knew he had absolutely no axe to grind and had complete faith in his integrity.

Many years later, I would have another opportunity to see the trust he inspired among his peers. Rahul and I were part of the first industry delegation that travelled with Prime Minister Narasimha Rao for the G-15 Summit to Caracas in 2004. We went out to dinner one evening with the presidents of Associated Chambers of Commerce and Industry of India (ASSOCHAM) and Federation of Indian Chambers of Commerce and Industry (FICCI). In the course of our conversation, an idea was thrown up – a merger of the three associations. Everyone at the table was excited; we felt that the combined leverage would strengthen Indian industry. We also agreed that the only person capable of bringing this to fruition was Rahul Bajaj. Had this happened, it would have changed the course of business history in India. Unfortunately it didn't, and I won't go into the reasons why. But the fact that the heads of different industry associations reposed the faith they did in Rahul speaks volumes as to the man he was.

This is why I feel that the Bombay Club moniker did a great disservice to Rahul's world view. It made him seem afraid to lose his pre-liberalization monopoly. While it's true that in the days of the licence raj, he had a licence to manufacture, there was little he could do about the demand-and-supply situation in the market. If anything, he wanted to do away with the licensed capacity in order to be more efficient and give his customers a good deal.

When Rahul took over Bajaj Auto from his father, Indian manufacturing had to contend with the Monopolies and Restrictive Trade Practices (MRTP) Act, 1969. This legislation limited Bajaj Auto's production to only 48,000 scooters a year, even though the company could produce and distribute much more. His rift with the powers that be during that period is well-documented. He stood his ground before the MRTP Commission and, over time, increased his licensed production capacity. Rahul may have been named by Jawaharlal Nehru, but he did not have it easy during the Indira Gandhi years. His father Kamalnayan Bajaj had aligned himself with the Opposition when the Congress party split in 1969, and his uncle, Ramkrishna, had a less-than-ideal relationship with Mrs Gandhi.

Rahul Bajaj made a pitch for a level playing field for Indian manufacturing so it could fight foreign competition fair and square. He wanted indigenous industry, and not imports, to get a fillip in the new scheme of things. If foreign players could make inroads on the strength of imports, where was the impetus for them to collaborate with Indian manufacturers?

Today people talk about 'Make in India'. Rahul Bajaj wanted it thirty years ago. But unlike others, he was outspoken and fearless enough to table what he wanted. Which was why his was the sole face to be tarred by the accusation that he was protectionist. There are many things that one could say about Rahul, but not even his staunchest critic would say he had a personal agenda in advocating what he did.

He was ahead of his times in his ability to see the bigger picture, even if he was not always necessarily a part of it. The fact that Bajaj expanded successfully from hard-core manufacturing to the new-age services sector is proof of this. These are the traits that allowed him to build an iconic brand in Bajaj.

Once I asked him about the origin of the jingle '*Hamara Bajaj*'; it had almost become a national song at one point in time. He said it had sprung from his family's close ties with Gandhi-ji. Rahul grew up seeing the country's struggles in fighting for independence and in nation-building first-hand. He believed passionately in India and its destiny.

'*Yeh hamara mulk hai,*' he would say passionately, and that passion for all things Indian was what led to the brief for the jingle, which in turn led to the creation of the '*Hamara Bajaj*' tagline by the advertising legend Alyque Padamsee.

The overtly Indian hue he carried did not do justice to Rahul. It often overpowered the role he played in putting Indian business on the international stage. He was among the first to attend the Davos World Economic Forum (WEF). His friendship with Professor Klaus Schwab, founder of the WEF, laid the foundation for India's regular presence at the world's most influential gathering of business leaders.

He used his delivery and leveraged his personal network to change the way the world perceived India; I can't think of any Indian who had such an impact on the international stage as he did. Rahul earned his place as a leader in India's global journey, and it wasn't just because he headed a large company. It was inherently his intellect and his ability to nurture relationships that made him stand out among his peers.

Rahul was the chairperson of the strategic committee at the WEF and headed it for a good twelve years. He wanted me to take a leadership role at Davos and pushed me to step into his shoes. I was hesitant because they were big shoes to fill. But he was a natural mentor and gave me the confidence to step into them and step up. Rahul just brought out the best in people – most definitely in me.

Rahul had a unique philosophy about doing business. He believed you had to do it in a way that allowed you to sleep well at night and leave behind a legacy you could be proud of. I knew Rahul Bajaj for speaking the truth to power and for never shying away from expressing his disagreements in public, even with the government, irrespective of who was in power.

Yet he had some great friends in the government; Sharad Pawar was one of his closest. However, even with friends he would argue and debate his point. He was a great friend to have – steadfast, loyal and intolerant of petty gossiping. I have seen him tick off several people when he felt they were overstepping their boundaries when discussing those he was close to. He would say that if there was something to be said of his friends, it had to be said to their face, not behind their backs.

Let me tell you he was great fun too! Every year at Davos, we ended up at the nightclub and Rahul would think nothing of swinging a leg until about 2.30 in the morning, even when he had a breakfast meeting or an important engagement the next day. Rahul was the type of person who could swing a leg as easily as he could swing an opinion. He loved good food and excellent wine. He was a man you would want next to you in good times and bad.

I miss him every day.

DHRUV M. SAWHNEY, Chairman and Managing Director, Triveni Group, and past President, Confederation of Indian Industry

Klaus Schwab

Rahul was not only one of the World Economic Forum's (WEF's) earliest supporters in India, but also a very dear and personal friend. His commitment to the vision of the forum, combined with his love for his country, laid the foundation for a unique partnership with India – one which continues to this day. Rahul gave his time generously to the forum. He was the first Indian member of the International Business Council and the first Indian to co-chair an annual meeting of the WEF.

Rahul's contribution to Indian and global business, his focus on social impact and his larger-than-life ways will always be remembered. And the legacy he leaves behind serves as an example for generations to come.

PROFESSOR KLAUS SCHWAB, *Founder and Executive Chairman, World Economic Forum, the International Organisation for Public-Private Cooperation*

Chanda Singh

I first met Rahul in the mid-1980s when my husband Avininder Singh (Timmy) joined the Confederation of Indian Industry (CII). I remember thinking he was an incredibly tall man; he had a presence which made him stand head and shoulders above others.

He was already 'The Rahul Bajaj' when Timmy and I got to know him. The man's reputation preceded him and clouded people's judgement of him. But there was a considerable difference between perception and reality when you got to know him well. Of course, he was a straight talker who fearlessly said it as he saw it, but that alone was not the sum and substance of who he was. There were many facets to Rahul Bajaj, but I am not sure how many people saw that.

I remember chatting with him informally at a CII event in Goa. We got talking about our families, and since both of us had close relatives who had been active in the freedom movement, the conversation veered towards history and politics. My grandfather had given up practising law to join the freedom movement and had gone on to become the general secretary for the Congress in Punjab under Lala Lajpat Rai. Rahul's grandfather, Jamnalal Bajaj, was called Gandhi-ji's fifth son. We talked a lot about his grandfather's relationship with the Mahatma and the influence of Gandhi-ji on so many people. Rahul was so strongly associated with business that people often failed to see that he was very mindful of his Gandhian legacy. Every inch of the man was of, for and about India – minus the jingoism, of course.

Rahul became close friends with Timmy over the years and I was fortunate to be included in his affection. He was warm, kind and generous to a fault. There was a teasing way about him, which endeared him to people. And he was not averse to letting his hair down after a hard day's work.

In 1994, my husband was invited to speak on the environment in relation to corporate social responsibility at Davos. I accompanied him. It was the first time at Davos for both of us. Rahul, on the other hand, was the old Davos hand who had represented India and Indian industry there umpteen times. His energy and enthusiasm were legendary – he walked the extra mile to ensure that everyone had the total Davos experience, including a taste of its fun and boozy underbelly.

He would march the group from one nightclub to another and make sure there was mirth and merriment. Wherever we went, we could hear loud greetings of 'Hello Rahul', 'Bonjour Rahul', 'Good evening, Mr Bajaj'. It was quite something. He had clearly made his mark, not just on the Davos organization, but also on all the people who worked and lived there.

Connecting to people came easily to the man.

There are a couple of lines from Kipling's *If,* which seem so apt for Rahul:

> *If you can talk with crowds and keep your virtue, Or walk with Kings – nor lose the common touch, If neither foes nor loving friends can hurt you, If all men count with you, but none too much . . .*

Rahul met both the king and the commoner on equal grounds, literally. I saw him interact with then Prince Charles at the tenth anniversary meet of Bharatiya Yuva Shakti. The British royal was there in his capacity as a patron of the organization. There was none of the fawning that often marks these interactions. Rahul showed the same friendliness and equanimity while interacting with the future king of England as he did while engaging with young CII executives. I remember seeing him walking into many CII dinner evenings and stopping to have a chat with everyone he met on the way. It was amazing; he knew each person by name.

It's fair to say that the CII staff adored him. They looked up to him, notwithstanding his penchant for straight talk. I know his bluntness got him into trouble many times, but you knew where you stood with him. Somehow, his public persona did not do justice to his deeply compassionate nature and his loyalty to his friends.

A deep and abiding memory I have is of the morning my husband passed away in hospital. It was a bleak December morning when I walked out of the ICU to meet my father, who was standing right outside. Behind him stood Rahul. Even in that moment of utter sadness, Rahul's presence struck me. He gave me a smile and a nod, and that was enough for me to know he cared about us. A couple of days later, he came home just to tell me that he was there should I ever need anything. And I remember thinking, that's what friends do – be there for each other.

Though my association with Rahul Bajaj began through my husband, I was fortunate to call him a friend for the rest of his life. Rahul may not be there in person any more, but the iconic Bajaj will always remain in the hearts of all he touched.

CHANDA SINGH, *Editor and Publisher, World Affairs, The Journal of International Issues*

Ashok Soota

Rahul Bajaj first burst into my consciousness when I was an aspiring young manager at Usha Fan Industries. We lived in times of shortage and long waiting periods, thanks to the licence raj. The waiting period for a Bajaj scooter was ten years and Rahul had been spending a vast amount of his time in the corridors of Delhi to get his licensed capacity increased.

This was when Rahul finally lost patience and declared that he was going to bust his licence agreement and the government was free to put him in jail. Of course, he didn't land in jail and Bajaj was allowed to grow. The system itself didn't change, as I realized when I joined Wipro Infotech as president in 1984 to find we had licensed capacity of a princely ₹6 crore for computer manufacture! The image that remained in my mind of Rahul was that of a fearless leader who would fight against all constraints. I also remembered thinking that Rahul was leading a business with integrity and was not afraid of raids from entities like the Department of Revenue Intelligence and Enforcement Directorate, who were quick to land up at your premises if you rubbed the government the wrong way. Rahul's bold and fearless approach became the foundation of my admiration for him.

My personal connect with Rahul began in 1986, when I became Confederation of Indian Industry's (CII's) state president for Karnataka and a member of the CII national council. The contact became more personalized when I finally became a member of the president's council from 2001 onwards. From my very first CII national council (NC) meeting, I realized that Rahul was already a colossus at the CII. In the years that followed, I also observed that he was present at each and every NC meeting and never missed a single one.

One couldn't help but also notice that at the NC meetings Rahul quite frequently had the last word. The reason, I believe, was that he was knowledgeable and did his homework. I was amazed at how well informed he was on so many matters beyond just trade and industry. Prior to the 2019 state elections, sitting in a small group discussion after a president's council meeting, he declared his pulse was that Congress would win in all three states – Rajasthan, Madhya Pradesh and Chhattisgarh. His views were met with strong disagreement by many of the participants, who were strong BJP supporters. A few months later, we all realized that he was correct. He also went on to say that these victories would not translate into gains in the national election, where too he turned out to be spot on.

When I became active at the CII, Rahul was already referred to as the 'owner'. I am not sure who conferred on him this sobriquet, nor how it originated and endured. Commitment was certainly a factor, but many other past presidents were also committed. To me the reason was that Rahul saw the CII as part of his extended family, very much the way he saw the Bajaj enterprise. He was devoted to the cause of the CII, what it stood for and did, and what he could do to ensure it retained its premier status amongst industry associations.

The above point struck me powerfully when I was elected CII president in 2002. The only person I sought to call on for advice was Rahul, and I reached out to him for a meeting in Pune. He responded to say that we could meet in the day and he would also host a dinner at his residence. I was overwhelmed because MindTree was a fledgling entity and here was the giant Rahul Bajaj hosting a dinner for me. The message was that the CII was important and he was hosting the dinner for the CII president. But Tarun Das, CII director general (DG), who controlled much of a CII president's time, called to say I was needed in Delhi for a dinner meeting with a foreign delegation. Still, we managed a leisurely meeting in Rahul's office. His advice to me included:

- Don't be timid or hesitate to freely express your views even if it is criticism of the government;
- Continue your association with the CII after your time as president. Throughout the presidency, people are on a career path. Continued association shows your deep involvement in CII's mission.

My next personal interaction with Rahul happened in 2003, on my sole visit to Davos where he was a regular visitor. As president of the CII that year, I was given the responsibility of finding a successor to Tarun. This was never going to be an easy task, since Tarun had built the CII into a formidable organization with his forty-plus years of leadership and had nurtured many presidents during his tenure. In fact, one felt that CII presidents came and went, but only Tarun and Rahul remained forever. One fine morning at Davos, I found myself walking with Rahul on the icy strip that leads from the hotels to the Davos convention centre. He was elegant, as usual, in his stylish overcoat and towered above me. I took the opportunity to ask Rahul who he felt should be the next director general to succeed Tarun. His response, 'What's there to discuss? Srini is next senior-most and the correct choice.'

Tarun and I had done an elaborate exercise to evaluate potential successors to Tarun. Srini was not on top of that list. However, I took the 'owner's' words as a dictum. When I got back to Delhi, I called a president's council meeting and proposed Srini's name. Left with a choice, I feel Srini would have opted out, but he dutifully accepted the role. Unfortunately, two years downstream he was faced with a president who, I am told, was particularly difficult to deal with, and even harsh. This broke Srini's spirit. Later, there was a second infructuous attempt and another director general (DG) was appointed. Thankfully, this erroneous selection was not on my watch! Finally, and the third time round, the CII appointed the current incumbent, Chandrajit Banerjee, as DG in 2008. A few years later, at a president's council meeting, Rahul voiced what many of us felt: 'It was extremely difficult to succeed Tarun, but Chandrajit, you have admirably stepped into Tarun's shoes and handled the role with energy and expertise. Friends, a round of applause for Chandrajit.'

My final one-on-one interaction with Rahul was when I suddenly resigned from MindTree and started Happiest Minds. There was a CII annual general meeting (AGM) a few days later. He approached me with concern and said, 'Does this mean you are going to start all over again?' When I nodded in the affirmative, he said, 'It will be difficult, but I am sure you will make a success of it.' His words meant a lot to me. I was moved also by the empathy he displayed.

In this eulogy of Rahul, I have stated that he was a family man. Since I had limited personal knowledge of him and his family, what is my basis for saying this? First, he was an incredibly proud parent. Rajiv, his elder son, was known to have strong views, at times contrary to Rahul's. On multiple occasions, at CII meetings or in smaller group discussions, Rahul would refer to Rajiv's brilliance and his strategic thinking, much like a proud parent. I am sure he had equally warm feelings for Sanjiv, but he was now one of us as part of the CII community. However, you could sense his caring from the way he stepped back as Sanjiv became a CII office bearer, to give him space and his place under the sun.

It has often been stated that Rahul needed a lot of persuasion to enter the financial services industry. I would conjecture that he entered this segment to leave behind two vibrant businesses for each of his capable sons. Many industrialists neglect to make a division of their empires, while others leave a disproportionately large part to the elder son. The new financial services business became a hugely successful diversification for the Bajaj Group. This created two platforms, which Rajiv and Sanjiv are leading to sustain Rahul's legacy for perpetuity.

ASHOK SOOTA, *Founder and Executive Chairman, Happiest Minds Technologies Ltd, and past President, Confederation of Indian Industry*

Venu Srinivasan

Rahul Bajaj was a colossus in the Indian industry space. It was a weight he bore lightly, with delightful humour and chutzpah, combined with integrity.

We were competitors – Bajaj and TVS – in the two-wheeler space. And we fought hard for market share. And yet Rahul would always greet me with his hand on my shoulder saying, 'Hello Venu, how are you?' It would have been hard for onlookers to guess that we were competing fiercely with each other.

His ambition to dominate the two-wheeler space never came in the way of his warmth and large-heartedness towards me, and it was a courtesy that he extended to many peers and competitors in the industry. Even those he disagreed with.

Of course, Rahul's hallmark was his sharp tongue, his bold statements and his staunch belief that one should say it as it is. And thus, you knew that Rahul meant every word of what he said. And in doing so, he often won the admiration of even those he criticized.

The sweep of that included even the government and policymakers. Rahul was truly unafraid to bat for industry and business, and in great measure the success of the Confederation of Indian Industry (CII) as an industry body was because of his tireless lobbying to make sure the voice of automakers was heard.

His detractors often said that he had set up the Bombay Club to protect his own interests. What he did was to voice the sentiment that Indian industry needed a level playing field. It takes a certain courage to be unafraid to publicly question government policies.

Every scooter that rolled out of his factory bore the stamp of quality; it passed under Rahul's eagle eye. Everyone in the industry knew that Indians couldn't get enough of the Bajaj scooter, and it would have been both easy and tempting to cut corners, but he never did.

Rahul was a busy industrialist and a very successful one, but he didn't lose sight of the Gandhian values handed down to him by his grandfather, the great Jamnalal. Rahul lived large in his ideas and his vision, but with simplicity in his everyday life.

Rahul will always be known not just for the giant brand he built, but also for the values he lived by. And so, he will always be '*Hamara Bajaj*'.

VENU SRINIVASAN, *Chairman Emeritus, TVS Motor Company, and past President, Confederation of Indian Industry*

M.V. Subbiah

Rahul Bajaj exuded a captivating presence that commanded attention from all corners. Whether he was in a meeting with Confederation of Indian Industry (CII) members, politicians or bureaucrats, people would instinctively turn towards him. His towering stature, handsome looks and innate charisma were hard to miss.

He had the ability to put everyone around him at ease. And this contributed to his straightforwardness not causing harm. I often say that I started my career in the abrasives business and I am an abrasive man. But he was the opposite. He could always get his point across without hurting anyone.

He approached everyone the same way, regardless of their position, whether it was the prime minister or an ordinary person.

Once, when a CII meeting was held in Chennai, Chief Minister Jayalalithaa's entourage delayed everyone's programmes. Rahul said, 'Subbu, you owe us for this delay. So, we're coming to your house for idli and dosa.'

And he did come to my house. My cook doesn't speak English, and Rahul didn't know Tamil. Somehow, he communicated with my cook, and they all ate idli and dosa and had drinks until late into the night!

During the anti-Hindi agitations in Tamil Nadu, my Hindi teacher had to flee to the neighbouring state of Kerala with his four children. I recounted this incident to Rahul Bajaj on one occasion to illustrate why I was unable to speak Hindi. But he never forgot it. Every meeting we had with Hindi speakers, he became my voice, in a way that no one ever could.

Once we were in a meeting, representing the CII, with Mrs Indira Gandhi, former prime minister of India, when he stopped her midway with a request to speak in English. He said, 'Ma'am, you can go on saying whatever you want. I understand, but I don't think our president does. I think you should make an attempt to speak in English.'

Mrs Gandhi then tried to say that I should have learnt Hindi. He responded quickly, 'Why don't you ask him why he didn't learn Hindi? Subbu,' he turned to me, 'Tell her about your Hindi teacher and his four children.'

In another instance, we went to meet N.D. Tiwari when he was the industry minister. Tiwari started talking in Hindi. Rahul immediately intervened and asked, 'Minister-ji, do you want your message to reach the members of the CII or only those of us who understand what you're saying?

'We already informed you. Our president doesn't understand a word of Hindi. You're wasting your energy. He has to go and explain to the members what was discussed here. So, make an effort to speak in English.' Tiwari said he couldn't speak English fluently. Rahul then said, 'Whenever you get stuck, you let me know. I'll translate that.'

Even when we met with Rajiv Gandhi, the same Hindi issue came up. He just turned to me and said, 'Subbu, I think we can leave.' Of course, once Rahul emphasized the gap in linguistic understanding between Gandhi and me when it came to Hindi, the meeting went smoothly.

For those familiar with Rahul, his forthright nature would hardly come as a surprise, making the term 'outspoken' aptly descriptive of him.

Rahul's business strategies reflected his approach to life. He created a waiting list for scooters in India, a feat that was previously deemed impossible. He was twice elected as president of the CII. He was an ardent patriot who always defended India's interests when speaking with foreigners. His love for his country earned him the position of chairman of Indian Airlines.

I will always remember Rahul for his forthright nature, reassuring presence and open-minded approach to life.

M.V. SUBBIAH, former Chairman, Murugappa Group, and past President, Confederation of Indian Industry

B.R. Taneja

When I was asked to write about my association with and memories of Rahul Bajaj, I felt humbled as well as embarrassed. Despite the fact that I consider myself to be a reasonably upright and successful first-generation entrepreneur, I and all others who are like me believe that Rahul has played a role in whatever little we have achieved professionally and intellectually. His presence in the Indian corporate world was so dominant and engaging that it was impossible for me or anyone else to not be, in some way or other, influenced by his thoughts and approach to life in general and business in particular.

He was passionately engaging and ruthlessly honest in all his relationships. There were no 'holy cows' for him, and he did not believe that position, or economic or social status, could make a person 'untouchable'. He could take anyone head on without being apologetic, as long as he was convinced about the merit of the issue he was handling. And his issues were not limited to concerns about business growth but extended to those that had socio-economic and national ramifications.

His life has been among the most fascinating journeys that I have come across. Usually, people born into a privileged environment, for reasons of growing up within the confines of a secure, well-defined and class-conscious framework, tend to not reflect on issues concerning the underprivileged. This is more so of people from business families. Rahul was one of the few who was emotionally connected with people who needed support and took it upon himself to work to bring about policy intervention and changes.

Rahul was one of his kind that corporate India has given to the nation. He believed in creating a strong and engaging interface within corporate India. This was not for the limited purpose of generating increased opportunities or an enabling policy environment for his fraternity, but with the underlying objective of creating a growth-led trickle-down effect for people living on the fringes and on a constant lookout for succour from the state.

In addition to maintaining the highest professional and ethical standards, and looking at issues from the holistic perspective of the societal impact that a solution could have, Rahul never compromised on his freedom of expression. His brutal honesty could be an embarrassment for people who deserved to be embarrassed, and a huge inspiration for people who deserved his attention and affection. Very few people have this great ability to think objectively and express their views without mincing words or being bothered about the repercussions.

Most of us who knew him admired this quality, because he said what he meant and this was not something one found in people associated with the corporate world. His brutal honesty and straightforwardness reflected in a conversation I had with him after I sent him a copy of *Diminishing India – Decades of Brazen Political Apathy*, a book I had authored. While the others I had sent the book to called up to compliment me and mentioned that they had browsed through a few pages and found it very interesting and looked forward to reading it in full, Rahul mentioned that he still had about 200 other books that were waiting to be read and he did not know when he would be reading mine.

This was the level of honesty he displayed in his social interactions, and it was only those who knew him well and/or were sensitized to his approach who would appreciate this. There are large groups of people from various walks of life who loved him for this, and everyone looked to him as a role model for his value-driven convictions and the courage to take on even the high and mighty. While a large part of the Indian corporate world spends considerable time in business development and personal image building, my personal take is that Rahul would have been the last person to compromise on his convictions and approach for the sake of personal or corporate gains. He was absolutely fearless and did not believe in appeasement of any kind. In his scheme of things, he could see large bands of black and white, and the fuzzy grey band was either not there or was insignificantly narrow. I wonder if the famous American actor John Wayne was inspired by Rahul when he said, 'If everything isn't black and white, I say "why the hell not".'

I have had the good fortune of being a beneficiary of his friendship and spending some time with him. As a person, despite his enviable lineage, he was down to earth, relatable, objective, socially conscious, fearless, respectful, emotional and informal in his approach. Whenever we had the good fortune of hosting him, we noticed he loved to slowly sip his small vodka and could be seen enjoying the spicy (chatpata) snacks we served. His love for chatpata food was only a reflection of his extremely lively (chatpata) personality and how he wanted people to enjoy things that were local, easily available and affordable – remember '*Hamara Bajaj*'! I guess he managed to evolve into a corporate maverick not because he was heading the Bajaj empire but in spite of that.

Rahul's concern for social etiquette and his penchant for choosing his company was remarkable. If he was coming to our place and was running late by ten minutes, he would call up to inform us. Interestingly, he would always ask us who the other invitees were. If he found that the list was large, he would politely excuse himself. He loved intense interactions and was fond of discussion and debate, and he always looked forward to getting convinced by or being able to convince others.

I couldn't resist talking to a couple of people who knew Rahul over years to seek their inputs. I talked to Sam Bhadha, a veteran in the hospitality sector, and his comments only reinforced my understanding of Rahul. He said Rahul 'always chose the St James and the Lexington at London and New York, as these were Indian hotels'. He added that 'humility was a great quality that he possessed' and that he would 'address all associates by name and thank them for their services and give them a handshake on departure'. He went on to add that 'even after retirement he kept in touch and always enquired about my health and family'.

Another person who gave me something to share about Rahul is Gautam Patwa, a US-based consultant. He met Rahul about twenty-five years back at Deepak Parekh's Christmas party, and he confessed that he was introduced to a person that he was in awe of till he met him. Upon Patwa addressing him as Mr Bajaj, Rahul immediately said, 'Call me Rahul.' Their acquaintance grew into a friendship, and when Rahul was appointed the chairman of the Indian Institute of Technology Bombay (IITB), Gautam suggested to him that 'Indian corporations should donate funds to IITs for naming rights to buildings and hostels'. Rahul liked the idea, and over time, Patwa said, 'IITB has become the beneficiary of substantial donations from Indian corporations and alumni.' Patwa added that he was 'happy to read that the Rahul Bajaj Technology Innovation Centre was inaugurated at IITB on 10 June 2022, which would have been Rahul's eighty-fourth birthday'.

I am sure that Rahul would be at his articulate and irreverent best even up there, and made as he is, would have given some food for thought to the Creator as well!

Love you Rahul, for what you were and what you have left behind for us to emulate.

B.R. TANEJA, *Founder Managing Director, Indian Seamless Metal Tubes Limited*

Dinesh Trivedi

I would have never ever imagined that one day I would have to write a piece in remembrance of the great Padma Bhushan Rahul Bajaj-ji, but such are the ways of the Almighty. No amount of write-ups can ever describe the man that Rahul Bajaj was, and even to make an attempt to do so is not easy.

I don't even know where to begin, so let me begin from the very beginning. My first meeting with him was way back in the 1980s, when he was appointed the chairman of Indian Airlines. It was my passion and love for aviation that got me to know more about him, but I really came to know him one on one in 2006, when he became a member of Parliament in the Rajya Sabha, where I had been a member since 1990, and again from 2002 onwards.

His election to the upper house itself was very significant. He was elected to fill in the vacancy caused by the untimely and unfortunate death of Pramod Mahajan. As an independent candidate, he had support from the Nationalist Congress Party, the Bharatiya Janata Party and the Shiv Sena, and comfortably secured 195 votes where he needed only 145. His famous statement upon being elected member of Parliament was, 'I will represent Indian industry but not represent the two-wheeler industry. I will not let a conflict of interest occur.' This he very carefully followed, and in spite of getting several opportunities as a member of Parliament to intervene on behalf of his industry, he refrained from it.

Right from the very first meeting with him, as they say, we 'hit it off', though Rahul-ji was much older than me and certainly much more experienced and wiser than I was. Most of the time we used to be together in Parliament, whether inside the chamber of the house or in the Central Hall of Parliament. So intimate was our friendship that almost every evening we used to be together, either at casual dinners or social functions, which were aplenty in Delhi. The other wise man who would also join us was the late Suresh Neotia, a philosopher, statesman and the founder of Ambuja Cement. Between those two wise men I found myself to be very fortunate, as from our conversations I would learn a lot, not only about current affairs but also about their philosophy of life.

Rahul Bajaj would introduce me to people as his mentor in Parliament and would say, 'I am learning how to conduct myself in Parliament from Dinesh Trivedi'; whereas the fact was that he was the one who would point out my shortcomings and subtly guide me on matters of public importance. I still remember him telling me not to bend to reach out to the mike when I used to preside over the Rajya Sabha as one of the panel members of presiding officers.

The Singur movement in 2006 was a turning point in the political and economic history of West Bengal. At the time I was a lone member of the Trinamool Congress (TMC) in the upper house and used to take up the issues related to Singur almost every day. I became the focal point in Delhi and elsewhere in the country in discussions on it. During those days, Rahul Bajaj genuinely wanted to know from me what was going on, and we would land up having discussions and at times heated arguments on the subject. Rahul Bajaj only had the interest of the country at heart, and having been born in Kolkata, his love for Bengal was natural. Interestingly, there were baseless rumours doing the rounds in the country that the Bajaj group of industries was behind the financing of the Singur movement!

Once we were having tea and snacks in the Central Hall with Rahul Bajaj, and some of our other colleagues in Parliament from across the party also joined us. When the bill came (which was very nominal), I insisted that I pay it, and jokingly said that otherwise rumours of Rahul Bajaj financing the Singur movement would be substantiated, at which all had a hearty laugh. That incident was narrated by Rahul Bajaj many a time to make people laugh. So great was his love for me that even on a TV show he mentioned me to say that he knew at least one MP who never went to the well of the house.

I had the opportunity to watch closely many notable industrialists in the Rajya Sabha, but Rahul Bajaj was an example of perfection. He hardly missed a day in Parliament. He was among the first to come to Parliament every day and the last to leave, waiting till the session ended for the day. His participation, right from question hour to the substantial speeches on various subjects, has gone down in the pages of the history of Parliament. Members belonging to political parties across the board respected Rahul Bajaj for the man he was. His patriotism came out clearly in every speech of his. He was among the first who would talk about self-reliance for India, and that was what made him known as a man of conviction. Rahul Bajaj would never miss out an opportunity to fearlessly and objectively criticize policies of the government that he thought were not good for the country. He did this in a most dignified way, so as not to offend any individual.

He was a man with an eye for detail, and he would talk at length even about his travel plans. He was gracious enough to visit us in Boston, where my son was receiving his master's degree in aerospace from the Massachusetts Institute of Technology.

Till his final journey, I was fortunate to be in touch with him and would literally spend hours on the phone with him. His zeal for life and his ever wanting to know more made Rahul Bajaj a household name – not only '*Hamara Bajaj*' but '*Hamara Rahul Bajaj*'.

The picture of that tall, handsome man in his spotless, well-starched kurta–pyjama will always remain fresh in my memory, and I see him smiling as I conclude. Thank you ever so much Rahul-bhai, for being part of my life. Without you and Suresh Neotia around, life is not the same.

DINESH TRIVEDI, *former Railway Minister*

Rajiv Bajaj

Was doing my yoga. Felt it. Wrote it.

My father is a great guy.

My father is a great guy not because he can talk on just about everything but because he walks his talk.

My father is a great guy not because he's always right but because he never hesitates to speak up against what's wrong.

My father is a great guy not because he always agreed with his father but because he never let his differences affect their relationship.

My father is a great guy not because he worshipped his mother but because he put her before himself to the very end.

My father is a great guy not because he was a tall boxer but because he never looked down upon anyone as being smaller.

My father is a great guy not because he married my mum but because she wouldn't have married anyone less.

My father is a great guy not because he built a great company but because he chose to live amongst those that he built it with.

My father is a great guy not because he is brilliant but because he did what he thought best so as to be the best at what he did.

My father is a great guy not because he's emotional but because he dropped everything to be at the vet's clinic when a dog was unwell.

My father is a great guy not because he was a great teacher but because he gave me the opportunity of a lifetime.

My father is a great guy not because he's rich but because he never made anyone else poor in any manner.

My father is a great guy not because of all that he's achieved but because he did it while sleeping well.

My father is a great guy not because he is decisive but because he asked endless questions when a tree was to be cut.

My father is a great guy not because he's strong but because every time mum was unwell his breath would stop.

My father is a great guy not because he gave his wealth away but because no deed was too tiny to be worthy of his support.

My father is a great guy not because he gave me life but because he always said that I was free to live as I wished to.

RAJIV BAJAJ, *Managing Director, Bajaj Auto Ltd.*

Acknowledgements

First, to all the contributors, for taking time out to respond and write. Without them there would be no book; and their response was far beyond our expectations.

Second, Rajiv Bajaj, for permission to publish in this book his personal poem on his father.

Third, the Bajaj family, for their approval to the idea of this book, consisting of contributions by friends from different segments of society whose lives had been touched in some way by Rahul Bajaj.

Fourth, Mohandas Keyyath, Rahul's personal assistant for decades, who was invaluable when it came to putting together this work. Not only did he point us to the right people, but he often picked up the phone himself to request a contribution. As Mohan writes in his personal piece, it was his boss who taught him how to get others to do what one wanted, happily. Mohan learnt from the best!

Fifth, Sophia Biju Mathew, for her constant support, for coordinating all the work and for being a dependable person. She was central to putting the book together.

Sixth, Vignesh Kumar, for his considerable diligence and work in the support team. He has done invaluable work.

Seventh, Shahana Chaudhury, who who helped some authors' put their thoughts together.

A Note on the Editors

Tarun Das is the former director general of the Confederation of Indian Industry (CII).

Kiran Pasricha is the former CEO of Ananta Aspen Centre.